Beauty and Holiness

Beauty and Holiness

THE DIALOGUE BETWEEN
AESTHETICS AND RELIGION

James Alfred Martin, Jr.

Princeton University Press

Princeton, New Jersey

Copyright © 1990 by Princeton University Press
Published by Princeton University Press, 41 William Street,
Princeton, New Jersey 08540
In the United Kingdom: Princeton University Press, Oxford

Library of Congress Cataloging-in-Publication Data
Martin, James Alfred, 1917–
Beauty and holiness : the dialogue between aesthetics and religion /
James Alfred Martin, Jr.
p.   cm.
Includes bibliographical references.
ISBN 0-691-07357-0
1. Aesthetics—Religious aspects. 2. Art and religion.
I. Title.
BL65.A4M35   1990
200′1—dc20   89-12835

This book has been composed in Linotron Weiss

Princeton University Press books are printed on acid-free paper,
and meet the guidelines for permanence and durability of the
Committee on Production Guidelines for Book Longevity of the
Council on Library Resources

Printed in the United States of America by Princeton University Press,
Princeton, New Jersey
10 9 8 7 6 5 4 3 2 1

Contents

4-2-90

Preface

What is art? What is religion? What is beauty? What is holiness? May systematic reflection of each pair of questions aid in finding responsible answers to all of them? I believe that it may, and I hope to show why I think so in this book.

I have arrived at this conviction through many years of reflection on the history and philosophy of religion, and on basic issues of theory and method in the humanistic disciplines. Many people have influenced these reflections through the years. My undergraduate mentor at Wake Forest, A. C. Reid, combined a classic philosophical sensibility with the prizing of excellence in all human creativity. My mentor in graduate studies at Duke, Alban Gregory Widgery, was a British philosopher of "the old school" who coupled a philosophical approach to fundamental human concerns with stimulating informal discussions of matters of taste in the fine arts. He also encouraged me to write a master's essay on James McCosh, President of Princeton at a time when the integrity of pursuit of the liberal arts was challenged by methodological imperialisms both theological and pseudo-scientific.

In the course of doctoral studies at Union Theological Seminary and Columbia University I learned much from Paul Tillich, Reinhold Niebuhr, and David E. Roberts at Union; and from John Herman Randall, Jr., Herbert Schneider, Horace Friess, and James Gutmann at Columbia. Tillich was completing his systematic theology and developing his theology of culture. Informal evening gatherings in his home frequently included among the guests persons from the world of art. At the Niebuhrs' one met T. S. Eliot, W. H. Auden, Arnold Toynbee, and other persons who made signal contributions to cultural analysis and sensibility. Randall brought both a keen intellect and a synoptic vision to his monumental exposition of the history of Western philosophy. Schneider brought a similar breadth of interest to his work on American thought, from a philosophical position in aesthetics that he shared with Erwin Edman. Friess and Gutmann had done distinguished

work in German Romantic philosophy, from which continuing reflection on the relation of aesthetic to religious apprehensions and articulations of reality emerged.

Military service in the United States Navy afforded initial contact
with the cultures of China and Japan. The interest stimulated by brief
visits to these countries after the conclusion of the Second World War
was further channeled through participation in the East-West Philosophers Conference at the University of Hawaii in 1949. Among the
participants who made significant contributions to my reflections on the
subject of this book were D. T. Suzuki, T. M. P. Mahadevan, and Wing-
tsit Chan. There were further contacts with Suzuki in the United
States and with Chan during the years when he was a member of the
faculty of Dartmouth and I was a member of the faculty of Amherst,
and in many years of participation in the Columbia University Seminar
on Oriental Thought and Religion.

As a member of the Department of Philosophy and Religion at
Amherst I developed courses in religion that combined a multi-cultural
approach with attention to the relation of music and the visual arts to
both Western and Eastern traditions. My colleagues in the department, Sterling P. Lamprecht and Gail Kennedy, brought the perspective of American humanistic naturalism to the analysis of historical and
contemporary issues in human culture. Robert Frost was a frequent
visitor, and his inimitable conversations frequently evoked reflections
on the relation of aesthetic to religious sensibility.

When I was invited to join the faculty of Union Theological Seminary, with a mandate to pursue systematic reflection on the role of
religion in higher education, the context of this reflection was further
enhanced by a four-month study tour, sponsored by the Rockefeller
Foundation, of resources for the study of religion in cultures of the
Near East, the Middle East, and Asia. This project, which entailed
visits to universities and to religious thinkers in Egypt, Lebanon, Pa-
kistan, India, Southeast Asia, Taiwan, and Japan, further strengthened
my conviction that the cultural roots of concepts of both art and religion, and of their intrinsic relatedness, must be responsibly addressed
in any viable view of the subject of this book.

Pursuing this aim as a member of a theological faculty increased
both my appreciation of the integrity and importance of theological
approaches to the issues involved here and my awareness of the distinctive cultural roots of theological positions that are often prema-
turely universalized. Among the colleagues at Union who were especially sympathetic with and supportive of my interests were Daniel
Day Williams, Robert T. Handy, and Roger L. Shinn.

When I moved from primary identification with Union's theological faculty to primary identification with Columbia's undergraduate faculties and the Graduate School of Arts and Sciences, I was able to aid in the development of a program in religious studies that is both interdisciplinary and cross-cultural. In the process I learned much from many colleagues, including Joseph L. Blau, preeminent student of the varieties of modern Judaism; Alex Wayman, distinguished Buddhologist; Ainslee Embree, stimulating interpreter of Indian thought and culture; and William Theodore de Bary, who is not only a leading scholar of the Neo-Confucian tradition but also a pioneer in the development of resources and rationale for the inclusion of Oriental humanities in any responsible liberal arts curriculum.

My work in theory and method in the study of religion at Columbia led to the development of graduate seminars on aesthetics and religion that were attended by students engaged in a variety of specializations in religious studies and aesthetics. I am grateful to these students, and to members of similar seminars at the University of Virginia and Wake Forest University, for many insights that I have attempted to incorporate in this book. I am also indebted to Cathie Brettschneider, religion editor of Princeton University Press, for her interest in and encouragement of this project as well as for her valuable editorial guidance. Kimberly P. Wood exercised both skill and patience in preparing the manuscript. And I am especially indebted to Nell Gifford Martin, who is not only an astute student of art history and religious thought but also a stimulating colleague and beloved companion.

Beauty and Holiness

INTRODUCTION

*T*HE TITLE of this book expresses its unique intent. I believe that responsible discussion of the relation of art to religion must address some fundamental questions of theory and method that are frequently overlooked or inadequately addressed in works on religious art, "religion and art," or "art in religion." Any worthwhile discussion of religion, whether in relation to art or to any other human phenomenon, entails or presupposes a theory of what religion is, or is taken to be, in that discussion. Any worthwhile discussion of art, whether historical or critical, entails or presupposes a theory of what art is—in other words, more broadly, a theory of aesthetics. To specify the referents of general concepts it is necessary to specify also the distinguishing evaluative criteria that control the application of the general concepts. I believe that the concept that is in this sense categorical for art is beauty, and that the concept that is in the same sense categorical for religion is holiness. Art has to do with beauty; the unique focus of religion is holiness.

But the concepts of beauty and holiness, like the concepts of art and religion, have a history. To understand the meaning of these concepts it is necessary to understand their history. In this book I offer such a history, to provide the necessary background for understanding and evaluating modern discussion of the concepts. I then deal with some of the major issues raised in that discussion. Included in contemporary debate is the view espoused by many that all four concepts—beauty, holiness, art, and religion—have outlived their usefulness in an intellectual milieu that includes vivid awareness of cultural and methodological pluralisms in the context of what is often called "postmodern" sensibility. I address this claim and offer a constructive response. The book is about the relations of art to religion when these are analyzed in terms of the categorical concepts beauty and holiness. The focus is therefore on aesthetic theory, on the one hand, and on theory of religion on the other, and on the dialogue between these in the ongoing search for understanding the relation of beauty to holi-

3

ness. The dialogical character of the discussion is exhibited in the historical and expository chapters, and it is given formal philosophical expression in the concluding chapter.

In Western thought the discipline from which much of the conceptuality germane to our subject has emerged is philosophy—or, more narrowly, aesthetics and philosophy of religion. These two disciplines did not emerge in Western thought, however, until that period of Western intellectual history broadly called the Enlightenment. There were, however, in the East long traditions of richly nuanced relations of what would later be called "art" and "religion," addressed academically under the rubrics "aesthetics" and "philosophy of religion" as a result of the impact of Western thought.

I begin the book, therefore, with a chapter that describes what we may now call "classical" understandings of the relation of holiness to beauty in Western thought. In a later chapter I offer a brief description of some of the major analogous concepts in Eastern thought. That chapter is even more selective and condensed than are the various chapters that deal with developments in the West. To have dealt as extensively with salient features of Eastern thought as I have dealt with features of Western thought would require additional expertise in areas that have received scholarly attention in the West for only a few generations, and another book at least as long as this one. The inclusion of even a brief chapter on Eastern traditions, however, affirms the importance of taking into account distinctive contributions of Eastern practice and theory.

Chapter One opens with an account of attitudes toward our subject that are expressed in the Biblical corpus that has played a central role in three religious traditions—Judaism, Christianity, and Islam—and in Western culture. This is followed by a sampling of major positions on the subject incorporated in the classical Greek philosophical tradition, with a concentration on the views of Plato and Aristotle. It should be noted that these accounts are offered only as condensed "samplings" and do not seek to deal in detail with the rich complexity of the thought of the philosophers concerned. I then turn to attitudes toward our subject expressed in the classical tradition of Christendom that set the parameters of much Western thought for many centuries. Here the concentration is on Augustine as heir of both the Biblical tradition and Plato, and on Thomas Aquinas as heir of the Biblical and Christian traditions and of Aristotle. The first chapter concludes with a discussion of a representative of Calvinistic Protestant thought, Jonathan Edwards, who combined a Platonic conception of beauty with the empiricism of John Locke to produce an empirical philosophical theology that may be unsurpassed in American thought. Edwards was, for reasons that I indicate, still within the classical tradition, though he lived in a century that would experience calls for new thought-forms. Both Judaism and Islam developed analogous but distinctive responses to the issues faced in Western Christendom. It was the classical thought of Western Christianity, however, often in interaction with the other two traditions, that played the major role in setting the agenda for modern Western discussion of our subject.

The second chapter begins with an account of some of the primary factors involved in the emergence of new habits of thought in the eighteenth and nineteenth centuries in the West. These are epitomized in the changing roles of rhetoric and logic in inquiry and in the articulation of basic human concerns. They are reflected in complementary visions of "the new science" exemplified in Bacon's *New Organon* and Vico's *Scienza Nuova*. From analyses of these factors I turn to the responses of David Hume and Immanuel Kant to the challenges posed to some of the basic assumptions of classical Western thought. I show that Hume not only dealt creatively with problems entailed in judgments of taste but also made an important contribution to the development of theories of religion and its history. I then show that Kant, who was "awakened from his dogmatic slumbers" by the writings of Hume, fashioned a critical philosophy in which the first fully developed philosophical theory of aesthetics played a central role. His analysis of the concept of beauty as the distinctive aesthetic category, as this analysis has been refined by Mary Mothersill in her book *Beauty Restored*,[1] provides a rationale for that category on which I elaborate in a later chapter. At this juncture I note that many of the same intellectual interests that gave rise to aesthetic theory and theories of religion were operative in the rise of art history as a field of inquiry, and I describe the basic concepts employed by its founders.

Next I turn to a summary of the thought of key figures in the German Romantic philosophical tradition that provided the impetus for much modern reflection on the relation of aesthetic to religious modes of apprehending and articulating reality. Special attention is given to Schiller, Schlegel, Schelling, and Schleiermacher. The chapter concludes with an account of aspects of the thought of Hegel that have been of paramount importance in defining the terms of modern discussion of art and religion.

The third chapter begins with a discussion of the meanings of *theory* when that concept is employed in religious studies and other humanistic disciplines. This discussion sets the stage for an exposition of the relation of beauty to holiness in the theories of religion formulated by Rudolf Otto, Mircea Eliade, Gerardus van der Leeuw, Paul Tillich, and Clifford Geertz. These figures are chosen because each represents a distinctive and widely influential viewpoint. I focus on the relation of aesthetic to religious sensibility in the formulation of each theory, and on the relation of beauty to holiness set forth in each.

Chapter Four presents a comparable analysis of the relation of aesthetics to religion in the thought of five modern philosophers: George Santayana, John Dewey, Alfred North Whitehead, Martin Heidegger, and Ludwig Wittgenstein. I show why poetry and religion play central roles in Santayana's vision of the quest for human beatitude. I then show that the aesthetic and the religious components of experience perform analogous functions in the thought of Dewey. The use of aesthetic categories in Whitehead's cosmology, and in his appraisal of the meaning of "religion in the making," is then described. Next I show that within the complexities of Heidegger's thought there is an insistence on the importance of poetic and religious, if not mystical, insight in discernment of the authentic "voice of Being." Finally I indicate why I believe that Wittgenstein, who epitomizes "the linguistic turn" in modern philosophy, provides the most fruitful way of describing and appraising the languages of art and religion and their "family resemblances."

In the fifth chapter I present a brief account of some of the chief features of the historical relations of art to religion, and of beauty to holiness, in the cultures of India, China, and Japan. Though this account is even more condensed and selective than are the accounts given in preceding chapters of developments in Western thought, it is intended to highlight similarities as well as differences between "Eastern" and "Western" thinking. I note the significance of the relative homogeneity, until recent times, of Eastern cultures in their formulations of the conceptual relationships on which this book focuses. I then discuss the problems entailed in the use of the concepts "art" and "religion," as these concepts have been developed and formulated in the West, for the analysis of Eastern cultures, and I offer alternative, functionally equivalent concepts to be used for this purpose. Major themes of Hindu, Buddhist, Taoist, Confucian, and Shinto thought are briefly summarized. I then analyze the meaning of the aesthetic notion of *rasa* in Hindu thought, along with Buddhist modifications of this concept in the light of the Buddhist doctrine of "dependent origination." I stress the interrelatedness of nonhuman and human nature in Chinese and Japanese expressions of transcendence, and I describe the Chinese *wen-jen-hua* aesthetic theory, along with the Japanese concepts of *yūgen, aware, miyabi,* and *sabi.*

Chapter Six employs the findings of a UNESCO Commission's study of "Main Trends in Aesthetics and the Sciences of Art" to outline areas in which scholars of art and aesthetics and of religion confront similar problems at the present time. These include problems of the relation of theory to practice; problems entailed by the awareness of cultural pluralism and the differing status of art and religion in different cultures, "developed" and "developing"; the general problem of universal claims in relation to pluralistic agendas; specific problems involved in "comparative" studies in all humanistic disciplines; and the special relevance of social-scientific studies for the elucidation of issues in both aesthetics and religion. After this summary of common problems I return to the matter of establishing categorical concepts for art and religion, and I develop the appeal of Mary Mothersill for the "restoration" of the concept of beauty as distinctive for aesthetics. I also propose that Mothersill's analysis of aesthetic judgment provides a model for the analysis of religious judgment.

I turn finally in this sixth chapter to Arthur Danto's claim that we have come to "the end of art," and Wilfred Cantwell Smith's claim that we should come to the "end of religion" in contemporary discussion of the concerns of this book. I then summarize several important responses to Danto's position and question whether the historical data and theoretical exigencies support Smith's claim. Insights into the viability of both claims, and into possible alternative positions, are found, I maintain, in discussions clustering around certain contemporary theories of literary criticism, especially those of Jacques Derrida and Mikhail Bakhtin. I agree with Giles Gunn that the culture of criticism stands in a symbiotic relationship with the criticism of culture.[2] I therefore highlight what I believe to be important implications of "deconstruction" for our subject and affirm the value of the "dialogical principle" espoused by Bakhtin for an ongoing discussion of the issues set forth in this book.

The concluding chapter outlines some of the issues that set the parameters for this ongoing discussion. These include the problem of universalizing strategies that are rooted in culturally founded, if not culturally embedded, concepts and procedures; the debate about "foundationalism" and "contextualism" in modern philosophy; and the problem of "canonization" in art and religion. These problems must be addressed academically, I maintain, through disciplines that are or should be multimethodological and cross-cultural. Both the study of art and the study of religion should exhibit in microcosm what a modern liberal arts curriculum should exhibit in macrocosm. Each of these two fields of study has much to learn from the other in the pursuit of common educational goals.

In view of the fact that much of the conceptuality in terms of which basic issues are addressed in both fields is philosophical, I conclude with a brief sketch of a philosophical stance that I believe to be most productive in dealing with these issues. I call it "dialogic neo-pragmatism." The dialogic emphasis builds on the insights of Bakhtin; the pragmatic cast is in the tradition of James and Dewey as modified by Joseph Margolis, Richard Rorty, Richard Bernstein, and Justus Buchler.

This volume represents a very broad approach to our subject, even though its unique focus is on specific problems of theory and method. Scholars who are specialists in one or more of the areas of inquiry that it takes into account may deem some of the discussion of matters in their fields to be somewhat elementary. I believe, however, that focusing on the relations of art and religion, or of beauty and holiness, in each instance may suggest leads for further specialized research. By setting forth several dimensions of our subject in one volume, I hope to encourage art historians, historians of religion, theologians, aestheticians, and philosophers of religion to become better informed about the concerns of other disciplines that have an important bearing on the pursuit of common interests. Each of them should be stimulated to develop more thoughtfully nuanced positions on the subject of this book.

But the book is not addressed exclusively, or even primarily, to specialists in the various disciplines in which attention to its subject matter is appropriate. It is addressed also to the general reader who surmises that there are important relations between art and religion and who seeks a context in which to think through what these relations are. This book is therefore an invitation to readers with a wide variety of interests to participate in the ongoing dialogue between aesthetics and religion, and to think more deeply on the relation of beauty to holiness.

CHAPTER ONE

The Holiness of Beauty and the Beauty of Holiness:

Classical Western Formulations

THE BIBLE

*I*T IS IN the King James Version of the Bible that we encounter the Psalmist's injunction to "worship the Lord in the beauty of holiness" (Psalm 29:2). It is significant, however, that other versions translate the passage "in the splendour of Holiness," with the note "or holy vestments,"[1] and others render it "in holy array"[2] or "festival attire."[3] Immediately we are made aware of the fact that the Biblical word translated "beauty" in the English of the King James Version does not designate a concept of beauty that is synonymous with that which originated in Greek thought, was absorbed in the Christian tradition, and eventually became the original definitive category of that species of systematic reflection we call aesthetics. Indeed, the question could be raised whether there is a *concept* of beauty as such in the Hebraic sources of the Western tradition.

It is true that English translations of the Bible employ the word "beauty" to designate outward comeliness or handsomeness, or, as Gerhard von Rad puts it, "the experience of beauty common to all men."

> Like all civilized peoples, Israel was aware of the beauty of man and his bodily form (Gen. 6:2, 12:11, 24:16); she was aware of the beauty of the moon (Song of Sol. 6:10); like others, she was able to sense a speech, or a form of expression as beautiful (Prov. 15:26, 16:24; Ezek. 33:32). But where the primitive instinct in Israel created works of art on a grand scale, the case is already different. . . . Israel's artistic *charisma* lay in the realm of narrative and poetry . . . [yet] admittedly, as far as we can see, Israel lacked all critical reflection on the phenomenon of beauty and on artistic reproduction as such.[4]

In the Psalmist's injunction, then, it is to the concept of *holiness* that we should look for insight into the use of the term "beauty," whether specifically identified, as in this instance, with characteristics of cultic vestments or more generally related to the broader notion of

9

"splendor." "Her most intensive encounter with beauty was in the religious sphere," von Rad continues, "and because of this concentration of the experience of beauty upon the *credenda*, Israel occupies a special place in the history of aesthetics."[5] Use of the term "aesthetics" may be an anachronism here, but it is consonant with later emphases on the affective quality of aesthetic experience and on the focus of its expression. In this case the quality is that of "delight" in the goods of creation and the ways of God in history; the focus of the expression is God's "glory"; and the point of aesthetic renderings of experience is "to glorify God." Some of Israel's literature, von Rad notes, "brims over in sheer delight in God's creation (Ps. 114, 143; Job 9:3ff., 26:5ff.). All agree that in this creation all is splendid, splendid even without purpose." The "highest" beauty, however, is in the unmerited redemptive work of God in history. "For Israel, beauty was something that happened rather than something that existed."[6]

If the focus of Israel's artistic creation is the glory of God, and its purpose is to glorify God, what is "the glory of God"? In early use *kābōd* was the dazzling heavenly fire that accompanied a manifestation of God's presence (Exodus 24:16ff.). In the Hebraic tradition, however, there was early resistance to understanding a theophany as in any sense compromising the otherness or transcendence—the holiness (*qādōs̆*)—of the divine. Sometimes, therefore, the "glory" was perceived as a *reflection* of the transcendent (1 Kings 8:11); or it was an otherworldly brilliance, "the heavenly robe or light in which glory is clothed which, though fatal to mortal eyes, must with the divine triumph fill the whole earth (Ezekiel 38:18; Isaiah 6:3, 40:5, 60:1ff.)."[7] Glory, then, was a concept intermediate between the divine transcendence and those manifestations of divine immanence that, in other cultures and other times, would be the focus of aesthetic interpretation. Here again, however, for Israel the natural and the historical are intertwined, and it is the triumph of the divine purpose in history that eventuates in a full experience of the divine glory in the whole earth.

The concept of glory in its earliest form is, however, morally neutral. It is with the emergence of the prophetic tradition that the term becomes charged with moral significance, and this understanding of the term would continue to be a part of its meaning in the subsequent history of those traditions in the West that are indebted to Biblical sources. Assimilated to the concept of holiness, it would apply to a "holy people" obedient to God's "holy will." "Nevertheless," says Walter Eichrodt, "it was the priestly use of the word which predominated, and had the decisive influence on the LXX and on Hellenistic as well as Rabbinic Judaism."[8] In the messianic tradition there was a merging of the priestly and prophetic strands in the figure of divine glory who, in bringing the historical process to fulfillment, would at the same time bring all of creation into participation in the divine glory.

Even so, to the extent that the concept of glory was expressible in terms of beauty, there was always a sense of the demonic possibilities in beauty—"the demonic element in beauty, which blinds the eyes, and seduces men to rebellion against the Lord's anointed."[9] The beautiful could become not only idolatrous or the occasion of idolatry (worship of the created rather than of the Creator); it could have power that opposed the divine purpose in history. This suspicion of beauty would also be a part of the legacy of Biblical religion to its inheriting traditions in the West. We shall be comparing this view with, among others, that of Plato and the inheritors of his vision, in which, although "earthly" beauties can never be the highest good, Beauty is the chief propaedeutic to the Good.

If, in the Hebraic milieu from which came the Psalmist's injunction to "worship the Lord in the beauty of holiness," the accent is on holiness, does this mean that religion, as contrasted with aesthetics, was of central concern for the Biblical community? No. As Wilfred Cantwell Smith points out, and Biblical scholars agree,

> Classical Hebrew has no word signifying "religion." Except perhaps a solitary Persian intrusion at the very end of its development (Daniel 6:6), the Old Testament is innocent of this concept and its term. The phrase "the fear of the Lord" is the closest approach in the sense of personal piety. Clearly it does not designate a system, sociological or ideological; and it cannot have a plural. In the New Testament the great word is *pistis*, faith. . . . In addition, St. Paul in passing uses once a term, *threskeia* (rite, ritual, observance) (Acts 26:5), to designate apparently a religious community characterized by its normative ways and some would even say a religion as a systematic pattern.[10]

St. Jerome, Smith notes, "introduced the term *religio* at a few places in his Latin translation of the Bible, fixing it therefore in the Western Christian tradition."[11]

In this respect, as we shall see, the people of Biblical culture were not different from those of other classical cultures; in none of them was there a sense of a system of specific beliefs and practices within the culture as constituting the "religion" of that culture. So, in terms of the subject of this book, we would have to say that if in Biblical Israel it was holiness rather than beauty that was of central concern, this does not mean that religion rather than aesthetics was a primary focus of attention. Was it the Greeks, then, who celebrated the holiness of beauty and made beauty a central concern of their religion?

PLATO (427?–347 B.C.E.)

The Greeks had both practical and theoretical interests that were different from those that informed the Hebraic sense of a holy people engaged in the work of glorification of God in history. And in the case of the Greeks both the practical and the theoretical became ingredients in the understanding of art and beauty. Unlike the Hebrews, the Greeks concentrated from early times on various forms of "know-how" (*technē*) in a range of undertakings. These included the know-how or "craft" of the cobbler, the builder, the trainer of horses—anyone who had expertise in a practice conducive to human well-being, physical or spiritual. They included medical arts (*technai*) and arts of divination. And they included a form of know-how that entailed a special type of "making" that was known as *poiesis*. The distinction between *poiesis* and other forms of know-how, seen as a matter of kind and not simply of degree, would in later centuries become one of the bases for distinguishing the "fine" arts from the other arts. *Poiesis* was seen by the Greeks to be both more important and more problematic than other forms of art understood as *technē*. Its importance would be symbolized by the choice of *poiesis* as the term for the divine "making" portrayed in Genesis, in the definitive translation of the Hebraic scriptures into Greek. This was consonant with the traditional Greek admiration of the poet—an admiration shared, as we have noted, by the Hebrews. In the case of the Greeks the admiration would be for a Homer as maker and singer of epic, and for Aeschylus, Aristophanes, and Sophocles as makers of comedy and tragedy; in the case of the Hebrews it would be for David as the prototypical hymner of the glory of God. The use of *poiesis* for divine making in the Septuagint's rendering of the beginning of things (Genesis) would also be consonant with Plato's assigning to divinity the work of the *demiurgos*: the work of incarnating eternal forms in temporal formations. And it is consonant with the Greek fascination with the kind of "energy" or work that is the task of the poet.

But it was also Plato who warned against the seductive powers of poets, who are, in his view, at best imitators of a world that is itself an imitation of the truly real. This reminds us that *mimesis*, which can be translated "imitation" or "representation," was seen to be the unique intent of the artist. But imitation is not presentation, and reproduction is not production, in the normative senses of these terms. We shall see that the mimetic theory of aesthetic creation would become a major type of critical theory after aesthetics emerged as a specific form of systematic reflection.

What, in the typical Greek view, is the kind of making that is artistic creation? Basically, it is a *forming* or *shaping*—the forming or shaping of clay by a potter, of marble by a sculptor, of a building by an architect, and of words in relation to other words by a poet. This activity of forming entails the envisionment of forms by the artist and the incarnation of these forms in the materials with which the artist works. (Aristotle would note that the material is as truly a "cause" of anything as is its form.) The distinctive blend of forms-informing-materials in the work of each artist is peculiar to that artist. It was viewed by the Greeks as a gift (*charisma*) or an inspiration unique to the artist's "genius." Plato suggested that it might be a form of "divine madness."

There were for the Greeks certain standards of the kinds of formations that were considered to be most pleasing and therefore most to be prized. In general these were shapings or makings that exhibited harmony, proportion, symmetry, or balance—or, as Bernard Bosanquet put it, "the imaginative or sensuous expression of unity in variety."[12] Unordered variety threatened to induce Dionysian chaos; unvaried form threatened to produce Apollonian deadness (to borrow a contrast later celebrated by Nietzsche). Thus was born that "classical formalism" that would inform Kant's concept of beauty and would constitute, for Hegel and others, the norms of the highest achievements of art in the spiritual life of humankind.

We should not forget, however, that the process of making in itself was prized by the Greeks, and that it could be assimilated to a kind of making that Plato (in the *Phaedrus* and the *Republic*, for instance) and Aristotle (in the *Politics* and the *Nicomachean Ethics*) would value even more highly than the makings of poets—namely, the making of well-ordered states by political artists or statesmen. It was, after all, primarily the welfare of the *polis* that facilitated the welfare of the person. And it was concern for the welfare of the *polis* that partly underlay Plato's suspicion of the poets. The poets, he thought, even in their portrayals of the gods, and especially in their representations of both immoral and moral persons, might induce immoral if not impious behavior.

In reflections like these, Plato passed from analysis of the work of the artist to criticism of the artist's function in society. Many have noted a certain irony in this, since it was Plato the master artist of dialogue who employed this artistic medium to call into question the ultimate worth of art and of the artist in human affairs. Later critics, as we shall see, would question the validity of a fundamental and inclusive distinction between artist and critic. Many see the critic as artist and the artist as critic. Some say that the disappearance of the distinction between artist and critic means "the end of art." But this would be the case, I suggest, only if some classical understandings of the intent of art as *mimesis* were taken to be normative for all time.

Plato, in any case, was more interested in *theoria*, or vision, and in the theoretical appraisal of *praxis* and know-how of all sorts. It is in this context that we are to understand his notion of beauty, a notion that was to be of immense import for later Christian reflections on the holiness of beauty as an ingredient in the beauty of holiness. Plato was interested in forms as standards: the eternal forms or "essences" of all exemplifications in the temporal world of change. His basic model was mathematical, translated ontologically into "the problem of the one and the many." He made frequent use of the model of geometry. Triangularity as such, he noted, does not exist in the realm of space and time. All representations of triangularity are imperfect, because specific and changing. Yet it is only by "participation" in triangularity that triangular representations are possible. This notion of participation would, in turn, also become an important ingredient of subsequent reflection on the relation of artistic representation to the real.

Just as there is the "perfect" triangle (triangularity), so there must also be perfect ideas or forms or standards of truth and of justice, Plato thought. Cognitions arrived at by sense experience are derived from and applicable to only the changing world of appearance; moral judgments based on observations of the way humans actually behave can, in the last analysis, be only descriptive and not normative. There must be norms of truth and justice, and these norms, like those of mathematics, are eternal in their perfection. It is to these norms that humans must look if they are to achieve the goals of truly human life. But the "looking" is not merely passive or optional. It is infused and motivated by an active process that is in many respects like that of artistic creation; indeed, it is the basic drive underlying that and all other forms of creation. It is *eros*, or love. Artistic creation is good if and only to the extent that it takes its ordered place in the more fundamental work of love in relation to its ultimate object.

What is that ultimate object? Plato called it the Good. The term, however, does not connote for Plato simply the morally good. It is also the noetically good and, as later generations would say (but Plato did not), the aesthetically good. It is, in short, excellence itself, reflected in all expressions of excellence, including excellence of physical form that physically attracts, and excellence of intellectual formulation that intellectually attracts. And the highest and most powerful reflection of that total excellence or perfection which is the Good is the Beautiful.

Beauty is the chief propaedeutic to the Good. Beauty, in other words, is ingredient in the work of intelligence and in the constitution of the world that intelligence may comprehend in that supreme vision which is *theoria* and may enjoy in that supreme human good which is contemplation. For Plato contemplation is itself, however, only the closest approximation of that beatitude which would characterize the vision of the Good as such. To speak of that beatitude would be to speak of immortality and to speak in the language of myth, like the myth of the winged chariot in the *Phaedrus*. The most compelling articulation of the ascent to the Good through Beauty is found in the concluding words of the vision vouchsafed to Socrates in the *Symposium*.[13]

ARISTOTLE (384–322 B.C.E.)

Aristotle modified the Platonic vision, but perhaps not as radically as some modern Aristotelians may suggest. He brought to the vision a more comprehensive and more finely nuanced experience of the world and a more precise articulation of that experience. He, too, recognized the importance of forms, but he believed that forms are perceived only as materialized. Thus both matter and form are irreducible ingredients of things in the world. To understand anything in that world we must ask and answer four questions: From what did it come (what preceded it)? Of what is it made? What is it that is thus made? And for what is it made? The world is a making, a *physis* (nature), a growing—and we must ask these questions about this "growing." When we have answered these questions we have given the cause(s) of whatever is. The world itself, in other words, is seen as an initiating-forming-of-material for a purpose.

Those arts or *technai* that enhance the life of humans in the world by translating knowledge of the world into human practice are the practical or industrial arts: the crafts and "science" as *technical*. In a sense they are engaged in the imitation of nature—that is, they adapt the ways of nature to human ways, and human ways to the ways of nature, or nature-as-human to humanity-as-natural. *Mimesis*, in other words, is not limited to those arts that later would be called "the fine arts." These arts, however—the arts of *poiesis* engaged in the forming or shaping of various materials, including words—may provide a further enhancement of human life as an improvement on or vivification of first-order human/natural processes. They engage in *mimesis* of a distinctive, and distinctively human, kind. They are not to be denigrated or rendered suspect because they are thought to be mere "imitations of imitations," as in the Platonic vision. Both science and art are engaged in the work of imitation, and the world articulated in each is always a world of material formed. To know what material is formed in what way, from what precedent, and to what purpose is the goal of science. To vivify that world through the imaginative makings (*poiesis*) of humans is to enhance the quality of human life. In both processes— those of the intellect in science and those of the imagination in the poetic arts—there are three desiderata: (1) integrity, or unity, because the intellect is pleased in the fullness of being, "the joy of knowing"; (2) proportion, or harmony, because the intellect joys in order and consonance; and (3) clarity, or radiance, because the intellect joys in that light which causes intelligence to "see." Analogous exemplifications of integrity or unity, proportion or harmony, and clarity or radiance characterize well-made works of art.

We have only one analysis by Aristotle of a specific art form: the art of tragedy, in the *Poetics*. His designation of the essentials of a well- made tragedy—the "three unities" of plot, time, and place—was to have far-reaching influence in later dramatic creation and criticism, as were his notion of tragic event through error (later to be misunder- stood as a doctrine of "tragic flaw") and his understanding of the effect of well-made and well-performed tragedy as catharsis. Unlike Plato, Aristotle did not criticize "aesthetic" good in terms of moral or social good, but he did include moral considerations in the delineation of aesthetically effective ingredients in works of art. The "hero" of a well- made tragedy, for instance, must be neither too "good" nor too "evil"! And in the *Rhetoric* he defined the beautiful as that good which is pleas- ant because it is good. "Good," however, in this case may be simply synonymous with "excellent."

Like Plato, Aristotle concluded that perfect happiness is found in comtemplative activity. This, he asserts,

> will appear from the following consideration. . . . We assume the gods to be above all other beings blessed and happy; but what sort of actions must we assign to them? Will not the gods seem absurd if they make contracts and return deposits, and so on? Acts of a brave man, then, con- fronting dangers and running risks because it is noble to do so? To whom will they give? And what would their temperate acts be? Is not such praise tasteless, since they have no appetites. . . . Now if you take away from a living being action, and still more production, what is left but contempla- tion? Therefore the activity of God which surpasses all others in blessed- ness must be contemplative; and of human activities, therefore, that which is most akin to this must be most of the nature of happiness.[14]

But contemplation is an activity. What is the contemplative activ- ity of God? Briefly, in his metaphysics Aristotle employed the concept of *theos* as the focal principle of being. God is that "unmoved mover" which is the goal, and therefore the source, of all motion. In a metaphysic that envisions all of reality in terms of potentiality moving to actuality, God is Pure Act. And God's activity is "thinking on thinking."

Does this mean that in the case of Aristotle we have moved into the realm of religion—that in him the aesthetic, in kinship with the scientific, is seen in ultimately "religious" terms? One would be justified in such a conclusion only if one identified religion with theistic belief and believed that Aristotle was a theist. But religion, as this term is employed in post-Enlightenment Western thought, is not limited to theistic belief-forms, or to belief-forms as such. Its purport is broader, and at the same time more specific, than anything that would have occurred to Plato or Aristotle or any other Greek, just as it is in relation to anything that would have occurred to Biblical Hebrews. The Greeks no more than the Hebrews thought of themselves as "having a religion." There were the Greek gods, to be sure, but they differed fundamentally from humans in only one respect: they were "immortal." As such, their power and their excellence, as well as their foibles, could exceed those of humans in degree but not in kind. They served to humanize nature and to naturalize the human. There were festivals and observances, and athletic contests as well as poetic and dramatic competitions were pan-Hellenic tributes to the gods and the excellence and mystery they embodied and evoked. But the Greeks did not think they had "a religion."

•

What did the early Christians, as heirs of both Jerusalem and Athens, think? As heirs of Jerusalem they had no more and no less a conception of "religion" than did their Hebraic forebears. Unlike the Greeks, but in continuity with the Hebrews, they did have a sense of being a distinctive people called to a distinctive task in working out the divine purpose in history. In performing that task they could agree that "pure religion and undefiled before God" (James 1:27, King James Version) is peculiarly sensitive to the needs of the powerless. But the term thus translated "religion" in the King James Version is the substance and measure of devotion to the God of heaven and earth in proclaiming divine ways in human history, rather than an aspect, segment, dimension, or compartment of personal or corporate life. This understanding differed from the more varied ways of relating the human to the nonhuman and ideal worlds that constituted Greek piety and celebration. It was in the Roman term *religio* that the Christians found a way of designating their own distinctive piety, and it was with the Roman sense of *pietas* that their Latin Fathers would write of "the true religion." The Latin *religio* embraced a sense of "the ties that bind" humans to the civil powers through the civic virtues, affirmed in cultic vows and oaths. This sense would be continued in Roman Catholic Christianity in the designation of those bound by special vows in their vocations as "the religious."

Then did the Christians, as heirs of Athens and Jerusalem, have an aesthetic? They shared with the people of Israel a profound sense of the divine *glory*, of its refraction in natural wonders, and especially of its manifestation in the "mighty deeds of God" in human history—climaxing, for them, in the Word made flesh. They also shared with Israel a wariness of visual representations of the divine glory, lest monotheism be compromised by idolatry. When Christianity spread through the agency of Greek-speaking evangelists Hellenistically nurtured, along the Roman seaways and roads of empire, the idioms and concepts of Greco-Roman philosophy would enrich the media employed for proclaiming and defending the new Wisdom of the Gospel. There was neither more nor less of an aesthetic theory in the Greek and Latin sources appropriated by the Christians than had been articulated in the rich variety of these sources themselves—Stoic, Platonic, Neoplatonic, Aristotelian, and others.

Would seminal Christian thinkers fashion from these sources a new "Christian" aesthetic? "It has frequently been said," notes Robert J. O'Connell, "that the attempt by Augustine and others in the early church to express the Christian mystery in the categories of Hellenic thought ranged from the heroically quixotic to something in the neighborhood of the perversely catastrophic."[15] There were resources in classical thought that were not fully apprehended or appropriated by the early Christian Fathers; some of these would come to light in the Western Renaissance and later. But the interpenetration of Hebraic and Hellenistic thought employed in the service of a distinctively Christian witness did result in some notable visions that would inspire Christendom for a millennium and beyond. The two that would be of most comprehensive and lasting importance are those of Augustine of Hippo and Thomas Aquinas—one, the heir of Plato as transmitted through the arresting Neoplatonic vision of Plotinus; the other, the heir of Aristotle as transmitted through Christian, Muslim, and Jewish sources.

AUGUSTINE (354–430 C.E.)

Augustine gives us a vivid account of his intellectual and spiritual pilgrimage in the *Confessions*. There he portrays an anguished search for intellectual certainty and spiritual wholeness. It was, he says, Cicero's *Hortensius* that first awakened him to philosophy as the route to intellectual certainty, and for a time he embraced some of the Stoic doctrines it espouses. Significantly, however, it was what we would now call the aesthetic appeal of Cicero's manner of portraying these doctrines that played a major role in Augustine's intellectual fascination with them. At the same time, he was enamored of the literary classics—Virgil in particular—and with the theater. He speaks little of visual art or of music as aesthetically appealing.

Stoicism, however, did not resolve for him what he saw as the dual problem of intellectual certainty and psychological wholeness. He found himself in ever-deepening personal conflict between intention and will, and in ever-deepening puzzlement over the reality of evil in the world—a reality that, he felt, Stoicism did not fully address. Thus he was led to the ethical and ontological dualism of the Manichees— a view that, as some modern commentators have noted, has exerted a perennial fascination in Western thought. Meanwhile he supported himself as a teacher of rhetoric and was thus impelled to appreciate verbal art, primarily for its persuasive powers but also in part for its varied manipulations of verbal symbols.

When he went to Milan to pursue his profession he was attracted by the homiletic skills of Bishop Ambrose and by his hymnody. Gradually he was led through these to reconsider the intellectual and spiritual claims of the Christian faith, embodied in the practice and admonitions of his mother Monica but abjured by his pagan father and previously considered naive by the sophisticated Augustine.

Meanwhile he found a compelling intellectual vision in the Neoplatonic work of Plotinus. Manichean dualism seemed inadequate in the light of Plotinus's vision of the One, emanating degrees of being and goodness in a hierarchy of being shading into nonbeing. The underlying unity provided moral foundations; forms of evil could be seen as forms of the absence of good. The whole could be seen as exhibiting a beauty that was in part an expression of the harmony of the whole, in part a richness of contrasting goods and evils. More important, the mathematical model of certainty extolled by Plato and incorporated into Plotinus's resolution of the problem of the One and the Many seemed to provide the cognitive foundations.

When he learned that Victorinus, whose translation of Plotinus had brought him intellectual satisfaction, had embraced Christianity, Augustine was impelled intellectually, as he had been drawn imaginatively by the power of Ambrose's preaching and hymnody, to reconsider the claims of the Christian faith. Significantly, this now involved a wrestling with the passions more than it involved intellectual debate. This fact, however, is not surprising when one considers that Augustine frequently described his intellectual quest for Truth in erotic terms; in this respect he emulated both Plotinus and Plotinus's master,

Plato. It was, however, the reading of a passage from St. Paul that served as a catalyst for Augustine's conversion to a Christian understanding of wholeness.

In his earliest postconversion reflections Augustine considered the relations of Beauty to Truth and Goodness—which, following Plato, he saw as ultimately one. In his *De Ordine* he asserts that beauty is a matter of *ratio*, or the relations of the parts of the beautiful object to each other and to the whole. This is akin to a "moment" of aesthetic judgment that Kant would later speak of as "purposiveness without purpose." Augustine speaks of it as equality, measure, or concord. The latter, we may note in anticipation, portends Jonathan Edwards's "Being's cordial consent to being." The notion of measure, however, relates more to the Platonic sense of *standard* of measurement, and it played a major role in Augustine's early conclusions about the nature of true beauty. Like later aestheticians, Augustine affirms that the experience of beauty occasions a distinctive kind of pleasure. In an earlier work, he distinguished between those pleasures derived from a sense of fittingness or *aptum* and those delights in harmony that entail a kind of detachment from practical ends and that characterize the experience of integral pleasure or *pulchra*—an anticipation, perhaps, of Kant's "moment" of aesthetic judgment that he calls "disinterested interest."

Even so, when Augustine goes on to inquire about true beauty, it is the mathematical character of *ratio* that most impresses him. Like Plato, he sees the arts that would later be called "practical," the *technai*, as inferior—even in the quality of pleasure-in-fittingness that they yield—to the truly liberating "liberal arts": the trivium and the quadrivium. It is the unique power of these intellectual "disciplines" to discipline the mind in increasingly clear, but increasingly abstract, thought, just as ascetic discipline, Augustine now believed, is required for the attainment of moral goodness. The model of clarity, again, is mathematics, and the certainty attained is, as it was for Plato, that of the analytic proposition, which alone could ground demonstrable knowledge.

It is in this light that we are to understand Augustine's only surviving work on what we would now think of as at least in part an "aesthetic" subject matter: music (*De Musica*).[16] For him music is a "science," not an art. Its essence lies in what we would now call musical theory. Thus in *De Musica* he develops an elaborate theory of grades of numbers and numerical relations, leading toward the purest apprehension of (mathematical) Truth. He notes the fact that in music these numbers are "sounded numbers," but the sounds are fundamentally media of numerical apprehension. Again, however, the notion of *measure*

intrigues him, and he employed the example of poetic measures as a springboard for reflection on time, in the *Confessions* and elsewhere. Reflection on time, in turn, evoked reflection on eternity, and at this stage in the development of his thought Augustine could think of time only as Plato's "moving image of eternity." The world of images is inferior cognitively and aesthetically, he thought, to the eternal Real of which they are images. Then is the eternal atemporal, like the "timeless" truths of analytic propositions, or is it "everlasting"? Augustine would wrestle with this dilemma for the rest of his life; both conceptions underlie typical expressions of his position. Meanwhile, the time-bound character of music could be seen only as exemplifying the soul's "fall" from eternity into time and its yearning for union (reunion?) with the (remembered or re-collected?) Eternal.

But what is the positive value of ultimately inadequate symbols, musical or otherwise? Why does the Eternal hide itself in temporal images, necessitating intellectual if not mystical ascent? In reflecting on this question Augustine reverts to the Neoplatonic affirmation of the value of a whole exhibiting contrasts of approximate goods and evils. Celebration of this beauty was now doubly required of the Christian Augustine who must also derive his anthropology from the book of *Genesis*, in which the whole of the created order is divinely declared to be good, and from the Fourth Gospel, which affirms that the Divine Word became flesh. The latter affirmation would lead Augustine through a quasi-dualistic doctrine of the Incarnation to a full affirmation of corporeal reality appropriate to the pre- and post-Resurrection *milieux*.

But Augustine the Christian was an heir of both Plato via Plotinus and of Moses and the prophets via Rabbi Jeshua of Nazareth confessed as Messias or Christos, the Anointed One. In both traditions, we have noted, there was affirmation as well as suspicion of aesthetic goods, especially those of the visual arts. In his postconversion single-mindedness Augustine could see in his earlier fascination with the arts only a substitution of image for reality and a worship of idols rather than the one true God. Why, he asks, did he weep for Dido and not for his own divided soul? Why did he thrill to theatrical drama and disdain the divine comedy? He was in fact, he says, worshipping idols; he was in fact distracted by images from the eternal Truth imaged in them.

And yet, just as we have noted irony in the fact that Plato, the master artist of dialogue, placed artists below philosophers in his vision of the ascent of the soul to the Good, and counseled philosophical censorship in his ideal Republic; just as there may be irony in Israel's suspicion of art coupled with its exaltation of David, Yahweh's master musician; so we may perceive irony in Augustine's ambivalence, if not pseudo-Philistinism, with respect to the arts. Augustine was himself a master rhetorician and, in the *Confessions*, a master exemplar of the creative imagination in adducing and combining images of the soul's quest for an attainment of Beatific Vision. Although his treatise *De Musica* is about music theory and the forms of harmony, and the teacher of rhetoric would subordinate poetry to grammar in a pedantic analysis of verse (an affliction still with us in some critical circles), Robert O'Connell may not be far from the mark when he writes:

> *Magnus, Domine;* "Great art Thou, Lord, and greatly to be praised": from its opening notes the symphonic power of Augustine's *Confessions* leaps to life. For the work is quite literally a symphony . . . meant to be read aloud, to be *heard* . . . a single, extended *exercitatio*, composed in a musical mode; at no point before the final book does he mean to resolve completely the tension set up in our minds—and imaginations—by this artful interweave of questions, hints, images, and suggestions, all pointing towards the meaning of man's life that he unfolds fully in Book XIII. [17]

O'Connell then proceeds to describe Augustine's artful use of images in the service of creative imagination, which has also been noted by Kenneth Burke in *The Rhetoric of Religion*. [18]

Is there any resolution of the conflict between Augustine the aesthetician and Augustine the artist? If there is it occurs, I believe, in the context of the tension/resolution of love as *eros* and love as *agape* in Augustine's thought as a whole. [19] Augustine was painfully aware of the power of physically erotic love; he, like Plato, would come to see this as at best a poor image of that more basic desire for truth and beatitude that motivates the human soul in its ascent to the Good. Like Plato, and like the mystics, he used a plethora of erotic images to describe this ascent, embracing the feminine as both alluring and maternal. His own beatitude, however, came only when he experienced this upward striving of *eros* met by the unmerited outpouring of divine *agape* that he understood to be both gracing and graceful.

Wrestling with the implications of the sovereignty of divine love thus understood would lead him into complex discussions of freedom of the will and about the character of divine destination in temporal terms. In his social anthropology it would lead him to contrast the beatitude of the City of God with the mixed goods of the City of Man. As he reflected further on the mystery of the Incarnation he would come to speak of carnate beauty in more positive terms. It is not clear, however, that he ever finally resolved the dilemmas of Plotinus accommodated to Paul. O'Connell maintains that

the logic Augustine eventually discerned as originating beyond, but dis-
coverable *within*, the very texture of his life experience . . . is not the
logic of Greek necessitarianism, but something far closer to Aristotle's
hints at "the possible which is possible or necessary," the seemingly (and
even possibly) mere chance happening which, viewed under a different
light, intimates an air of design after all. For if it be credible that God
does not toss dice with His universe, it is equally clear that his dealings
with mankind are scarcely governed by a logic which is mathematical.
How grasp the profoundly interpersonal cast of God's logic in dealing
with His children? Again, I am suggesting, an incarnate aesthetic may
well furnish a most appropriate key.[20]

If there is not an unambiguously "incarnate aesthetic" in Augustine,
is there one in Thomas Aquinas, who explicitly drew on an interpretation of Aristotle rather than Plato for many of his major philosophical assumptions?

THOMAS AQUINAS (1225–1274 C.E.)

"It has been suggested," note Katherine Gilbert and Helmut Kuhn in
their *History of Esthetics*, "that St. Thomas is to Augustine as Aristotle is
to Plato. The implication is that both in Greece and the Middle Ages
the later thinker dealt with goodness and beauty for man, and not with
beauty and goodness in the abstract, and that the later thinkers were
more lenient toward the human hunger for recreation and the place of
art as food for the hunger."[21] Although this observation is accurate to
some extent, it overlooks the many concepts that Thomas shares with
Augustine, and it underplays both the modification of Platonic concepts in Augustine's thought and the modification of Aristotelian concepts in Thomas's thought. We have noted some of the former in Augustine's adaptation of Plotinus's Neoplatonism. Similarly, although
Thomas appropriated the principal terminology of Aristotle, whose
scientific works had only recently become available to Western Christendom, his employment of that terminology differed at crucial points
from its employment in the original Aristotelian corpus. While he devoted considerable labor to writing commentaries on many of the
newly translated works of Aristotle, he was soon opposed by philosophers who claimed that he was not thoroughly and comprehensively
Aristotelian, as well as by theologians who found his employment of
Aristotelian concepts dangerous for Christian thought that had made
its peace with Plato.

Like Aristotle, Thomas opposed the Platonists by maintaining that
forms exist in nature only as materialized. Matter is an essential ingredient of all that is in the created order. Specific instances of matter are

the material ingredients of individual substances, and "prime matter" is
the inexhaustible source of all the instances of specific materials embodied in individual substances. One of the "causes" of anything that
is, as we noted in our exposition of Aristotle above, is "material cause":
the "of what" anything is that is. Thus in "explaining" a work of art,
due attention must be paid to the necessity imposed by the material.
Furthermore, the material media of the senses are fundamental ingredients of cognition; Thomas, like Aristotle, is in this sense an empiricist. His worldview is *at least* "materialist," though not "materialistic."

But his worldview is also "formalist," though not "formalistic."
Form plays a crucial role in his understanding of all that is. "Aquinas'
favorite expression for a form," says Anthony Kenny, "is 'that by
which, or in virtue of which, a thing is what it is' (*id quod aliquid est*). A
substantial form is that in virtue of which a thing is the *kind* of thing it
is; that, indeed, in virtue of which it exists at all."[22] Although form
may be abstracted from its material embodiment for intellectual operations, it must first be present in that from which it is abstracted.
Therefore, "What makes Peter, James, and John three men and not a
single man is their matter, and not their form; but the matter, in individuating the substances, also individuates their substantial forms.
Aquinas would have regarded as unacceptable the Platonic notion that
Peter, James, and John are all men by sharing in a common form of
Humanity."[23]

When Kenny speaks of form as that "in *virtue* of which" anything is
what it is he calls to mind those who have drawn attention to the *active*
role of form, as forming or formation. ("Virtue," it should be noted,
derives from *virtus*, which is strength or power.) Kenny himself finds
difficulties in Thomas's sense of form as something a substance "has,"
transferred into a notion of form as something *having* or causing material embodiment. Many students of Aristotle, however, believe that
Thomas is warranted in understanding form as active agency. As such
it is indeed not the eternal "timeless," and thus "unchanging," forms of
the Platonic vision. It may, however, be assimilable to some extent to
the outpouring activity of the One in Plotinus, appropriated, with
modification, by Augustine.

Plato required the action of a *demiurgos* for the materialization of
forms. Aristotle, and Thomas, turned to the concept of action itself,
assimilating past, present, and future action into the notion of *potency*,
realizing potentiality in actuality. The real is actuality that was for-
merly potentiality. Some would see in this formulation an illegitimate
transfer of the logical notion of *possibility* into an ontological notion of
potentiality. It seems clear, in any case, that Thomas found a basis in
Aristotle's worldview for making the potentiality/actuality continuum

ontologically fundamental. In doing so he further appropriated Aristotle's sense of "cause" as including the "for what" anything is, that is, the end-in-actuality of any potentiality exhibited in anything that is to be explained. This is "final" cause, just as that which initiates a specific process of actualization is "efficient" cause. What is initiated are formations of materials progressing from potentiality to actuality.

The process, then, is one of ends and means. Aristotle, in the *Nicomachean Ethics*, had enunciated the principle of "the golden mean" as a guide to the moral life that embodies the four "cardinal virtues" of prudence, temperance, justice, and fortitude. The exercise of prudence is a "moral art"; as prudence is to moral "doing," suggests Jacques Maritain, "art" is to practical "making"; it is *technē* or know-how, "good judgment" or habitual skill, *habitus*. The "truth" of the artwork, therefore, lies in the perfection of the thing made. This, however, is first in the mind of the maker, in the artist's imaginative envisionment of the "form" to be materialized; hence art is declared, as it had been by Augustine, to be an "intellectual virtue."[24] Although there appears to be a directness of action—a coalescing of end and means—in the "making" of the artist, and although art does not—like prudence—require deliberation, still, Maritain maintains, "art seems to be nothing other than a certain ordination of reason, by which human acts reach a determined end through a determined means (*Posterior Analytic* lib I lect. 1, No. 1)."[25] The artist does not operate without rules, but he or she has so assimilated these rules through practice that their application seems direct and effortless.

The criteriological category for artistic excellence, as for all excellence, is beauty. Thomas, like Aristotle, Augustine, and Plato, does not employ the term "beauty" as applying exclusively to what would later be called "purely aesthetic" goods. With respect to all excellence, beauty is understood in terms of its *effects*, "that which, being seen, pleases" (*id quod visum placet*) (*Summa Theologia* I, 5, 4, ad. 1). Understood in terms of its *essence* it is characterized by the three elements enunciated by Aristotle: integrity, proportion, and clarity.

It is in the criterion of clarity, we suggest, that Thomas enunciates a concept assimilable to that of "splendor" consonant with the Biblical "glory." Clarity is that, says Maritain, which "makes a form shine on matter";[26] the beautiful is "shining form." The use of the imagery of light is consonant with its use in Augustine and Plotinus, and with Plato's use of the image of the sun casting shadows in the cave of imperfect knowledge, in the Eleventh Book of the *Republic*. It is also consonant with the use of the imagery of fire as volatile source of light in Biblical expressions of the divine glory. Is is the source of "the order of splendor in things." For Thomas the Christian theologian, its paradigmatic expression is the Fourth Gospel's "Light that enlightens everyone who comes into the world," the Light that shone in a darkness that was not able to extinguish it.

And Saint Thomas was first and foremost a Christian theologian. He turned to Aristotle as a guide to those truths that, he believed, may in principle be known by all humans through the light of natural reason. These include, he believed, the existence of God, the immortality of the soul, and the natural perfection of human being in life in accord with the four cardinal virtues. Some philosophers have questioned his understanding of Aristotelian science as he employed what he believed to be its basic assumptions in constructing his five theistic proofs. Others have questioned the intelligibility of his doctrine of the human soul as a "rational soul" incorporating the functions of "vegetative" and "animal" soul in a unity that persists after the death of the body, to be reunited with a "resurrected body." Still others have questioned the intelligibility of his conception of God as being in which form/matter, potentiality/actuality, and essence/existence distinctions are collapsed into One whose essence *is* existence, Pure Act. The theological thrust behind Thomas's monumental employment of Aristotelian terminology in the construction of what he believed to be a universally intelligible worldview stems, however, from his conviction that reason does not supplant faith and faith does not render reason unnecessary or dangerous. Faith completes, through revealed truth, what reason may establish in its God-given work. There is a harmonious synthesis of faith and reason.

Central to that synthesis is the Triune God of Christian faith. In his doctrine of the Trinity Thomas says that beauty is attributed most fittingly to the Son, who has integrity (perfection in Himself); proportion (as the "express image" of the Father); and radiance, because He is the Light that enlightens everyone who comes into the world. In Jesus as the Christ, the Son (the Word) became flesh. The significance of Creation itself is, as a modern theologian who incorporated both Thomistic and Heideggerian themes in his thought suggested,[27] to be understood in the light of that central datum. It is that Mystery which is expressed or re-presented in the Eucharist, Thomas believed. In his attempt to articulate or refract that Mystery in the language of Aristotelian metaphysics as he understood it, he said that in the Eucharist there is a transubstantiation of the substance of bread and the substance of wine into the Body and Blood of Christ, though the "accidents," the sensory perceptible qualities, remain those of bread and wine. Some philosophers who believe that they are more faithful to Aristotelian meanings find the concept of transubstantiation thus formulated unintelligible, whether "substance/accidents" is assimilated to "subject/predicates" constructions or simply affirmed as ontologically specific. To speak of continuing accidents whose substantial matrix has changed is, they feel, at best highly problematic. This, however, may miss the point of Thomas's principal concern as a Christian theologian, which was to delineate and celebrate the Christian vision as he understood it. And it is in this connection that Thomas the meticulous philosophical theologian on a few occasions became a poet.

Thomas Gilby O.P. maintains that although Thomas enunciated no formal poetics, and certainly no formal aesthetic theory in the modern sense, the concreteness and dynamism of the world as he construed it reflect "poetic experience."[28] The concreteness, I suggest, is that of Aristotelian empirical realism pressed into the service of Christian theology, and the dynamism of continuity derives from Thomas's understanding of Aristotelian science and ontology employed in the same service. In any event, it is fitting to conclude our brief exposition of aspects of Thomas's thought that relate the holiness of beauty to the beauty of holiness with a sample of the work of Thomas the poet, in a eucharistic hymn:

> Word made flesh, the bread he taketh,
> By his word his Flesh to be,
> Wine his sacred Blood he maketh,
> Though the senses fail to see,
> Faith alone the true heart waketh
> To behold the mystery.
> Therefore we, before him bending,
> This great Sacrament revere;
> Types and shadows have their ending,
> For the newer rite is here;
> Faith, our outward sense befriending,
> Makes our inward vision clear.[29]

We will see the theme of "types and shadows" elaborated by Jonathan Edwards. If the Word did become flesh, as those in the tradition celebrated by Thomas believe, both the heights and the depths of the created order are affirmed and illumined by that fact. The divine and the human realms are then not discontinuous; the universe is a "sacramental universe," and artists are engaged in sacramental celebration.

The viability of the Thomistic synthesis was soon to be challenged by a series of intellectual, religious, and cultural developments. The Aristotelian science that it had embraced in its understanding of nature would be challenged, and eventually deposed, by the emergence of more powerful tools of mathematical analysis and expression, on the one hand, and by increasing insistence on the importance of the observational ingredient in scientific inquiry, on the other. For both, there were powerful new instruments: analytical geometry and calculus for the one; telescopes, microscopes, and other observational devices for the other. Finally, with the appearance of Newton's *Principia* came a comprehensive challenge to teleological understandings of the universe.

Concurrently, the theological synthesis of faith and reason and of scripture and tradition was challenged by the Protestant affirmation of *sola fide, sola scriptura*, salvation by grace apprehended in faith guided by scripture. Whereas for Luther and Lutherans this would still permit affirmation of the divine glory manifested in the created order, and celebration of that glory in architecture, music, and narrative painting, for many Calvinists if not for Calvin himself fear of idolatry in the visual arts, or in all aesthetic pleasures in and for themselves, would radically qualify a sober and selective enjoyment of these goods.

Social realities were also changing. The rise of capitalism and nationalism, along with awareness of exotic "primitive" cultures in the New World, would challenge the feudal European culture to which medieval Christian moral theology and polity had been specifically addressed, and in whose terms moral and ecclesiastical precepts had been formulated. How, in the revolutionary world of eighteenth-century Western Christendom, were the relations of the holiness of beauty to the beauty of holiness to be conceived or reconceived? The life and thought of the American philosophical theologian Jonathan Edwards provide both a register of the new currents of thought and an impressive attempt to forge a philosophical theology that would do justice to the new science as well as to Reformation theology in the setting of the New World. In the process, he affirmed the holiness of beauty as both source and measure of the beauty of holiness.

JONATHAN EDWARDS (1703–1758)

Edwards was the heir of Plato as transmitted through the Cambridge Platonists More and Cudworth, tutors of many Puritan divines. But while he was reading Cudworth's *The True Intellectual System of the Universe* he also read John Locke's *Essay on Human Understanding*. And Locke had said that the purpose of his *Essay* was "to prepare the ground before the incomparable Mr. Newton." Edwards emerged from the experience a Platonic empiricist, committed to Newtonian cosmology as the vehicle for conceiving God's relation to the created order. At the same time he reasserted the Calvinistic proclamation of the sovereignty of God and divine glory and insisted on visible fruits of experiential religion.

Did Edwards develop a theory of aesthetics in his impressive synthesis of the old and the new? We have previously observed that "aesthetic" may refer primarily to a mode of apprehending the real, or primarily to a mode of articulating the real. Edwards's epistemology may be described as an "aesthetic realism" in the context of an empiricism based on a distinctive theory of experience. Certainly he sought to ground knowledge of the world and of God in experience. As Perry Miller notes in his Introduction to Edwards's *Images or Shadows of Divine Things*, "Although he is customarily represented as an arch-reactionary Calvinist, Edwards is properly to be described as the first American empiricist; yet from the beginning he recognized that empiricism meant a living relation between man and the world, not the dead schematic rationalism from which William James was later to attempt to rescue it. In this way of thinking, the image was no longer a detachable adornment on the surface of truth; it *was* the truth."[30]

Locke, as we shall see in the next chapter, distinguished between first-order sensory inscriptions on the *tabula rasa* of the mind, yielding knowledge of primary qualities, and second-order images, yielding knowledge of secondary qualities. Hume grounded all knowledge in "impressions," graded in terms of their "liveliness." Edwards, too, sought to ground knowledge in what he called "naked ideas." But these ideas are, he believed, apprehended through a faculty that other thinkers were to call imagination—a term Edwards reserved for what others (e.g., Coleridge) would call "fancy." And, like James in the future, he would insist that the *relations* between experiential data are as truly grounded ontologically as are the related data. Furthermore, Edwards would follow Hutcheson and other Scottish moralists in insisting that there is *moral* "sensibility" as well as cognitive sensation, and that it is equally vivid and foundational in human experience. Like his eighteenth-century contemporary Kant, Edwards saw the link between the cognitive world of sense perception and conceptual determination and the moral world of freedom to lie in the realm of feeling—or, as he put it, the *affections*. Like Hume, he saw sensory experience as characterized by degrees of "liveliness"; like his Platonic forebears he understood the freedom of the will to lie in its affective "inclinations" toward apparent or real good. And the heart of religious apprehension of the real, he affirmed, lies precisely in what Calvin had called "the sense of the heart" and Edwards called "the religious affections."

How could the religious affections ground both true knowledge of the world and true virtue? In answering this question Edwards utilized, as had Augustine, the resources of rhetoric, understood as the science of both spoken and written language. Christian exegetes had long made use of an elaborately developed system of the various "senses" of scripture, and Puritan divines were skilled in the homiletical employment of a system of "types" and "tropes" to relate the literature of the Hebrew Bible to what they affirmed to be its fulfillment in the events described in the literature of the New Covenant. Edwards made the daring and powerful move of employing the notion of types and tropes to portray the world of nature described in science as a world of "images or shadows of divine things." The images, however, were not to be deprecated or undervalued, and the shadows attested to the reality of the divine light. To understand the world in terms of Christian imagery was, in short, to understand the world as it really is, with empirical directness. "To Edwards," says Perry Miller, "his 'Images of Divine Things' was what the *Prelude* was to Wordsworth, a secret and sustained attempt to work out a new sense of the divinity of nature and the naturalness of divinity. He was obliged by the logic of his situation to undertake an investigation of the visible world as though no man had seen it before him."[31]

There would, however, be no Plotinian/Augustinian call for ascent *through* the images to the unalloyed real; the divine reality was to be experienced concretely, here and now, in an incomparable "sweetness" of affective "taste." Edwards would take seriously the Biblical injunction to "taste and see that the Lord is good"[32]—to taste and see the divine goodness directly in the created order described by Newton, and in the "amiableness" of moral inclination attuned to the divine will. Such experience, however, should not give rise to romantic poetic fantasies or the unbridled enthusiasms of the Pietists. Calvinistic sobriety best attested to the awesomeness of the divine glory reflected in both the splendors of the world and in splendid character. And the controlling term for conceptual expression of the divine sovereignty and glory was, for Edwards, not goodness or righteousness but beauty. His "aesthetic realism" in epistemology and ethics led naturally to the favored employment of an aesthetic term in speaking of the divine.

God, he said, is "primary beauty." As for Plato, primary beauty constitutes the standard and measure of all other, reflected and derived, beauties. But primary beauty is not static in its eternal realm. As for Plotinus and Augustine, it is eternally active (cf. Thomas's *actus purus?*) in bestowing being—and therefore truth, beauty, and goodness—on all that is not itself. Edwards characterized it as "Being's cordial consent to being." Its work, as the Septuagint translation of the first chapter of Genesis put it, is that of the kind of "making" which is "*poiesis.*" The divine *poiesis*, however, creates all from nothing.

The world created by the divine *poiesis* exhibits "secondary beauty." Like the Platonists, Edwards saw the marks of this in *ratio*, in proportion and harmony: the harmonious whole of the natural order and of its parts to each other, and approximations of the social harmony of the City of God in the true communities of God's people in the world—a harmony for which Edwards the preacher and pastor labored mightily in a New World that, some thought, might become the New Jerusalem. Perception of these "secondary beauties" is open to the "natural sensibility" of humans created in the image of God—that natural sensibility that grounds scientific as well as moral and aesthetic apprehensions of the real.

Perception of the primary beauty that is God, however, requires "spiritual sensibility." Only through spiritual sensibility can one perceive what may be termed "the supernatural in the natural." And this spiritual sensibility cannot be achieved as a human work extending the limits of "natural sensibility." It can occur only as the free gift of God—as the work of grace. The Christian gospel, Edwards believed, is the proclamation of the effectual work of that grace. The sovereignty of God, then, is manifested in the secondary beauty of the created order. It is, however, chiefly manifested in the work of grace that facilitates perception of that primary beauty that places the secondary beauty of the world in authentic perspective. It does not facilitate a "flight of the alone to the Alone" or engender the ascent of mystic vision. It engenders works of prudence and charity in the world, by humans whose "chief end is to glorify God and enjoy Him forever."

Is there, then, an aesthetic theory in Edwards's work? No, not in the sense that would characterize such theory in the thought of other eighteenth- and nineteenth-century philosophers, to which we will turn in the next chapter. Edwards did not analyze the qualities of what would be called "aesthetic pleasure" as such or delineate the "moments" of aesthetic judgment. Baumgarten, in 1750, coined the term "aesthetics" and Kant, in 1790, delineated the "moments" of aesthetic judgment. As for what would later be called uniquely "aesthetic" media, Edwards said little about the visual arts—consonant, perhaps, with his Calvinism and the cultural resources of Western Massachusetts in the eighteenth century.[33] He did, though, enjoy and commend music—not, however, for its exhibition of numerical harmony, à la Augustine, but for its hymnodic use in praising God. Hymns also embodied poetry, and Edwards praised poetry employed in the service of God. Milton, naturally, was a favorite.

But it was from the beauties of nature that Edwards perhaps derived the greatest degree of what could be called aesthetic pleasure. His *Images or Shadows* continued a lifelong practice of describing in writing the beauties of nature—beginning with a description of the beauties of a spider when he was twelve years old. That use of "imagery" is far more revealing of Edwards's aesthetic theology than is his much-quoted sermon, "Sinners in the Hands of An Angry God," depicting a spider held over flames of fire. Edwards was, however, a powerful preacher. Like Augustine's Ambrose, he was a master of at least one art—homiletics. And homiletics may utilize all the literary arts, along with the spoken cadences of rhetoric. Edwards the preacher, philosopher, and theologian both brought together in his life and thought many of the intellectual, religious, and cultural developments of the eighteenth century and anticipated many others that would receive more extensive and systematic treatment by some seminal thinkers to whom we will turn in the next chapter.

I have included Edwards's ideas among the classical Western formulations of the relation of the holiness of beauty to the beauty of holiness because he, like the other thinkers whose views I have described in this chapter, could assimilate the logic of scientific cognition to the logic of rhetorical persuasion. Others in the eighteenth century believed that the Newtonian science Edwards admired had quite different implications. In the next chapter we will see what these implications were thought to be, and how systematic reflection on them led to sharper distinctions between apprehensions of reality based on controlled observation, quantitatively expressed, and apprehensions rooted in feeling or volition, expressed in more complex imagery or nonverbally. Critical reflection on these distinctions led to critical philosophy and to the emergence of theories of aesthetics and religion.

CHAPTER TWO

The Emergence of Aesthetics and
Religion in Western Thought

WE HAVE SEEN that Jonathan Edwards exemplified a classical response to some of the currents of thought of the eighteenth century in his celebration of both beauty and holiness. The forms of art that he prized most were literature, rhetoric, and music. Yet Alasdair MacIntyre has pointed out that when, in the musical culture of the Enlightenment, "the Catholic Mass becomes a genre available for concert performances by Protestants, when we listen to the scripture because of what Bach wrote rather than because of what St. Matthew wrote, then sacred texts are being preserved in a form in which the traditional links with belief have been broken, even in some measure for those who count themselves believers . . . . a traditional distinction between the religious and the aesthetic has been blurred."[1] MacIntyre is correct in his perception of the relation of the aesthetic to the religious in the Enlightenment, but he is wrong in saying that it was in this cultural milieu that "the traditional distinction between the religious and the aesthetic was blurred." On the contrary, it was in this period that the distinction between the aesthetic and the religious was first formalized in aesthetic theory and in theories of religion.

Many factors were at work in the emergence of this distinction. The discovery of the New World of the Americas and the rediscovery of older cultures of Asia engendered a critical awareness of distinctive features of the "Western" culture of "Christendom." For Montaigne in the sixteenth century this growing awareness of other cultures and other ways of life would lead to a moderate humanism that retained a cultural place for Christian orthodoxy.[2] For Leibniz and, later, Hume, it would engender a search for "natural religion" in all cultures, with a concomitant universal concept of "religion" as such.[3] At the same time, aesthetic judgments would be assigned to the domain of "taste," and the question would be raised whether there is a *sensus communis* underlying all such judgments. Pursuit of these questions contributed to the emergence of a concept of religion as a specific dimension or component of life and thought, with a distinctive referent (God, the divine, the holy), and of aesthetics as critical reflection on judgments of taste in relation to a distinctively aesthetic category, beauty. At the same time, the social revolution occasioned by the rise of capitalism and nationalism called into question the traditional moral sanctions of Christianity and precipitated a quest for a social science of the good society. The achievements of mathematical theory combined with refined observational techniques to forge powerful new tools of scientific inquiry that generated a new cosmology. New times, it was said, called for a "new science," and the new science called for a rethinking and revision of the traditional structures and categories of philosophy and theology.

But there were two visions of what the new science should be. One was articulated by Giambattista Vico in his work called *The New Science* (*Scienza Nuova*); the other was articulated in the seventeenth century by Francis Bacon in *The New Organon* and developed in the eighteenth century by Issac Newton, John Locke, and David Hume, among others. Both visions reflected a sea change in sensibility that Michel Foucault has described in these words:

> When the *Logique de Port Royal* states that a sign can be inherent in what it designates *or* separate from it, it is demonstrating that the sign, in the Classical Age [Foucault's term for the period under discussion] is no longer charged with the task of keeping the world close to itself and inherent in its own forms, but, on the contrary, that of spreading it out, or juxtaposing it over an indefinitely open surface, and of taking up from that point the endless deployment of substitutes in which we conceive of it. And it is by this means that it is offered simultaneously to analysis and combination, and can be ordered from beginning to end. . . . It is the sign that enables things to become distinct, to preserve themselves within their own identities, to dissociate themselves or bind themselves together. Western reason is entering the age of judgment.[4]

Edwards's "images and shadows of divine things" would no longer be perceptible in a scientific description of the world, which would necessarily be limited to phenomena that could be expressed mathematically. And Immanuel Kant would see that the character of judgment would be the central issue in any philosophical system that would come to grips reasonably with the procedures and implications of the new science. "The age of judgment" emerged, Foucault contends,

> when activity of mind . . . will no longer consist of *drawing things together*, in setting out on a quest for everything that might reveal some sort of kinship, attraction, or secretly shared nature with them, but in . . . *discriminating*, that is, in establishing their identities, then the inevitability of

the connections with all the successive degrees of a series. In this sense, discrimination imposes on comparison the primary and fundamental investigation of differences, providing oneself by intuition with a direct representation of things, and apprehending clearly the inevitable connection between one element in a series and that which immediately follows it. . . . On the one hand there will be erudition, the perusal of written works, the interplay of their authors' opinions. . . . Over against this history, and lacking any common unit of measurement with it, are the confident judgments we are able to make by means of intuitions and their serial connection.[5]

What was being left out in all this? Foucault maintains that on the borders of, and in a sense underlying, the new grids of identity and difference there remain vast areas of "The Same of The Other" that were to be articulated by madmen and poets (but not in the manner of the "divine madness" of Plato's poets). Don Quixote appears as "the negative of the Renaissance." "At the other end of the cultural arena, but brought close by sympathy, the poet is he who, beneath the named, constantly stated differences, discovers the buried kinship between things, their scattered resemblances. . . . [I]n the language of the poet, the Sovereignty of The Same, so difficult to express, eclipsed the distinctions between signs."[6]

The artistry of words (and of colors and of sounds and so on) thus becomes an alternative to—or a complement of—the precisions of mathematically expressed science. It was this artistry, traditionally embraced in the notion of "rhetoric," that Vico would place at the center of his expanded vision of *The New Science*. In the process he saw the analysis of past cultures as propadeutic to the analysis of contemporary cultures. Such analysis brings to light what he termed the *sensus communis*, the network of traditional values embedded in language and culture that humans inhabit by virtue of being human. Effective study of cultures past or present, he thought, should begin with religion and myth. The tradition of humanist rhetoric, he believed, exposes the religious roots of language and shows how eloquence both maintains and advances culture. Rhetoric, as Michael Mooney expressed it in the title of his Columbia doctoral dissertation on Vico, is *Wisdom Speaking*.[7] Donald P. Verene, in *Vico's Science of the Imagination*,[8] highlights the role of "imaginative universals" in Vico's work and maintains that these "begin with the holy, and then permeate language with a non-rational element." Verene, says John D. Schaeffer in his succinct review of the volume, "shows how religious experience is for Vico the *archē* of both language and culture. The non-rational element operates through persuasion, and as culture develops persuasion becomes objectified in rhetoric. . . . For Vico rhetoric means 'first philosophy.' "[9] Mooney goes further and attributes to Vico insights that were later developed by Weber, Marx, and other pioneers of sociology. These insights include the recognition that "society is a structure of sentiment and thought as well as a cluster of rites and forms, and that its gods and heroes, its customs and laws, its words and its sciences depend for their plausibility as much on the common and collective sense of the people as on the refined ideas of intellectuals."[10] We shall note the employment of some of these insights in contemporary social-scientific study of aesthetics and religion in the next chapter.

Meanwhile, we must consider the contrast between Vico's notion of the New Science, drawing on the tradition of rhetoric, and that of Bacon and his followers. Wilbur Samuel Howell has pointed out that issues posed by the transition from rhetoric to logic, and a specific understanding of the nature and role of the latter, were among the chief factors that gave rise to formally articulated theories of aesthetics and religion in the eighteenth century. Traditional logic, says Howell,

> had taught the methods of deductive analysis, had perfected itself in the machinery of testing propositions for consistency, and had served at the same time as the instrument by which truths could be arranged so as to become intelligible and convincing to other learned men. In short, traditional logic prided itself upon being a theory of learned enquiry and learned communication. Meanwhile, traditional rhetoric also prided itself upon having a share in these two same offices, its special purpose being to communicate truths through a process which, on the one hand, blended scientific conclusions with popular opinions and manners, and, on the other hand, transmitted the blend to the general public. The new science, as envisioned by its founder, Francis Bacon, considered its function to be that of subjecting physical and human facts to observation and experiment. . . . And logic, which had always claimed to be the theory of enquiry, began to incorporate the new methods in its doctrines and ended by becoming so enamored of them that it allowed them to crowd out the waning interest in the methods of learned communication. Meanwhile rhetoric began to see itself as the rightful claimant to the methods of learned communication and as the still unrivaled master of the arts of public discourse; and, by making these two activities its new concern, it came ultimately to think of itself as the art which governed all forms of verbal expression, whether popular or learned, persuasive or didactic, utilitarian or aesthetic.[11]

If rhetoric succeeded to the traditional tasks of logic with respect to the communication, as contrasted with the investigation, of truth, what discipline emerged to attempt a similar office with respect to nonverbal apprehension and articulation of the real? It was in 1750 that Alexander Gottlieb Baumgarten (1714–1762) coined the term "aesthetics" for this enterprise, though he still meant by that term sensuous as contrasted with nonsensuous knowledge. [12] It remained for Immanuel Kant to incorporate philosophical aesthetics as an integral—I would say fundamental—part of a philosophical system, and then to find in analysis of that form of *feeling* that may be designated "aesthetic apprehension" the clue to the nature of judgment itself.

DAVID HUME (1711–1776)

It was the writings of David Hume, said Kant, that "stirred him from his dogmatic slumbers." Hume, in turn, had carried the Lockean enterprise to what he believed to be its logical conclusion. He had resolutely restricted knowledge-claims to assertions clearly induced from "impressions"—primarily sensory, but including other transactions with the world experienced with singular "liveliness"—and "ideas" directly traceable to them. On this ground he could assign only varying degrees of probability to statements of matters of fact, expressed in contingent propositions. Necessary or analytic propositions obtained only in the realm of mathematics; only in that realm was demonstrable knowledge possible. In the famous conclusion of his *Enquiry Concerning Human Understanding* Hume said that

> the only objects of the abstract or demonstrable sciences are quantity and number, and that all attempts to extend this most perfect species of knowledge beyond these bounds are mere sophistry and illusion. As the component parts of quantity and number are entirely similar, their relations become intricate and involved; and nothing can be more curious, as well as useful, then to trace, by a variety of mediums, their equality or inequality, through their different appearances. But as all other ideas are clearly distinct and different from each other, we can never advance farther, by our utmost scrutiny, than to observe this diversity, and, by an obvious reflection, pronounce one thing not to be another. Or if there be any difficulty in these decisions, it proceeds entirely from the undeterminate meaning of words, which is corrected by juster definitions. . . . All other enquiries of men regard only matters of fact and existence, and these are evidently incapable of demonstration. Whatever *is* may *not be.* No negation of a fact can involve a contradiction. . . . The existence, therefore, of any being can only be proved by argument from its cause or its effect, and these arguments are founded entirely on experience. [13]

Here Hume is employing a concept that would be germane to all future discussions of aesthetics and religion: the concept of *experience.* The parameters of that discussion, as we shall see, would be largely determined by the theory of experience entailed by or assumed by participants in the discussion. For Hume experience is "the foundation of moral (probable) reasoning, which forms the greater part of human knowledge, and is the source of all human action and behavior. Moral (probable) reasonings are either concerning particular or general facts. All deliberations in life regard the former; as also all disputations in history, chronology, geography, and astronomy."[14]

At this point Hume introduces additional concepts that would be fundamental in the development of aesthetic theory: those of *sentiment* and *taste*. And a concept of taste, as we shall see, will prove to be fundamental in many future discussions of aesthetics and religion. "Morals and criticism," Hume says, "are not so properly objects of understanding as of taste and sentiment. *Beauty, whether moral or natural, is felt*, more properly than perceived. Or if we reason concerning it, and endeavor to fix its standard, we regard a new fact, to wit, the general taste of mankind, or some such fact, which may be the object of reasoning and enquiry."[15] Thus, he concludes, "When we run over our libraries, persuaded of these principles, what havoc must we make? If we take in hand any volume, of divinity or school metaphysics, for instance, let us ask: *Does it contain any abstract reasoning concerning quantity or number?* No. *Does it contain any experimental reasoning concerning matters of fact and existence?* No. Commit it then to the flames: For it can contain nothing but sophistry and illusion."[16] It would appear that the foundations of classical expressions of the relation of the holiness of beauty to the beauty of holiness were undermined by the currents of thought that were powerfully articulated in the paradigmatic work of Hume.

Hume had found, however, that certain foundations of "experimental reasoning" remained mysterious, within the context of his theory of experience and his epistemological strictures. Having reduced causality to sequentiality or what Aristotle called "efficient cause," he could account for its force only on the basis of "habit" or "custom." As John Herman Randall, Jr., once remarked, "If habit is second-nature, for Hume nature is first-habit." And, if "moral reasoning" is applied to the arena of human concern called "morals," then another kind of "sensibility" or "moral sentiment" must be a component of "experience" and be at work in the experiential/experimental-deliberative process. More significant for our inquiry is his statement that if beauty is "felt, more properly than perceived," then if we "reason concerning it" we encounter what are at least new "facts" called by the names "taste" and "sentiment." If taste is rooted in sentiment (what others would call "feeling"), then "good taste," said Hume in his essay "Of The Standard of Taste,"[17] must be based on "sound" analyses of "exact and clear" or "clear and distinct" instances of sentiment. Can such instances of *sentiment* form the materials of *judgment?* If they cannot, how can there be a "standard of taste"?

"There is a species of philosophy," says Hume,

> which represents the impossibility of ever attaining any exact standard of taste. The difference, it is said, is wide between judgment and sentiment. All sentiment is right; because sentiment has reference to nothing beyond itself, and is always real, whenever a man is conscious of it. But all deter-minations of understanding [the locus of judgment] are not right, because they all have references to something beyond themselves, to wit, real matters of fact, and are not always comfortable to that standard. Among a thousand different opinions men may entertain there is one, and but one, that is just and true, and the great difficulty is to fix and ascertain it. [18]

Where, then, may we turn for something analogous to a cognitive standard of *truth* in an aesthetic standard of *taste?* Hume's answer to this question suggests, I believe, the appeal to a prospective qualified so-cial judgment and confirmation that would later be incorporated in the philosophy of C. S. Peirce and in the work of some contemporary thinkers whose views we will examine in our discussion of issues of objectivity and subjectivity, or of "foundationalism and relativism," in art and religion, in Chapter Seven. For Hume the appeal is to an "ideal observer" or qualified judge.

There are, says Hume, five qualifications that should characterize such a judge. (1) He must be possessed of sound *understanding*, even though taste is rooted not in understanding but in sentiment. Such understanding or intelligence is required if the judge is to comprehend the purpose of the work judged and to perceive the consistency and uniformity of the whole. Such understanding or intelligence also aids in (2) minimizing the effect of prejudice on one's views—prejudice stemming from personal friendships, animosities, envy, self-interest, political views, and so forth. In addition to sound understanding, how-ever, there must be in matters of the affections what Hume termed (3) "delicacy of the imagination," or discriminating perception. This is re-quired for proper discrimination of all the ingredients in the work judged. "Delicacy of imagination" or discriminating perception (notice the interplay of sensory and affective elements here—as also in later talk of "sense and sensibility") may be further enhanced through (4) *practice.* "Nothing tends further to increase and improve [a person's 'delicacy of imagination']," says Hume, than "practice in a particular art, and the frequent survey or contemplation of a particular species of beauty." [19] Finally, the development of good judgment in matters of taste requires (5) constant *comparison* of a work with others in its genre and in other genres. Here Hume has articulated issues involved in comparative analysis, and in the assessment of the relation of theory to practice, that are at the center of contemporary discussion of the topic of this book.

All this, we may find ourselves saying in dialogue with Hume, is well and good with respect to general qualifications of good judges in general, but how are we to tell whether a specific individual is endowed with them in particular? Who is to say who is a good judge, and how? Well, said Hume, we must put forward the best arguments available to us in debating the question, keeping in mind the fact that there may be universal agreement about one matter—namely, matters of fact. We must also be charitable toward those who offer differing opinions. And, as a matter of *fact*, he claims, there does seem to be universal agreement about some exemplars of good taste, perhaps expressing a universal *sentiment*.[20]

In any case, says Hume—and a similar claim is crucial in subsequent discussions of art and religion, or of beauty and holiness—the general principles of taste reveal a certain uniformity of human nature.[21] Is there such a thing as "human nature"? If so, does it exhibit "uniformities"? Are they designated by such terms as *homo sapiens, homo ludens*, or *homo religiosus*? Are these uniform in the same sense as the uniformities of nonhuman nature? Are the assertions that there are such uniformities demonstrable? Or are they nondemonstrable assertions that nevertheless have logical entailments—that is, are they *principles*? What is *in principio*? Or is there nothing *in principio*—"no foundations, all the way down"? To this question also we will return in Chapter Seven.

Meanwhile we should note that even as Hume was defining issues that would be fundamental for future discussions of aesthetics, he was also employing concepts that would be fundamental in future discussions of religion. He was convinced that there is such a thing as "natural religion" inherent in "human nature" in all places and all times. This religion is characterized primarily by certain beliefs: in a supreme being, in moral law, and in a human destiny beyond death. Leibniz thought that it is clearly exemplified in the religious tradition of China. Hume added to the concept of natural religion the idea that just as there is a "natural history" of the components of nonhuman nature, so there might be a "natural history of religion" that would trace and classify the various types of religious belief and practice. Hume thought that this history reveals primarily the varieties of "superstition" and the baleful consequences for morality of the "warring of superstitions." His execution of the enterprise of the history of religion exhibits many assumptions and protocols of later endeavors in this field. A basic assumption is that whatever else religion may be, it is at least an expression of something universally human, and that this expression may be traced and classified in accord with what are believed to be the protocols of all historical inquiry. Another assumption is that there are rational criteria in terms of which one can judge the characteristics of "developed" or "undeveloped," "primitive" or "advanced" religions—can distinguish between "true religion" and "superstition"—and/or that there are moral criteria in terms of which one can appraise the moral worth of various religious traditions.

In Hume's most celebrated work on "natural religion," *Dialogues Concerning Natural Religion*, he subjects the claims of what he takes to be orthodox Christian belief to the test of his epistemological canons described above. The traditional "proofs of the existence of God" are found wanting, with the possible exception of the "teleological" argument for design in cosmology—and this with careful strictures with reference to any other religious claims that might be made in its name. The "conclusion" of the dialogues, however, is ambiguous and has been the subject of endless debate. On the surface it appears that Philo, the character in the dialogue who is most frequently taken to be the spokesman for Hume's views, asserts that philosophical skepticism is in fact a prerequisite of mature religious faith. This could lead to further exploration of the phenomenological character of "faith," and this lead has been followed by many later philosophers of religion. With Hume, however, it is never entirely clear just where his tongue is in relation to his cheek.

IMMANUEL KANT (1724–1804)

There is less doubt as to where Immanuel Kant stands on most of the major issues raised by Hume in Hume's discussion of matters of taste and of faith. When he was "aroused from his dogmatic slumbers" by the writings of Hume, Kant said, he was driven to ask three fundamental questions: What can I know? What ought I to do? For what may I hope? There are, I believe, two constants in Kant's pursuit of answers to these questions: imagination and judgment. Kant exhibited to a remarkable degree some aspects of what Hume termed "delicacy of imagination." He also saw that crucial to the successful pursuit of these questions is a sound theory of judgment.

In *The Critique of Pure Reason* Kant agrees with Hume that all knowledge is occasioned by sensory transactions with the appearances of things, and that these phenomena are all that are knowable. Of noumena, or "things in themselves," we have no critical knowledge. The initiating work of imagination is "intuition," or bare sensation. Sensory intuitions, however, present themselves immediately as *manifold*, through the "forms" of space and time. The latter Kant thought to be the "inner," the former the "outer" dimensions of the manifold. Out of this manifold, memory—the work of the inner sense—constitutes reproductive imagination, whose images are schematized in the "categories of the understanding": quantity, quality, relation, and modality. These categories yield determinate concepts, articulated in propositions, analytic or synthetic.

In all this work the power of judgment is central. Kant agrees with Locke that judgment *is* a "power" (*Urteilskraft*). It is the shaper and arbiter of imagination in all its works— perhaps even in the fundamental work of "intuition." (Would Kant agree with Wittgenstein that in a sense there must be "agreement in judgments" if *any* meaningful discourse is to occur?) "The significant and prominent place that Kant allots to judgment," notes Ernst Cassirer, "is of necessity rooted in the initial presupposition of his way of putting the problem. Judgment is the natural, factually demanded correlate of the object, since it expresses in the most general sense consummation of and demand for that combination to which the concept of the object has reduced us. The type and forms of synthetic unity are precisely what yield the forms of judgment."[22]

All the work of the understanding, however, is carried out in the context of "the transcendental unity of apperception," or self-world consciousness. Recognition of the interplay between self and world is as far as the "faculty" of understanding can take us—all we can know in a sense warranted by the new science of the eighteenth century as Kant understood it. The concepts of "self" (or soul) and "world" are themselves, however, "transcendental ideas" or ideals. We can never experience self or "I" as such; we experience only, as Hume had shown, a serialized manifold of data that constitute "me." Similarly, we never experience the world as a whole; we experience only those aspects of the world that present themselves through sensation and understanding for judgment. The notion of "the whole" is also a transcendental idea: it represents no object of knowledge but rather an ideal employed in the enterprise of inquiry, demanded by "reason" for the work of "understanding." Finally, reason also posits a grounding of self and world in a unified source of subjectivity and objectivity, or God. The traditional "proofs of the *existence* of God," however, are invalid, Kant thought. They all rest on the assumption that existence is a predicate; Hume and others had shown that this cannot be the case.

When we turn, however, from the data of "nature" (what can be scientifically *known*—note the methodological criterion of ontological status for nature) to the irreducible datum of "freedom," there is, Kant claimed in *The Critique of Practical Reason*, direct experience of the noumenal, because in the experience of freedom we *are* "the thing-itself":

persons. The experience of persons as moral agents is the immediate and irreducible experience of the incorrigible "dignity" or "itselfness" of freedom in personhood. When we proceed with the analyses and syntheses of "pure practical reason," the rationale of the *praxis* of persons, we discover the "categorical imperative": never to make an exception of self to the demand of moral law. We experience the freedom of self-imposed law.

Exploration of the demands of the life of practice, however, reveal "antinomies" of pure practical reason comparable to those of pure reason when the latter passes beyond the bounds of "understanding" or knowledge. How, for instance, is the necessary disinterestedness of moral virtue to be related to the quest for happiness, which is also a legitimate component of the *summum bonum?* A rational answer to this question, Kant believed, demands the postulation of freedom adjudicated by God in immortality, where worth and happiness are correlated. The fundamental "argument for the existence of God," Kant maintained, is the *moral* argument. God is a necessary postulate of pure practical reason. Religion, then, consists in "treating all duties as divine commands." In making this claim Kant was enunciating a basic presupposition of many subsequent theories of religion "within the limits of reason alone."

But what is the essential character of judgment itself, whether it be employed in the cognitive determinations of the First Critique or in the moral judgments of the Second Critique? For an answer to this question Kant turned to what Hume and many others would have deemed an unlikely domain: the domain of feeling and taste. Judgment, as analyzed in the Critique that bears that name, is neither essentially cognitive nor essentially practical. Pure judgment as such is exemplified in aesthetic judgment. Here it is expressive, not of the manifold of sensation, or the work of the understanding, or of moral determinations, but of feeling of pleasure or displeasure—roughly, Hume's "sentiment." (We should remember that "feeling," "pleasure and displeasure," or "pain" have, in the Kantian context, much richer meanings than they are likely to suggest in contemporary parlance. We shall emphasize this point again when we turn to later theories of religion that root religion in "feelings" of particular sorts.)

The controlling aesthetic category, beauty, is experienced when the free play of productive imagination and understanding—*"without a concept"*—articulated in aesthetic form results in a delight in ordering, produced by nature or by the creative artist (for Kant, the "genius") and enjoyed by persons of aesthetic sensibility and informed taste. As we shall see, Kant assumed that aesthetic sensibility is a universally human ingredient of a *sensus communis.* And although he agrees with

Hume that there are no *principles* of taste, in the sense of non-warrantable assertions with logical entailments, Kant claims there are nevertheless valid *judgments* of taste. How can this be?

Following the schema of the categories of the understanding—which are the correlates of the forms of judgment in traditional logic—Kant asserts that, with respect to quality, the aesthetic experience of beauty is an experience of *disinterested* pleasure. It is nonutilitarian. As such it is also, Kant says, an "emblem" of that disinterestedness that characterizes moral virtue in relation to "the good." With respect to quantity, it is singular, but of universal import. It thus exemplifies the universality of prima-facie contingent propositions that Kant attempted to analyze under the rubric "synthetic *a prioris*" in the First Critique. With respect to relation, the experience of beauty bespeaks a "purposiveness without purpose"—a non-utilitarian "fitness." This provided the basis for Kant's subsequent analysis of "teleological judgment." And this, in turn, provided ground for the acceptance of scientific description as congruent with the structure of the world. Science makes sense, Kant says, if we understand nature as imitating art.

With respect to modality, aesthetic judgment is "private" or subjective, yet it inherently appeals to a *sensus communis*. It simply makes no sense to say—it is not faithful to aesthetic experience and judgment to say—"this appears only to me, or to another person, to be beautiful." No, it is simply and without qualification judged to be beautiful. We should note that Kant is not here making a claim whose validity could be confirmed or disconfirmed in a cosmic Gallup Poll, or in a survey of what Hume called "the facts" of empirically ascertainable instances of judgments of taste. He is, he believes, simply analyzing faithfully the character of authentic aesthetic judgment. In Chapter Six we will see how Kant's view of aesthetic judgment, as interpreted by a contemporary scholar, might shed light on the nature of religious judgment. [23] But first let us note Kant's analysis of what he took to be an aesthetic category distinct from that of beauty—namely, the category of the sublime. This analysis, we shall see, was to have far-reaching effects in some later theories of religion.

There was widespread interest in the notion of the sublime in the eighteenth and nineteenth centuries. [24] The concept originated in the domain of rhetoric and was attributed to Longinus (early first century C.E.). In this context it designated discourse of unusual power. In the eighteenth century its use was extended to certain kinds of experience of nature or of human exigency and was expressed in such terms as "awe" or "wonder." "Two things fill my soul with awe and wonder," said Kant, "the starry heavens above, and the moral law within." Kant's contemporary Burke and others had sought to designate a physiological source of feelings of the sublime, associating the peculiar "pleasure" it seems to embody with a feeling of safety in otherwise fearful situations—as in beholding the majesty of a mountain or the terror of an abyss. Kant eschewed the reduction of the experience of the sublime to empirically ascertainable pleasures and pains translated into securities and fears. He saw the experience of the sublime as a generic form of aesthetic experience, irreducible to explanation in terms of forms of non-aesthetic experience.

How, then, does the experience of the sublime differ from the experience of beauty? For Kant the sublime, experienced as either "mathematical" (the "sense of the infinite"—a "sense" to be employed in later influential theories of religion) or "dynamic" (awesome overpoweringness), appears to be the antithesis of beauty. Where beauty is formal, limited, and related to discursive—even playful—understanding, encouraging the furtherance of life, the sublime appears formless and wild; it arrests life and "performs an outrage on the imagination."[25] It "forces us to abandon our merely empirical sensibility and draws us to a higher realm."[26] It seems to be a conduit of "the supersensible." For Kant, however, the experience of the sublime is not mystical intuition. As F. X. J. Coleman observes, in discussing Kant, "Man is not possessed of any privileged access to what might lie beyond the world of appearances. Kant never wavers on this point."[27] Yet the experience of the sublime is not "mere feeling," totally noncognitive. Its import is both moral and cognitive. "Moral knowledge is presupposed by feelings of the sublime, as opposed to outbursts of enthusiasm or swoonings. Just as the feeling of *achtung*, or moral respect [reverence?] logically follows from the thought of the moral law, so the feelings of the sublime follow from certain cognitive states."[28] Awe and wonder, Kant had said, characterize both the experience of "the moral law within" and the experience of "the starry heavens above." But the experience of awe and wonder does not provide privileged access to the supersensible. The experience of the sublime attests, not to the "glory of God," but to the dignity of humans, whose power of reason can posit that which imagination cannot encompass. Iris Murdoch says that Kant's theory of the sublime "ought to be Kant's theory of tragedy."[29]

In any case, Kant would not identify the experience of the sublime as a uniquely "religious experience" providing access to the divine. For him such access was a correlate of the postulates of practical reason. At only one other place in his *Critique of Judgment* does he suggest a notion that might have been developed into an aesthetic bridge to the divine. That is the notion of what he called "aesthetic *ideas*," which, he suggests, seem to embody both a conceptual and a nonconceptual function. But Kant did not develop this possibility. It remained for others to follow such a lead and to claim that the experience of the sublime is analogous to, if not identical with, the experience of the holy. We shall trace some of these developments later in this chapter and in the following chapter.

THE EMERGENCE OF ART HISTORY

First, as we pursue the dialogue between aesthetics and religion we note the fact that the same eighteenth-century sensibility that led Hume and others to conceive a "natural history of religion" led others, principally in Germany, to conceive a "history of art"—a historical account of another distinctive human phenomenon. In this process the emphasis was at times on the aesthetic as primarily a unique *mode of apprehension of the real;* at others, on the aesthetic as a unique *mode of articulation of the real.* We shall see these varying though complementary emphases expressed also in some major theories of art and religion to which we will turn in the latter part of this chapter and in the next chapter. In all these enterprises recognition of the importance of "the new science," in both Vico's sense of this term and Bacon's, played a central role.

J. J. Winkelmann typifies the developments that would lead to the formulation of a scholarly enterprise called art history. Like Bacon, he insisted on the importance of direct contact with the data to be described and interpreted; like Vico he saw human culture as amenable to a narrative account organized around "periods" and degrees of complexity, with certain periods as exemplary if not normative for understanding the narrative as a whole.

"It may seem strange," says Bernard Bosanquet, "to set the name of Winkelmann beside that of Bacon. But no one can read the constant diatribes of the former against mere 'book-learning,' or against the work of 'scribes,' in comparison with the knowledge of the educated eye, without feeling their motive to be fundamentally the same as that of Bacon, the eagerness for contact with reality at first hand."[30] For Bacon that reality was nature, principally nonhuman; for Winkelmann it was the concrete reality of works of art that expressed the highest achievements of human nature. In the eighteenth century explorers and archeologists brought to light a wide range of data from ancient, Middle Eastern, and Far Eastern cultures. Lord Elgin brought marbles from the Parthenon; excavations of Herculaneum and Pompeii presented fresh data from a classical past; work in Egypt would initiate a new understanding of ancient Egyptian culture. Eventually Schliemann would set out to discover the Troy of Homer. These were among the data to which art historians should attend in firsthand observation, said those who wished to follow Winkelmann's lead. The conviction remained, however, that all these data should be interpreted in a narrative history employing a specific developmental scheme for its framework. These assumptions were at work in both the emerging discipline of the history of art and the emerging discipline of the history of religion.

Consequent upon the recognition by Winkelmann of the importance of firsthand acquaintance with the data of cultural artifacts, writes Bosanquet,

> is the conception of art as something that has a history and phases of its own—a growth and decline—corresponding to and rooted in the history and condition of peoples. Let us take for example his conception of history as ἰστορία, a research and a system, not a chronicle. "The history of Art aims at expounding its origin, growth, change, and fall, together with the diverse styles of peoples, ages, and artists, and at demonstrating this, as far as possible, from the extant works of antiquity." This attempt to trace a development extending through long ages in its essential causes and connection was, he affirmed, a new thing in the literature of art. [31]

If Hume could propose an evolutionary "natural" history of religion, Winkelmann could propose that the "earliest" works of art are formless and minimally distinct—like seeds of different plants! Against the background of this assumption he would see Greek art as an independent development, not borrowed from Oriental or "primitive" forms. Then, significantly, he suggests that this distinctiveness may be understood in terms of a difference of "climate" in Greece, by which he meant not only the salubrious physical climate of the area between the Orient and Northern Europe, but also the economic and political conditions of classical Greece that nurtured freedom, the *sine qua non* of artistic creativity and productivity.

Winkelmann saw four periods or phases in Greek art: The first moved from the "formless" beginnings to the generation before Phidias, in which the drawing was emphatic but hard and graceless. The second, "lofty" or "grand," style coincided with the freedom of the Greek Enlightenment (!), beginning with Phidias. Gracefulness came with Praxiteles and lasted into the early Hellenistic period. After that came the period of the "imitators," whose work was preeminently available for inspection in Rome. To the "high" or grand style he attributed many of the characteristics of the sublime as well as those of formal beauty. And it is the high style, he affirmed, that exemplifies "true beauty," or normative beauty.

This identification would lead Winkelmann to problems with the

relation of beauty to expression, and to strictures against Gothic art
and much other art in his own time. Even these, however, he would
see as authentic expressions of varying "climates." Here again we may
note that historians of religion would also present developmental
schemes in which one period of religious history or one form of religion would provide the key to understanding the historical narrative.
Hume, we have seen, spoke of the history of "warring superstitions" as
deviants of or antithetical to the "natural religion" of basic "enlightened" beliefs. Others, to whom we shall turn in the next chapter,
would see the evolution of the apprehension and articulation of "the
holy" as leading to normative embodiment in a version of Christianity
(Otto); in the religion of "archaic" *homo religiosus* and its rudiments in
living faiths (Eliade); in the "essence and manifestations" of religion
appraised from the perspective of a "high" theology (van der Leeuw);
or, among some nineteenth- and twentieth-century Romantics, in the
"original" and ultimately "inscrutable" "wisdom of the East."

The nascent discipline of art history itself, writes Micheal Podro,
proceeded through three stages:

> the first was the view, like that of Winkelmann, which accommodated
> alien art only as a deviant or precursor of the writer's own norm. This was
> enriched by allowing different criteria and so different norms, as when
> Hegal makes Greek art a supreme exemplification of art yet allows later
> art a greater status as an expression of the mind's freedom, or where the
> Germans identify Gothic art as their cultural heritage while still assuming
> the paradigmatic role of Greek art. There was then a third stage in which
> a general conception of art was constructed, of which particular arts were
> seen as modes or manifestations. In this last stage, rather than seeing ear-
> lier works as partial expressions of an ideal to which the writers them-
> selves subscribed, continuity with the sensibility of the present was main-
> tained by the concept of a universal artistic purpose shared by past and
> present. That purpose was seen in the way art exhibited the mind's free-
> dom. [32]

Podro notes that Karl Friedrich von Rumohr, rather than Winkelmann, "is most often thought of as the founder of modern archival
research in art history."[33] Winkelmann and those under his influence,
Rumohr thought, tended, in their emphasis on freedom, "to treat
works of art as expressions of moral ideas." (Recall Kant's praise of art
as providing "emblems" of the dignity of freely imposed moral law.) A
work of visual art, Rumohr said, does not have "as its content a non-
visual idea . . . a mere exemplification of something known in language." Furthermore, Rumohr amplified Winkelmann's concept of
"climate" into a more highly nuanced sense of art's participation in
communal life: "For art," said Rumohr, "is moved by the same laws, the

same standards underlie its evaluations, as in every other free activity of the mind. Thus the same considerations must direct our judgment on the merit or demerit of works of art . . . as on the value of value-lessness of other human products. In art, as in life generally, energy, intensity, scope, goodness and gentleness, acuity and clarity about its own purpose make a proper claim on our approval."[34]

"The sense of art as part of social life," notes Podro, "is underlined in Rumohr's remarks on his own procedures as a historian. 'Not un-commonly, historical relations are illuminated infinitely better by the citing of sources than the most consummate elaboration.' "[35] There are two ways in which the distance from Hegel, to whose views we will turn below, may be remarked on here. The first is the decision to work from the exemplary particular, and the second is in choosing what it is that should be exemplified. What needs to be exemplified, in Ru-mohr's view, are such factors as "commercial practice in public com-missions, the relations of artists to their patrons and contemporaries, and the artist's technical procedures."[36] With Rumohr art history was embarked on a course that historians of religion would follow when they incorporated into their narratives the findings of sociologists of religion and cultural anthropologists.

Noting that German pioneers of art history were responding in various ways, and being compared to, Hegel, we return to an account of the development of general philosophies of art and of religion in the light of the Kantian legacy to nineteenth-century German thought. We turn first to the group called "Romantics," whose views played a major role in the development of theories of aesthetics and religion.

FRIEDRICH VON SCHILLER (1759–1805)

We begin with the aesthetic theory of Friedrich von Schiller, poet and dramatist, whose work influenced Goethe and Beethoven (who incor-porated Schiller's *Ode to Joy* in his Ninth Symphony). A major state-ment of his aesthetic theory appears in a work with a significant title: *On the Aesthetic Education of Man.*[37] The metaphor of "education" pro-vides a revealing key to an account of human development; others would see the history of religions as the story of the religious educa-tion of humanity—or, in theological idiom, as "progressive revela-tion."

Schiller begins with the Kantian harmony of feeling and reason in the Third Critique but prescinds from Kant's insistence that aesthetic judgments are "subjective" so far as the strict dictates of cognitive un-derstanding, and of "objectivity" in that sense, are concerned. This would be, suggests Schiller, a typical *philosopher's* view. But the practice of the artist reveals that in the work of art, and in aesthetic judgment concerning it, feeling and reason are coordinated, or in "reciprocal subordination." Beauty is objective, because reflection is prerequisite to its experience; but it is also subjective because its perception is dependent on feeling. In art, therefore, the full range of human apprehension of the real is epitomized.

But if feeling and reason are unified in art, it is only because in reality they have equal ontological status—only because they exhibit equally warranted capacities for both independence and coordination. What actually occurs in experience must have been possible in experience. It is therefore art that plays the central role in advancing humankind from savagery to civilization. It does this when the "play impulse," freed from the necessities of mere survival, produces artistic "semblance" (*schein*) that is "honest"—that is, semblance that announces itself as semblance but claims an independent status as expressive of a · paradigmatic human value. Here is a reversal of Plato's view of the value of *mimesis*.

In the process of the aesthetic education of humanity two major forms of art (illustrated, for Schiller, first in forms of poetry) appear. These Schiller labels "naive" and "sentimental." Whereas the former achieves its greatness, as in the classical forms of antiquity, by *limitation*, the latter, exemplified in forms of contemporary art, bespeaks the infinity of feeling. But the two are not to be thought of as discontinuous or antithetical; they illustrate a continuum of universal aesthetic sensibility and achievement, the achievement that is humankind's crowning glory.

FRIEDRICH VON SCHLEGEL (1772–1829)

Schiller's contemporary, Friedrich von Schlegel, was the leader of a group that included his brother August Wilhelm, the poets Hölderlin and Novalis, and Friedrich Schleiermacher, who joined them as a young theological student in Berlin in 1796. Schlegel was not a systematic philosopher; he was primarily a critic of the arts. In this respect he foreshadowed the impact of literary and other critics on contemporary reflection on art and religion that we will note in Chapter Six. In the course of his critical reflections, however, he enunciated some views that were to have considerable influence on subsequent thinkers.

The fundamental apprehension of reality, he said, occurs in "intellectual intuition," similar to aesthetic intuition. Philosophical systems, he maintained, always begin in the middle, like epic poetry, and intellectual intuition is "the categorical imperative of theory." The role of the philosopher is not to explain the world but to articulate a vision of the world that may foster felicitous contemplation. In this task art and religion are of paramount importance, because in the work of the artist there is a synthesis of the finite and the infinite. But each artist presents a unique vision, a vision that often is prophetic of emerging sensibilities in culture.

This means that artists have a religious vocation. In the service of divinity, Schlegel said, individuals must realize their uniqueness as singular confluences of the finite and the infinite, for the sake of an ideal community of fully realized individuals. The task of the religious person is to make his or her life a work of art; the task of the artist is to make his or her pursuit of beauty an offering to the divine.[38]

FRIEDRICH WILHELM JOSEPH SCHELLING (1775–1854)

Friedrich Wilhelm Joseph Schelling incorporated insights shared with Kant, Schiller, Schlegel, and Schleiermacher—and with Fichte, Jacob Boehme, and George Friederich Creuzer—into a program for philosophy that culminated in a program for *Religionswissenschaft*, or the History of Religions.

Historians of philosophy have debated the question of how many visions or re-visions of the world were created by Schelling in his long career. These successive visions or re-visions are frequently described in terms of "systems" or of "periods" of his thought, each exemplified in a paradigmatic work. Typically they are described as (1) a period of discipleship and criticism of Fichte (1794–1797); (2) Philosophy of Nature (1797–1800); (3) Transcendental Idealism (1800); (4) Philosophy of Identity (1801–1804); (5) Philosophy of Art (1802–1803) and Philosophy of Religion (1804 or 1806–1834), the latter subdivided into Philosophy of Freedom (1804 or 1806–1815) and Philosophy of Mythology and Revelation (1827–1854). Robert F. Brown[39] is correct, however, in affirming the consensus of recent scholarship that there are in fact only two major "periods" or styles of philosophizing in Schelling's oeuvre. The works prior to 1806 are described by Schelling as "negative" philosophy, and those from the long period after 1806 are described by him as "positive" philosophy. The sequence, however, does not signify discontinuity between the second and first periods, or in the developments expressed in the first period. In some respects like modern process philosophers and pragmatists, Schelling saw the philosophical enterprise as an ongoing and open quest for the most adequate vision of a world in which temporality and freedom are "givens." John Herman Randall, Jr., is also correct in seeing Schelling's attitude toward the philosophical quest to be that of the creative artist, freshly working and reworking materials presented by all the ranges of human apprehension of the real into more adequate—but never fully adequate—visions.

Schelling first produced a philosophy of nature, in which—drawing to some extent on leads suggested in Kant's *Critique of Teleological Judgment* (which, in turn, used the model of aesthetic judgment as a clue to the congruence of scientific description with the phenomena of nature)—he moved from the Newtonian mechanistic view of nature to a more organic view centering on forms of organization of dynamic processes. These, in turn, he accounted for in terms of a primary undifferentiated force (cf. Whitehead's "Creativity" as described in Chapter Four) that he called will or freedom. This force or will differentiates itself in positive and negative forms, from whose interactions comes the varied reality of the natural world. In humans this force achieves self-consciousness; humans are microcosms of the macrocosmos (later, for him, theocosmos). The creative drive of primordial will, freedom, or "Spirit," is at work in both human and nonhuman nature. And, as Kant suggested in *The Critique of Judgment*—though Kant restricted its import as "merely subjective"—Schelling saw in aesthetic judgment and in the work of the creative artist (Kant's "genius") the paradigmatic formulation of natural and human creativity. It is in the aesthetic self-awareness of the artist that humans, philosophically speaking, apprehend the nature of ultimate reality. It is, therefore, the philosophy of art that should be the "organon" of all philosophy.

In agreement with Schlegel, Schelling went on to affirm that the artist is also an instrument of divine revelation. As Randall puts it,

> A work of art is inexhaustible, it contains in its perfection far more than the artist consciously put into it. The artist is literally inspired; just as in history unconscious and impersonal forces work through the conscious deeds of men, so in the artistic genius there is revealed a force greater than himself that through him creates the infinite and eternal. It is his proud Fate to serve freely as the tool of the supreme Artist. What he produces is indeed infinite, and capable of endless meanings; yet it is also a finite and harmonious whole, a genuine synthesis of Nature and freedom. Beauty is thus a finite embodiment of the Infinite, a union of free activity and the inexhaustible resources of Nature.[40]

There remain, however, the age-old questions of how, from the undifferentiated One, polarity and variety emerge, and—more dauntingly—why there is anything at all, One or Many. In the pursuit of answers to these questions Schelling exhibited affinities with aspects of Augustinian Neoplatonism, but he ultimately turned to Biblical voluntarism for his final "answers," couched in the terms of theology and revelation. Augustine had combined the Hebraic emphasis on the freedom of the divine will with the Platonic emphasis on the emanation of penultimate reality from the divine ultimate, an emanation apprehended in the deductive work of reason. Reality, Schelling affirmed in his later or "positive" philosophy, is indeed accessible to the power of reason, and rational dialectic exhibits the dynamic structure of the real. But the sheer fact of *existence—that* anything is—cannot, as the empiricists had forcefully shown, be deduced from rational norms and operations. There is an irrationality or nonrationality in the "givenness" of the empirical world. So the work of reason in describing nature, as Hume had insisted, must also entail patient and disciplined observation and experiment. Temporality and novelty set parameters for purely speculative rationalism.

But why is the world such that both the dialectical work of pure reason and the experimental work of scientific inquiry obtain? Why is there a "given" in the structure of reality? With this ontological question Schelling associated also the question of "the problem of evil." Why is there irrational or "surd" evil in the world?

In pursuit of answers to these questions Schelling drew heavily on the mystical theology (if Boehme's work can be classified as an "-ology" of any sort) of Jacob Boehme. "Underneath" all, Boehme affirmed, is not merely a rational-ontological *ground;* the ground itself is an expression of a "groundless," an *ungrund,* or sheer "free-willedness." Associated in mystical theology with the Godhead, the ultimate may be seen as a dynamic but self-contained entity that confronts its own eternally given "Other" in an ongoing process of redemption. The world of human experience reflects the dynamic structures of the Godhead. The resultant view is not so much a pantheism as what Charles Hartshorne would later call a pan-en-theism. In any case, the most direct experience of the divine Real is that of mystical ecstasy (*ek-stasis*). This is the theologically expressed correlate of the aesthetic self-awareness of the artist. The human drama may then be interpreted through the classical Christian motifs of Creation, Fall, Redemption, and Eschatological Fulfillment. These motifs Schelling pursued in a never-completed work on *The Ages of the World,* assimilated to the work of Father (Creator from undifferentiated abyss), Son (Redeemer), and Spirit (ongoing and dynamic agent of world redemption).

Although there is a shift from philosophical to theological terminology, Schelling viewed the work of reason that reveals the basic structures of reality as positive. It is "negated" or transcended only at the point of limit-questions about "why there is anything at all" and why, within that which is, there is irrational evil. Only in this respect does the work of reason have "negative" import or limitation. It is that work which was explored in the first, brief but highly productive, period of Schelling's career. For a "positive" answer to the unanswered questions of reason, Schelling later concluded, one must turn to divine revelation. But revelation itself is "positive" in the sense that it is a sheer and undeductible "given."

In his view of the history of religions Schelling saw mythology as the first stage (as did Vico). Mythology, he believed—along with Georg Friedrich Creuzer (1771–1858)—shows that all primitive myths reveal traces of an original monotheism. In his study of the deities of Samothrace Schelling assumed that all the great myths of the religions of the world express an archetypal awareness of the threefold potencies of the divine nature, representing them symbolically as individual deities.[41] The age of revelation in the definitive sense, however,

> is the time of Christianity, the personal appearance of God in history as the Son. The mode of human awareness here is called "revelation" because it depends on the divine initiative. The future will be the age of the Spirit, when the actualization of God's life in history will be completed. This will be the end of history, the definitive restoration of fallen consciousness, and of all being, to the communion of God. In this way Schelling brings the doctrine of potencies together with the trinitarian theology. History for Schelling is fundamentally the history of religion.[42]

Schelling was unwilling, however, to identify completely the work of revelation with the Christian church in its current historical embodiment. Fulfillment will come, he said, in "the Johannine Church of the future," in which "the world will be born anew in the Logos that is God."[43]

FRIEDRICH DANIEL ERNST SCHLEIERMACHER (1768–1834)

If Schelling could pursue an artistic philosophical vision to find the goals of philosophy fulfilled in the history of religions, it was his older contemporary, Friedrich Daniel Ernst Schleiermacher, who would develop a theory of religion as such—a theory of an "essence" that is manifested in various historical forms, a theory that he first articulated in his *On Religion: Speeches to Its Cultured Despisers*.[44] This book, says Wilfred Cantwell Smith, "would seem to be the first book written on religion as such—not on a particular kind or instance and not incidentally, but explicitly religion itself as a generic something."[45] Certainly it is the first statement of a theory of religion in that family of theories that George Lindbeck has labeled "experiential-expressive."[46] In that family are many of the most influential contemporary theories of religion, some of which we will examine in the next chapter. When other theories emerged in the social sciences they were heavily influenced by assumptions incorporated in "experiential-expressive" theories. How, then, did Schleiermacher arrive at the formulation of his theory, and what is the role of aesthetic apprehension and articulation in it?

Schleiermacher was a student of F. A. Wolff, leader of the classical revival in Germany, and of E. A. Eberhard, an exponent of Greek philosophy who opposed the critical philosophy of Kant. At Eberhard's instigation Schleiermacher translated Aristotle's *Ethics* and began a translation of Plato that was to become the standard German translation. Through his classical and literary studies he became immersed in problems of interpretation, and he is widely regarded as a pioneer in the enterprise of hermeneutics, the science of interpretation. In 1799 he published his *Soliloquies*, a popular and forceful statement of Romantic sensibility.[47] In 1804 he was appointed professor of philosophy and theology at Halle, and in 1810 he became the first head of the theological faculty at the new University of Berlin, where he taught for the remainder of his life. Among his lectures was a course on aesthetics, in which Paul Bernabeo finds a "family resemblance" to his theory of religion.[48] His major work there, however, was to be his systematic Christian theology, a work that was to have enormous influence in nineteenth- and twentieth-century Christian religious thought.

In Schleiermacher's thinking we find many echoes of themes we have encountered in Schiller, Schlegel, and Schelling: themes of unity-in-multiplicity, which is apprehended in affective intuition, and designation of such intuition as providing privileged access to the identity of thought and being, which are seen as split only in the processes of reason in relation to the real—in the relation of "subjects" to "objects." The first of the *Soliloquies* contrasts the "ordinary man" who is immersed in the "outer" world with the "spiritual" man who sees that world as symbolic of a nature that he shares with that world. Whereas the "ordinary person" is immersed in transient existence, "He alone enjoys freedom and eternity who knows what man is and the world is."[49] The second Soliloquy abjures the Kantian exaltation of conscience in favor of a sense of identification with the "essence" of humanity as such. In the light of that identification one may discern "receptive" natures—"who develop one's inner humanity into distinctness, expressing it in manifold acts"—and "creative" natures who project their distinctive humanity into works of art. Schleiermacher, in contrast with Schelling, counted himself among the "receptive" natures. "I have so emphatically eschewed anything that makes the artist,

I have so eagerly made my own whatever serves the culture of Self, whatever confirms and hastens its development."[50]

The third meditation extends the reflection to two different conceptions of humanity's task in civilization. One seeks control over nature; the other sees the goods of civilization in deeper identifications with nature and in the goods of human fellowship. The fourth meditation addresses the question of human destiny and contrasts the person who is ever anxious about specific outcomes of personal projects with the soul who seeks to view the shifting changes of fortune as congruent with a higher or deeper creative order. (Schleiermacher had earlier found nurture in Spinoza. Perhaps there are here Romantic echoes of Spinoza's "intellectual love of God.") In the fifth meditation both the goods of age and those of youth are affirmed to be ingredients of an ever young and growing life that seeks to offer to its fellows only mature and seasoned contributions to culture.

In this ambience what, then, is the nature of religion—assuming, as Schleiermacher did, that religion is something that *has* a "nature" which can be designated in a definition and articulated in a theory? "The contemplation of the pious," he says (and piety or reverence, we have noted, has long been designated the distinctively religious attitude or disposition),

> is the immediate consciousness of the universal existence of all finite things, in and through the Infinite, and of all temporal things in and through the eternal. Religion is to seek this and find it in all that lives and moves, in all growth and change, in all doing and suffering. It is to have life and to know life *in immediate feeling*, only as such an existence in the Infinite and Eternal. Where this is found religion is satisfied, where it hides itself there is for her unrest and anguish, extremity and death. Wherefore it is a life in the infinite nature of the Whole, in the One and in the All, in God, having and possessing all things in God, and God in all. Yet religion is not knowledge and science. It is itself an affection, a revelation of the Infinite in the finite, God being seen in it and it in God.[51]

Later Schleiermacher would define religion as "sense and taste of the Infinite." The Infinite, however, expresses itself in an infinite variety of ways.

> There is in religion such a capacity for unlimited manysidedness in judgment and in contemplation as is nowhere else to be found. I will not except even morality and philosophy, not at least so much of them as remains after religion is taken. . . . The man who thinks methodically, and acts from principle and design, and will accomplish this or that in the world, unavoidably circumscribes himself, and makes everything that does not forward him an object of antipathy. Only when the free impulse

of seeing, and of living is directed towards the Infinite and goes into the Infinite, is the mind set in unbounded liberty.[52]

Note that Schleiermacher seems to use "the Infinite," "the Whole," and "God" interchangeably. Focus on the latter designation has led to endless debate as to whether Schleiermacher is or is not a "pantheist." He denied this, affirming that the Absolute is "the world" for thought, "God" for religion. The world is unity including antitheses; God is unity excluding antitheses. Knowledge of God is the *terminus ad quo* of knowledge; knowledge of the world is the *terminus ad quem*. Knowledge of God is only *mediated* by the world; God and world are not identical. As a Christian theologian, or simply as an inhabitant of Western culture in his time and place, Schleiermacher would naturally use the term "God" for the ultimate. His general view of religion, however, could accommodate other designations.

Indeed, Schleiermacher said that "religion" *exists* concretely only in *the religions* of humankind, and that the religions of humankind are to religion as the forms of music are to music as such.

> Religion thus fashions itself with endless variety, down even to the single personality. Each form again is a whole and capable of an endless number of characteristic manifestations. . . . Were I to compare religion in this respect with anything it would be music, which indeed is otherwise closely connected with it. Music is one great whole; it is a special, self-contained revelation of the world. Yet the music of each people is a whole by itself, which again is divided into different characteristic forms, till we come to the genius and style of the individual. Each actual instance of this inner revelation in the individual contains all these unities. Yet while nothing is possible for a musician, except in and through the unity of the music of his people, and the unity of music generally, he presents it in the charm of sound with all the pleasures and joyousness of boundless caprice, according as his life stirs in him, and the world influences him. In the same way, despite the necessary elements in its structure, religion is, in its individual manifestations whereby it displays itself immediately in life, from nothing farther removed than from semblance or imitation.[53]

There is authenticity and integrity in all religions. Nevertheless, just as the forms of music may be classified in a morphology of music, so religions may be classified in a morphology of religion. Schleiermacher himself went on to offer such a classification, and it was guided by confessional as well as by descriptive aims and evaluations.[54] Does art have any special role to play in evoking a sense of "God-consciousness" or "feeling of absolute dependence," as he would term religious experience in his later work? "If it is true that there are sudden conversions whereby in men, thinking of nothing less than of lifting themselves above the finite, in a moment, as by an immediate, inward illumination, the sense for the highest comes forth and surprises them by its splendor, I believe that more than anything else the sight of a great and sublime work of art can accomplish this miracle."[55]

GEORG WILHELM FRIEDRICH HEGEL (1770–1831)

Schleiermacher's theory of religion exhibits motifs shared with Schiller, Schlegel, Schelling, and others who epitomize what Germans called *die Romantik*. It was the goal of his contemporary and early colleague Georg Wilhelm Friedrich Hegel to incorporate Romantic insights and sensibilities into a system that also honored the classical identification of thought and being—to proclaim that "whatever is rational is real, and whatever is real is rational." In the process, the understanding of both rationality and reality were altered in a way that was to have enormous and far-reaching consequences, not only for philosophy itself, but also for political theory and practice, both "left" and "right"; for the understanding of social and cultural phenomena through the social sciences; and, with respect to the concerns of this book, for the understanding of art and religion, of beauty and holiness.

There are those who would see in the Hegelian understanding of art and religion the end of both as they were traditionally understood and evaluated. We will examine the validity of this view in Chapter Six. But first we turn to a summary of a few of the themes in Hegel's thought that form the context of his views of art and religion. We do this with full recognition of the fact that there are perhaps as many interpretations of Hegel as there are interpreters, and that many modern schools of philosophy claim that they are the "natural" and responsible executors of the Hegelian program in the modern world. The remarkable thing about the richness of Hegel's thought is that each interpretive claimant can find some legitimate ground in the Hegelian achievement for the plausibility of the claimant's interpretation.

Hegel wished to do justice to all those forms of human experience that appeared to be excluded from reality or from comprehension within the parameters of Newtonian science and its implications as these were understood by the British empiricists and in Kant's critical philosophy. These forms of experience were, however, celebrated in the emphasis on affective intellectual intuition heralded by the Romantics, including the distinctive features and functions of art and religion that were revealed from their perspective. At the same time Hegel wished to be faithful to the classical philosophical task of achieving synoptic vision—a synoptic vision that would, in the spirit of Aristotle, take full account of concrete realities as they actually present themselves in human experience and are interpreted in critical thought. The result, for him, was a more catholic understanding of the many facets of human experience in a variety of social contexts, and of ultimate reality as the totality of experience.

That totality, however, is always "not yet." Temporality, novelty, and change, as the Romantics had affirmed, are "givens" of experience and therefore of reality. Rational understanding of human experience as this is embodied in human cultures, therefore, can at best encompass an understanding of the present in the light of its past. It cannot predict the future. Speculations about the future, however, may be tempered and guided by an understanding of how past and present came to be. "The owl of Minerva takes its flight only when the shades of night are gathering."[56]

The pattern of such understanding is the implicate of recognition of the partial and incomplete character of every formulation of present insight or "explanation." The inadequacy of every affirmation is experientially revealed. This revelation is presented as the "negation," or circumscription, of the affirmation. But apprehension of the negation itself generates a more adequate and commodious affirmation. In logical terms, thesis begets antithesis which begets synthesis. Classical formal logic had enshrined the "principle of (non-)contradiction" in its canon: what is true or false is so "eternally"—that is, as a "timeless" implicate of given logical (or mathematical) operation or demonstration. Thus, Being could be deduced from demonstrable sets of propositions. Experience, said Hegel, reveals that this is not the case—or at least that it is the case only in a formally circumscribed sense. In the ongoingness of thought and being, if the rational is the real and the real is the rational, *and* temporality is a given, then Being entails or generates "nonbeing" (contingency), which in turn generates a fresh constellation of Being through and in the process of *becoming*. Being is to nonbeing in becoming as thesis is to antithesis in the generation of synthesis.

The Hegelian logic is "the logic of events." Logical characterization of the real is of a Real that is the ideal totality of all becomings and syntheses, the ultimate context of all contexts. Hegel spoke of this, in various contexts, as "Idea," "the Absolute," or "the Whole," and of its operations as those of "Spirit," conscious or unconscious. In reality as human experience, "Spirit" becomes "Objective," "for and in itself" and "for us." From a theological point of view the Absolute may be called God. From the point of view of the enterprise of rational human understanding the operations of Spirit exhibit affinities with what social scientists call "the developments of culture." Although Hegel spoke of the Absolute also as "Self," or an individual, it was the

"Self" of the totality of experience, not the selves of individual experiencers, that he had in mind. Experience is for him inherently *social*.

But if the operations of Spirit are perceived in what social science calls "culture," it is "world culture" that Hegel has in mind. World culture is, however, the projected totality of distinctive human cultures, each realizing or epitomizing "culture" in authentic ways relative to specific times and places. Thus it may be said with some warrant, as many are now saying, that Hegel's understanding of culture either entails or permits a strong sense of cultural pluralism, if not cultural relativism. Others maintain that Hegel saw the fulfillment of culture in a projected idealized version of features of German culture, as described or imagined in the perspective of his own time and place. To this claim it may be said in rejoinder that if the affirmation of cultural relativism is valid, that would be the only way in which Hegel *could* see the matter. The true import of his vision is of an indefinitely endless variety of cultures appearing in an inherently open-ended world process of cultures. In this process relatively stable but never "final" constellations may be apprehended in an act of understanding that is "beyond relativism and objectivism." We will return to this claim, and its implications for the study of the relations of holiness to beauty, in Chapter Seven.

First we must summarize briefly the philosophies of art and of religion that emerged from the Hegelian vision. Of paramount importance for subsequent discussions of art and of religion is the fact that for Hegel both "art" and "religion" are distinctive *concepts* or "ideas" whose "nature" or "essence" can be conceptually unfolded—universal ideas that are historically embodied in specific cultural configurations. This conviction is perhaps Hegel's chief legacy to ensuing philosophies of art and philosophies of religion, or histories of art and histories of religion.

Hegel focuses his discussion of aesthetics, not on the nature of aesthetic judgment, as did Kant, but on the concept of the beautiful. This is consonant with his emphasis on the concreteness of specific concepts as constituents of both understanding and, in a sense, of that which is understood. "The concept of the beautiful and of art," he said, "is a presupposition given by the system of philosophy."[57] Its "idea" is not other than that which is unfolded in the science of logic. Beauty is, he said, the "appearance" (*schein*) of this idea in sensuous reality." The idea, however, *must* appear; in itself it does not exist. Beauty is the immediate, direct mode of its appearance. Of course "idea" may also be grasped in thought, but with more difficulty. Thus "when the truth in this its external existence is present to consciousness immediately, and when this concept remains immediately in unity with its external appearance, the idea is not only true but beautiful."[58]

Hegel agrees with Kant that if anything is judged to be beautiful, this is not because of its utility or its "charm." He disagrees with Kant in the latter's general exaltation of natural over humanly created beauty. Although nonhuman nature has its beauties, which Hegel enumerates, it is clear to him that the beauty of art is "higher" than that of nature, because "the beauty of art is beauty born of the spirit and born again, and the higher the spirit and its productions stand above nature and its phenomena, the higher too is the beauty of art above that of nature. In a *formal* sense, in fact, even a wicked fancy that pops into a man's head is higher than any product of nature, because in such a fancy spirituality and freedom are always present."[59] The artist, therefore, has a lofty vocation because, as child of both nature and awakened spirit, he or she employs productive or projective imagination to remold natural forms into unique expressions of individualized spiritual being. Given his prizing of artistic over natural beauty, Hegel severely criticizes the traditional understanding of art as *mimesis*. Art is "ideal," in that it unites idea with particularity in individuality.

Art, therefore, can render even the tragic and the "ugly" in a holistic "completeness" or serenity. How, and in what forms, has art done this in various cultures and historical periods? There are, Hegel thought, three paradigmatic ways. One he labels "symbolic." In its "Oriental" phase it is, he said, largely unconscious of the idea it is striving to portray. In the first instance it is like the "undifferentiated" or "formless" type described by Schelling. Next above this is "fantastic" symbolism, in which sensuous content and spiritual meaning are distinguishably present but confused. He thought that much Hindu art is of this type. In Egyptian art there is an advance into a sense of mystery or of the sublime, describable only in symbolic terms. Indeed, the Absolute is itself, in terms of aesthetic categories, sublime. It is symbolized religiously in pantheistic, polytheistic, or monotheistic religious traditions.

The second style (and "period") of art is the classic, in which the natural and the moral are brought into complete harmony, and the ideal world appears as a community of humanized gods and divinized humans. Its aim is to depict the balanced and harmonious confluence of the moral and the natural, the human and the divine. Though, as we shall see, Hegel does not view this period as the culmination of art, there is no doubt that it always had for him a wistful attraction. "In this respect, amongst the fundamental characteristics of the ideal we may put at the top this serene peace and bliss, this self-enjoyment in its own achievedness and satisfaction. The ideal work of art confronts us like a blessed god."[60]

The third phase of art, emerging from the inadequacies of the first two in dialectical fashion, is the "modern"—which is, for Hegel, the Romantic—phase. Following the implications of the Christian doctrine of the Incarnation as understood by Hegel, in which the "inwardness" of the divine in the human is stressed, art now turns, in his view, inward for its inspiration and finds its material in the heights and depths of human life. It creates music and poetry, and religious figures are humanized in sentiment. The infinite and the universal return, but no longer as opposed to the individual and the finite. The synthesis of "Oriental" and "Classic" is achieved.

Note that Hegel finds each of the three phases of art to be epitomized in their presentations of the divine. This is consonant with his view of the supremely idealizing function of art. He eschews all didactic or moral evaluations, "for art has above all to make the divine the center of its representations."[61] We must remember, however, that for Hegel "the divine" is a very large and commodious concept. "God" is Spirit, which, in the last analysis, is Truth. Hegel saw the history of religions as evolving from "natural" religion, which was for him dependence on and subservience to nature, to the sublime mystery symbolized in Egyptian art, thence to the humanized serenity of Greek religion, thence to the Hebraic accent on the transcendental unity and personality of the divine, and finally to Christianity. The Christian concept of the Trinity itself, he believed, recapitulates the threefold history of religions. The Father represents the pure identity of the Absolute. The generation of the Son by the Father is the final religious expression of difference within identity, in the infinitely variegated realizations of Spirit in the world. The Holy Spirit of the Trinity, "who proceeds from the Father and the Son," is the religious manifestation of the return of difference into identity or community.

There is a fundamental difference between Hegel's view of the work of the Spirit and that of Schelling. Schelling, we have observed, saw the task of the history of philosophy fulfilled in the "positive" realities of the history of religions. For Hegel, too, history is religious history, but it is the history of religion understood quite differently in relation to the history of philosophy. For Hegel the threefold expression of "objective Spirit" in human culture culminates neither in art nor in religion but in philosophy. The sequence of the dialectic in culture is art—religion—philosophy. Art renders Idea in sensuous appearance. Religion, through its historical phases, makes the Idea concrete in a variety of traditions that are the highest and most immediate expressions of the Idea accessible to humans. But "the vision in which consciousness has to depend upon senses passes into a self-mediating knowledge—into *revelation*. Thus the principle which gives the idea its content is that it embodies intelligence, and as 'absolute' it is for the spirit."[62] And the most profound embodiment of that which is for religion "revelation" is to be found in philosophy. In philosophy revelation is transmuted into thought—the complete rationalization of the totality of being.

Arthur Danto claims that Hegel thereby initiated "the philosophical disenfranchisement of art."[63] Did he also thereby initiate the philosophical disenfranchisement of religion? Did the nineteenth century, which began with the emergence of aesthetics and theories of religion, end with the eclipse of their subject matter?

Certainly the enterprise of art history underwent a change at the end of the nineteenth century. In 1895 Alois Riegl (b. 1858) joined Franz Wickhoff in the Faculty of Art History of the University of Vienna, where he remained until his death in 1905. Riegl agreed with his eighteenth-century predecessors that art historians must begin with careful observation of the data they seek to interpret. But he went on to insist that they must faithfully describe them in their given "coherence" rather than impose standards of coherence that seem most natural to the historian and to the historian's own culture. The aim is to uncover the *kunstwollen*, or visual intentions, of the artist in the integrity of whatever period provides the cultural milieu of the artist's work. In this process Riegl and others of his time drew on what they believed to be an emerging general philosophical psychology of perception, in which the notions of standard norms for all artistic perception would be abandoned. In the light of these convictions the basic idea of a developmental structure controlling the historian's narrative would be radically called into question. The result, says Podro, is that "so far from seeing earlier stages as mere preludes or incomplete forms of some final triumph, he insists on all stages as of equal value."[64] Successors to Riegl in art history would go on to question whether evaluation itself is an appropriate ingredient in the work of the art historian. The notion of "canon" would be challenged, and eventually it would be affirmed that all styles, forms, and types of art objects have the same claim to legitimacy in the purely descriptive work of the art historian. This would raise the question whether art itself can be defined except by the individual artist—or by the vagaries of the marketplace.

Similar developments would occur in the field of the history of religions. There would be insistence that the work of the historian of religions is also descriptive, not evaluative. Developmental schemes resting on philosophical or theological assumptions must, it would be said, be abjured. In the next chapter we shall look at influential modern theorists who claim to be objectively descriptive (e.g., Otto, Tillich) but seek at the same time to provide narrative accounts controlled by a structure of development in religious history—an account that may be incompatible with a purely descriptive agenda. We shall then see that others (e.g., Eliade, van der Leeuw) have called for empathetic observational accounts of religious phenomena as they actually appear in various times and cultures, interpreted in typologies or morphologies that allegedly emerge from the data themselves. We shall see that these enterprises grew out of a variety of theological and philosophical concerns and assumptions about the "nature" or "essence" of religion that are legacies of the nineteenth century. Finally we will sample the work of a theorist of religion from social science (Geertz) who also strives for objective neutrality in his organization and interpretation of the data, but whose theory rests on specific critical assumptions.

In Chapter Six we shall address the claims of some contemporary scholars that all the frameworks of narrative description employed in the history and interpretation of both art and religion, as well as all previous identifications of beauty and holiness as categories of interpretation, are dissolved in a "postmodern" sensibility. If this is the case, then perhaps the posture of philosophical thought typified by Hegel did lead to developments in the understanding of culture that would eventuate in the "end" of both art and religion, as these had been identified in the nineteenth century, and in modern theories of art and religion that built on nineteenth-century foundations.

CHAPTER THREE

Holiness and Beauty in Modern Theories of Religion

*I*T IS appropriate to begin this chapter with some remarks about the use of the term "theories" in its heading, because the use of the term itself encapsulates many of the questions posed by developments of thought in the nineteenth and early twentieth centuries to which we alluded in Chapter Two.

The term has an ancient and honorable history, stemming from the prizing of *theoria*, or synoptic vision, in Greek thought. This understanding of the term is reflected in contemporary uses of the term "view(s)" to indicate one's overall perspective on a particular subject or subject matter. A more refined use of the term theory emerged in reflection on the ingredients of inquiry in the natural sciences. One such ingredient is mathematical theory, and mathematical theory is perhaps the most "elegant" or "pure" of all types of theory, because it expresses internal relations of relatively clear concepts of entities whose significance is not dependent on types of observation. More general theories in natural science normally contain some non-observational terms, but their function as general explanatory schemes entails relations to experimental laws derived from experimental operations on observable "givens" or "data." Relations to the observables are expressed in "correspondence rules." Some philosophers of science would espouse possible reduction of theories to the laws they incorporate, whereas others see them as performing specific heuristic or functional roles in the total process of scientific inquiry.

As the nineteenth-century aspiration toward a "social science" of the good society developed, there were those who believed that there could be general unified theories of social science that would assimilate the specialized theories of specific social sciences in unitary explanatory schemes. Echoes of this aspiration are found in the aspirations of other scholars toward general or unified theories of art or religion. The fulfillment of such aspirations in the social sciences proved to be elusive or illusive, and contemporary social scientists eschew them in favor of stronger but more limited theories employed in specific types of social science. Reference to more general theoretical guides may, however, be incorporated in various ways of approaching the data: (1) developmental approaches, employing notions of "growth" or "evolution" in the description and explanation of change in the data; (2) "social-systems" approaches, employing concepts of equilibrium-disequilibrium, or mechanical or biological analogies, in describing relations of "ideal types" of social phenomena; (3) structuralist approaches, employing binary or other concepts to express compositional relations; or (4) functionalist approaches, stressing the operative significance of specific social behavior within and between specific social structures. There are appropriations, or at least echoes, of each of these social-scientific models in contemporary theories of art and religion. If Hegel's *geist* is interpreted through the concepts of society or culture in social science, then the relations of art or religion to culture may be articulated in the idioms of sociology or cultural anthropology. In this chapter we will examine one suggestive and influential theory of art and religion in cultural anthropology.

In the preceding paragraph we employed the concept of "interpretation." In Chapter Two we noted that Schleiermacher—building on canons of Biblical exegesis and the interpretation of classical texts—moved toward a general philosophy of interpretation as such, or hermeneutics. The hermeneutical enterprise was first directed to the interpretation of *texts*, but it was then extended to the interpretation of nonverbal data as well. Some twentieth-century scholars of art history and art criticism draw heavily on developments in hermeneutics in their historical and critical work. We will pay special attention to some of these in Chapter Six. Meanwhile, we note the fact that many of the pioneers of modern theories of religion were engaged in the general task of hermeneutics. They thought that, whatever else they might be doing, they were offering interpretations of religion that would lead to a proper understanding of what religion is. The question must then be raised whether such understandings (or theories) were or are thought to be normative (what religion "really" is or *ought* to be) or neutrally and "objectively" descriptive or explanatory. Three of the theorists of religion whose views we shall examine in this chapter were also theologians. What is the relation of a theological stance to the character of the theory of religion espoused by those who take such a stance—and vice versa?

This question evokes a more basic one, namely, in what sense is the term theory of religion itself warrantable, if protocols for the use of the concept of theory are to be consonant with those of its use in natural or social science? In pursuing this question further we must advert to the use of another term, "criticism," in the humanities. The

employment of this term in the humanities is perhaps as imprecise—
or at least as varied—as is employment of the term theory in the humanistic disciplines, where we are offered both "critical theories" and
"theories of criticism." A standard dictionary definition of criticism so
employed may reveal the multiplicity of issues involved in the practice
of criticism in the humanities: "the art of judging with knowledge and
propriety the beauty or faults of works of art or literature."[1] Practitioners of criticism expatiate on what the "art" is and how it works; on
what is "propriety" and who are its proprietors; on what is "good judgment"; and on whether "beauty" or "faults" are appropriate categories
of evaluative judgment. As we shall see in Chapter Six, a variety of
substitutes have been proposed for the latter: "aesthetic merit," "literary worth," "authenticity," and "integrity," among others. At this point
it is interesting to note that the notion of criticism has not been widely
employed in "religious studies" with respect to the generic concerns of
that field or discipline, as contrasted with its more specific uses in
enterprises such as forms of "Biblical criticism," "historical criticism,"
and so forth.

Use of the term "historical" in the preceding sentence flags a variety of questions that are germane to both art history and the history
of religions. We cannot here go into the complexities of the development of concepts of history as a field of inquiry in the nineteenth
century or the continuing debate about whether or to what extent history is to be understood through the canons of social science. We
simply note both the complexities and the importance of the issues for
more detailed analyses of the concepts of art history and/or the history
of religions. We return instead to our initial question about the use of
the term theory in art history, in art criticism, or with respect to general or comprehensive (normative?) "views" of religion.

The present state of discussion of this issue in all these endeavors
is ably captured in the statement of Stephen Knapp and Walter Benn
Michaels that "theory" in art and literature (and religion, I would add)
is to be understood minimally as "the attempt to govern the interpretation of particular texts [substitute comparable phenomena in art and
religion] by appealing to an account of interpretation in general." In
art history this appeal may take one of two, not unrelated, forms: "reference to the rules of writing art history," or "references to rules which
explain how art [or religion] develops." Theory in this sense is to be
contrasted with "practice," "which denotes those passages or works in
art history [cf. history of religions] which do not make reference to
the same two topics."[2]

It is with these caveats and qualifications, then, that we turn in
this chapter to five influential accounts of religion that function in

religious studies as theories in the sense specified above. The ambiguities inherent in this use of theory may be endemic to the field or discipline of religious studies itself, a field that—as Philip Ashby said of the discipline called history of religions—may in its present state be "an area of scholarly pursuit in search of a definition of itself."[3] Perhaps the same could be said of the field of art history. It is the thesis of this book that this search may be enhanced by closer attention to analogies between issues in aesthetic theory and in theories of religion. In the following exposition we will note, with respect to category formation, that just as the category "beauty" has sometimes been replaced by other—but, we will maintain, functionally equivalent—categories in aesthetics, so the category "holiness" has sometimes been replaced by "the sacred," "the ultimate," "transcendence," "mystery," or, in some recent discussion, "alterity." Even so, it is my conviction that examination of the relations of holiness by any other name to beauty by any other name in theories of religion may contribute to a better understanding of both aesthetics (and, by implication, art history or criticism) and religion in their various dimensions.

I have chosen to examine the views of Rudolf Otto, Mircea Eliade, Gerardus van der Leeuw, Paul Tillich, and Clifford Geertz because the theories of religion offered by these scholars are widely influential, not only in religious studies but also in many other disciplines when the latter attempt to describe and assess what they take to be religious phenomena. Otto is perhaps principally responsible for the extensive employment of the concept of "the holy" or "holiness" as the distinctive religious category in current discussion. Eliade maintained that he incorporated Otto's insights in what he believed to be a more adequate category, "the sacred." Tillich derived from his existentialist philosophical theology a concept of religion as "ultimate concern" that has been employed both in popular cultural analysis and by some practitioners of various academic disciplines. Van der Leeuw has been the most influential expositor of one type of phenomenological approach to the understanding of religion. Clifford Geertz has employed a form of cultural anthropological analysis to interpret both religious phenomena and aesthetic phenomena.

I will not attempt to give a summary of all the major components of the views espoused by these scholars. I will concentrate, instead, on two things: (1) the role of concepts and procedures analogous to concepts and procedures employed in aesthetics in their theories of religion and (2) the religious significance of aesthetic phenomena in the light of their theories of religion. These two matters are frequently conflated in popular discussions linking art and religion. I will concentrate primarily on the first of these and will refer only briefly to the second, as a way of further explicating the theoretical issues addressed in the first. It is these theoretical issues, I maintain, that pose the necessary "prior questions" for responsible or fruitful discussion of religious art, or art in religion, or religion in art. Much current discussion of the latter topics has been carried on with insufficient awareness of either crucial issues in theories of religion, on the one hand, or crucial issues in aesthetics or theories of art, on the other.

RUDOLF OTTO (1869–1937)

Otto's earliest works were explicitly theological: a doctoral dissertation on Spirit and Word in Luther and a book on Luther's doctrine of the Holy Spirit. In 1898 he published a new edition of Schleiermacher's *Speeches*. Turn-of-the-century interest in the concept of evolution is reflected in his *Darwinism and Religion* (1909); we shall note Otto's own appropriation of a concept of evolution in his theory of religion. Meanwhile, he expressed his philosophical affinity with the neo-Kantian position of Jacob Friedrich Fries in a work published in 1889, *Kantich-Fries'sche Religionsphilosophie* (Eng. trans. *Philosophy of Religion*, 1931). In his statement of his theory of religion in *The Idea of the Holy* there are a number of appeals to Fries's concept of *ahnung*—presentiment, surmise, intuition, or, as Otto would put it in religious terms, "divination," as a mode of apprehending reality shared by aesthetics and religion. A further theme of *The Idea of the Holy* is presaged in an article on the folk psychology of Wilhelm Wundt, published in *Theologische Rundschau* in 1910. There Otto raised the question whether there is a universal *sensus numinis* at the root in all religion.

In 1916 Otto published his first work on Indian thought, *Dipika des Nivasa: ein Indische Heilslehre*, followed by *West-Östliche Mystik* in 1926 (Eng. trans. *Mysticism East and West*, 1932) and in 1930 *Indiens Gnadenreligion und das Christentum* (Eng. trans. *India's Religion of Grace*, 1930). The first two employ a pan-religious concept of mysticism, in differentiating between forms of mysticism, and the third employs a concept central to Christianity—grace—to interpret the *bhakti* movements in Hinduism. The earlier works aspire to objective descriptive analysis, and the later works evoke questions about the impact of apologetic concerns on the protocols of description.[4]

All these interests and influences converge in Otto's presentation of his seminal theory of religion. His aim was to formulate categories in terms of which all religion may be understood. The very title of his major work, however, may contain an ambiguity: *Das Heilige*. Is "the holy" an ontological or a psychological category, or both? It is perhaps revealing that the English translation of the book is titled *The Idea of the Holy,* which perhaps leaves the question open. Certainly the question has been endlessly debated by scholars in various fields who find Otto's work suggestive and fruitful.

The thesis of the book is fairly straightforward. Because, however, Otto especially stresses the significance of what he saw as one "moment" or dimension of the holy, a moment he labeled "the numinous," it has been popularly assumed that Otto equated the holy with the numinous. Actually he is at great pains to indicate that "the holy" is a concept embracing both rational and nonrational aspects or dimensions. In this respect, we may note, it may bear some similarity to the concept of beauty as employed by Kant. In any case, Otto asserts that Western thought has typically and perhaps exhaustively articulated the holy in terms of rational concepts. If the concept of God is so articulated, to God are attributed the "omni-" qualities of omniscience, omnipotence, and so forth. If the natural is the ordinary, then God as the paradigmatically extra-ordinary is affirmed to be "super-natural." Otto does not wish to deny or denigrate any of this. He is convinced, however, that rational concepts and the articulation of divinity in terms of them leaves out the equally important moment of the numinous, from the Latin *numen* ("supernatural" entities).

What, then, is the numinous? Literally, of course, we cannot say, because to "say" is to employ concepts. We may recall that Kant had said that aesthetic judgment also operates "without a concept." The *sensus numinis* may be evoked in various ways, but it cannot be rationally produced. Does this mean that it is "irrational"? No, it is neither rational nor irrational, it is simply nonrational, "other" than rational. Indeed, Otto would say that its impact is of that which is *"totally* other." May the numinous, then, be verbally articulated in any way? Yes, but the articulation must simultaneously affirm the impossibility of full rational articulation. So Otto proposes to designate the numinous as the *mysterium tremendum et fascinans.*

Mysterium bespeaks *mystery,* and the mysterious is to be distinguished from the problematic; the "unknowable" is to be distinguished from all cognitive possibilities encapsulated in the ordinary uses of the term "knowledge." It is this sense of mystery, Otto affirms, that underlies the authentically religious sense of "miracle," in which the force of miracles is not their inexplicability in terms of natural law but their affective impact as "signs" of the divine—their reception in awe and wonder.

Mysterium is therefore also *tremendum:* un-canny (not to be "kenned"), awe-ful, over-powering, "daunting," evoking that distinctive kind of "fear" that is termed in Biblical language "the fear of the Lord"—the overpowering sense of divine majesty that Jonathan Edwards celebrated in his sermons and in his theology. The mystery of *religion* as a pervasive human phenomenon, however, is signaled in the fact that that which is *mysterium tremendum* is also *fascinans*. That which is experienced in holy fear is also the source of religious bliss in apprehension of the Infinite. Just as Kant did not base his affirmation of the *sensus communis* in aesthetics on any possible empirical confirmation of universality in matters of taste, so Otto did not view the affirmation of the *sensus numinis* as a "proved" (or provable?) conclusion of empirical observation of historical data. It is rather, he said, *a priori*. Its logical functioning, however, is not that of Kant's *a prioris*. And it is also not something that is observably "innate" in all humans—something of which all human beings are at all times aware. It is rather, he said, something that is a *potentiality* in all humans—something that is *latent* in human nature, which may be evoked by the objective or subjective constituents of those phenomena that are appropriately labeled "religious." Some humans are more sensitive to the numinous than are others; in some its confluence with the rational and moral nonnuminous constituents of the holy is more perfectly realized than it is in others. These persons are the prophets, saints, and sages of the world's religions. Their function in the world of religion is similar to that of the "genius" in the aesthetic world, as that function is interpreted by Kant and others and appropriated for religion by Schleiermacher. "The same thing is very evident in the sphere of art: what appears in the multitude as mere receptiveness, the capacity of response and judgment by trained aesthetic taste, reappears in the *artist* as invention, creation, composition, the original production of genius. . . . It is very similar in the domain of the religious consciousness, religious production and revelation.[5]

It is within this framework that Otto constructs a scheme for interpreting the history of religions. The sense of the numinous, he says (reflecting the interest in "associationism" in psychology), evokes associated analogies and feelings. These cannot be expressed in pure concepts; they present themselves in what Otto called "ideograms," which he labeled—significantly, for our purposes—"illustrative substitutes for concepts." Kant, we recall, had said that aesthetic judgment operates "without a concept." But among the ideas in Kant's ideal world are what he called "aesthetical ideas." These, he seemed to say, function in ways that are in some respects like the functioning of concepts and in other respects not.

In his interpretation of the history of religions Otto employs a scheme that is "evolutionary" in a sense that appears to be both "historical," with analogies to "natural" evolution, and dialectical, à la Hegel. In its terms he traces the evolution of religious sensibility from its "cruder" phases to its ideally perfect expression, which turns out to be its expression in Christianity. The historian and theorist of religion is also the theologian.

But on what ground may it be affirmed that the *sensus numinis* is inherent in human nature? We have seen that both Hume and Kant assigned some important human concerns to the realm of "taste," and that Schleiermacher spoke of the "sense and taste of the Infinite."

In the religious sphere the "highest" expression is, Otto holds, that of the prophet: "The prophet corresponds in the religious sphere to the creative artist in that of art." Otto the theologian then goes on to speak of the work of the prophet as embodying the work of the Spirit, and to say that "we can look beyond the Prophet, to one in whom is found the Spirit in all its plenitude, and who at the same time in His Person and in His performance is become most completely the object of divination, in whom Holiness is recognized apparent. Such a one is more than Prophet. He is the Son."[6]

We may here only note the fact that, in terms of the basi ingredients of Otto's theory of religion, the theological interpretations and affirmations are acknowledged to entail a "more." What is "more" and what is "less" in theological theories of religion and/or religious theories of theology? Otto here exemplifies issues that are topics of ongoing contemporary discussion. We cannot pursue them here, nor can we pursue the further logical-epistemologial issues involved in Otto's use of the term *a priori*. We go on to note, instead, other points in his argument at which he uses analogies from philosophical aesthetics.

We have said that both the aesthetic and the religious are viewed as incorporating distinctive modes of apprehension of the real and distinctive modes of articulation of the real. Both apprehension and articulation are entailed in aesthetic and in religious *judgments*. Speaking of religious judgment, Otto says:

> There is a precisely parallel process in another department of judgment, that of aesthetic taste. While the taste is still crude, a feeling or forefeeling of the beautiful begins to stir, which must come from an *a priori* conception of beauty already present, else it could not occur at all. The man of crude taste . . . *misapplies* this obscure, dim conception of the beautiful. . . . And later . . . when his taste has been educated, the man . . . becomes qualified to see and to judge rightly, i.e. to recognize as beautiful the outward objects in which the "beauty" of which he has an inward notion and standard really "appears."[7]

There is, Otto affirms, a "faculty of cognizing" the beautiful, expressed in aesthetic judgments, that is "precisely parallel" to the religious "faculty of cognition" that he calls "divination." Note that the concept of a normative aesthetic category is alleged to function in aesthetic judgments as the concept of the holy functions in religious judgments. He then goes on to speak of the aesthetic and the religious apprehension of the real as "intuitions." This leads us to recall the concept of "intellectual intuitions" in some of the Romantic philosophers examined in Chapter Two, though here the parallel is not "precisely similar." Otto affirms that

> No intellectual, dialectical dissection or justification of such intuition is possible, nor indeed should any be attempted, for the essence most peculiar to it would only be destroyed. Rather it is once again to aesthetic judgments that we must look for the plainest analogy to it. And the faculty of judging . . . certainly belongs to that "judgment" (*Urteilskraft*) which Kant analyzes in his Third Critique, and in which he himself sets "aesthetic judgment" in antithesis to logical judgment. Only, we may not infer from this that the particular several judgments passed in this way need be judgments of "taste" in their *content*. Kant's distinction between the "aesthetic" and logical judgment did not mean to imply that the faculty of "aesthetic" judgment was a judgment upon "aesthetic" objects in the special narrow sense of the term "aesthetic," as being concerned with the beautiful. His primary intention is simply and in general terms to separate the faculty of judgment based upon feeling of whatever sort from that of the understanding, from discursive, conceptual thought and inference. . . . Kant employs sometimes another expression also to denote such obscure, dim principles of judgment, based upon pure feeling, viz. the phrase "not-unfolded" or "unexplicated concepts" (*unausgewickelte Begriffe*).[8]

Perhaps the employment of this latter term informs Otto's reflections on "development" in the history of religions.

It is not, however, the concept of the beautiful that is the aesthetic concept which is most suggestively analogous to that of the numinous in the holy; it is the concept of the sublime. "The connection of 'the sublime' and 'the holy' becomes firmly established as a legitimate schematization and is carried on into the highest forms of religious consciousness—a proof that there exists a hidden kinship between the numinous and the sublime which is something more than an accidental analogy, and to which Kant's *Critique of Judgment* bears distant witness."[9] And Otto had clear convictions about where the sublime appears in art as "the most effective means of representing the numinous." It is in architecture, he believed, that it first appeared, in monuments like Stonehenge and the Pyramids. He enumerates specifically

> The art of China, Japan, and Tibet, whose specific character has been determined by Taoism and Buddhism, surpasses all others in the unusual

richness and depth of such impressions of the "magical." In great art the point is reached at which we may no longer speak of the "magical" but are rather confronted with the numinous itself. . . . In no art, perhaps, is this more fully realized than in the great landscape painting and religious painting of China in the classical period of the T'ang and Sung dynasties.

For Westerners, however, "the Gothic appears as the most numinous of all types of art. This is due in the first place to its sublimity; but Worringer in his work, *Probleme der Gothik*, has done a real service in showing that the peculiar impressiveness of Gothic does not consist in its sublimity alone, but [shows its historical derivation from magic]. . . . But 'magic' is too low a word: the tower of the Cathedral of Ulm is emphatically not 'magical,' it is *numinous*."[10]

Neither the magical nor the sublime, however, affords more than "indirect" means of representing the numinous.

Of directer methods our Western art has only two, and they are in a noteworthy way *negative*, viz. *darkness* and *silence*. The darkness must be such as is enhanced and made all the more perceptible by some last vestige of brightness . . . the "mystical" effect begins with semi-darkness. Its impression is rendered complete if the factor of "the sublime" comes to unite with and supplement it. . . . *[S]ilence* is what corresponds to this in the language of musical sounds. . . . [Silence] is a spontaneous reaction to the feeling of the actual *numen praesens*.[11]

Oriental art, says Otto, offers, in addition to darkness and silence, emptiness and empty distances as direct means of producing "impressions" of the numinous.

Empty distance, remote vacancy, is, as it were, the sublime in the horizontal. Chinese architecture . . . makes a wise and striking use of this fact. . . . The imperial tombs of the Ming emperors at Nanking and Peking are, perhaps, the strongest examples of this. [But] still more interesting is the part played by the factor of void or emptiness in Chinese painting. There it has become a special art to paint empty space, to make it palatable, and to develop variations of this singular theme.[12]

This theme is to be understood in terms of the role of "nothingness" and "void" in forms of Buddhist thought—and perhaps in terms of the "negations" of Western "negative" and mystical theology. These, in turn, may be reminders that, in musical settings of the Christian mass, silence may be the most powerful expression of the climactic moment.[13]

We shall not enter into a discussion of Otto's "standards of taste" in these matters, or of other questions of art criticism (or religion criticism?) that they entail. Our purpose in this section has been to show the role of analogies from aesthetic theory in his theory of religion, and only briefly to illustrate some features of the theory by showing his application of it to appraisal of aesthetic data.

MIRCEA ELIADE (1907–1986)

In the introduction to one of his most widely influential books, *The Sacred and the Profane*, Mircea Eliade pays homage to Otto for his pioneering work in establishing the role of the numinous in a viable theory of religion. "After forty years," he says, "Otto's analyses have not lost their value." "But in the following pages," he continues "we adopt a different perspective. We propose to present the phenomenon of the sacred in all its complexity, and not only so far as it is *irrational*. What will concern us is not the relation between the rational and the nonrational elements of religion but the sacred in its entirety." And what is the sacred? "The first possible definition of the sacred is that it is the *opposite of the profane*. The aim of the following pages is to illustrate and define this opposition between the sacred and the profane."[14]

Eliade pursued this aim in myriad works, drawing on an encyclopedic knowledge of data from a wide range of cultures, from prehistoric to modern times. His method throughout is to define by illustration and to illustrate by definition. Data are interpreted as exemplifications, and examples are seen as instantiations of a basic theory of religion—a theory that entails an interpretation of cultural history and an ontological stance.

James Elkins, writing about theory and method in art history, notes that

> A very important kind of proof in art history has been characterized for the first time in print, as far as I am aware, by W.J.T. Mitchell in "Introduction: Pragmatic Theory" in *Against Theory*, p. 6. In distinguishing what "theory is" from what "theory is not," he gives inductive and deductive proof to theory and "adductive" to practice. Adduction is the practice of citation and exemplification. . . . Deduction proceeds from generals to particulars; induction, from particulars to generals, and adduction, from particulars to particulars. In art history, "adduction" is proof by aggregation; when a sufficient number of specific references are provided, a point is taken to be persuasive. The data need not be in direct relation to the point at hand; a point at the end of a paper may receive its weight from unconnected data cited earlier.[15]

Elkins goes on to suggest that to "round out" the forms of procedure employed in the theory and practice of art history, there may also be "transduction," which moves from generals to generals in the formation of "holistic" theories. Eliade, as a historian of religions, I suggest, most frequently employs the practice of "adduction" in support of theory expressed in the language of deductive or inductive proof, or of persuasion. His enterprise as a whole, however, may also be seen as exemplifying a "holistic" theory of religion utilizing the basic categories "sacred" and "profane."

To understand distinctive features of Eliade's theory we must be aware of two things: the cultural resources upon which he drew in its formulation, and the fact that he was both a historian of religions and an artist—a writer of novels, drama, and poetry. He understood the two vocations to be complementary aspects of his spiritual life. "While yet a young man," he wrote,

> I realized that no matter how captivated I might be by oriental studies and the history of religions, I would never be able to give up literature. For me, the writing of fiction—short stories, novellas, novels—was more than a "violon d'Ingres"; it was the only means I had of preserving my mental health, of avoiding neurosis. . . . I said to myself that my spiritual equilibrium—the condition that is indispensable for any creativity—was assured by the oscillation between research of a scientific nature and literary imagination. Like many others, I live alternately in a diurnal mode of the spirit and in a nocturnal one. I know, of course, that the two categories of spiritual activity have to do with the same "subject"—man—or, more precisely, with the mode of existence in the world specific to man, and his decision to adopt this mode of existence.[16]

Eliade employed his theory of religion to interpret aesthetic phenomena; he utilized his aesthetic sensibilities in the formulation of his theory of religion. Like a novelist fashioning or discerning a plot or narrative structure, or like a visual artist or composer of music creating or discerning patterns of relationship in her or his media, Eliade discerned patterns in the data of comparative religion.[17] Frequently his technique is that employed in the formation of a collage, building up layers of significance in an articulated whole. And, as his remarks about the "two categories of spiritual activity" having to do with "the same 'subject'—man—or, more precisely, with the mode of existence in the world specific to man, and his decision to adopt this mode of existence" indicate, he affirms that discernment of religious phenomena and aesthetic creativity stems from the same source: a primordial relation of the human to reality.[18]

What, then, are the sacred and the profane in Eliade's theory of religion? As is the case with Otto, it is not always clear whether or when Eliade uses these terms ontologically, phenomenologically, psychologically, or sociologically. In the passage quoted at the beginning of this section, he speaks of the "phenomenon" of the sacred. However else it may be characterized, the sacred is that which pervasively "appears" in human life; it has phenomenological significance, whether or not it has ontological significance. Eliade's term for such appearances is "hierophanies." He also speaks of the sacred and the profane as "two modes of being in the world," or two existential stances adopted with respect to the world. It is, he believes, clear that for "archaic" humans and "archaic" cultures hierophanies are also "ontophanies"—revelations of foundational reality. In Eliade's uses of the term archaic there would appear to be both a sense of antiquity and homogeneity and a sense of "foundation"—that which is the *archē* of all that is. "Archaic" humans are humans of earliest, or less complexly differentiated, societies; but such societies also exist within later or more complex social configurations. Eliade frequently cited the folk religion of contemporary Romanian or other societies as well as those societies once labeled "primitive" in some anthropological schemes.

It is in such societies that "religious man," *homo religiosus*, is most vividly present. For *homo religiosus* the sacred is that which is basic in being and power, providing order and orientation in and through "sacred space" and "sacred time." The sacred is that which establishes order in chaos. Sacred space and sacred time are nonhomogeneous; in them humans may renew their nurture in being and stability, passing through "breaks" in "profane" space and time, which is homogeneous. Techniques of passage from profane space and time to the sacred source to which Eliade devoted early and extensive attention are those employed in yogic discipline and shamanistic trance. He also highlights those "rites of passage" that enhance and empower the life of humans from birth, through the major transitions of life, to death. Initiation, renewal, and release or fulfillment are exemplified in these rites of passage.[19] The paradigm of profane space is geometrical space; profane space is repetitious and directionless. The character of profane time in relation to sacred time, in turn, is epitomized in "the myth of the eternal return"—return either to the beginning of a repetition of a cycle, or to the empowering and orienting "origin" of space and time. Sacred space represents or provides access to the origin and "original" of all time. Eliade offers many examples of objects and actions that perform these functions in a wide range of cultures. The sacred, in brief, engenders, orders, and centers.

The most deep-seated problem of *homo religiosus* living in profane space and time is, for Eliade, that of time. Whereas loss of orientation in sacred space results in chaotic or directionless life, it is the loss of renewal in sacred time that occasions the experience of what Eliade calls "the terrors of history." Much of his most forceful criticism of "modernity" stems from his rejection of the "historicism" that emerged in the West in the nineteenth century, which we noted in Chapter Two. Before the emergence of historicism, however, there were (and are) other "solutions" to the problems of time. In describing these, Eliade presents an interpretation of cultural history.

"Archaic" humans' escape from the chaos of the "terrors of history" was (is) effected through the media of sacred time that provide immersion in that which was "in the beginning," apprehended as "the eternal present." In Greece, India, and elsewhere, however, "elites" began to see the cyclical returns to origins as themselves embodiments of endless repetition. In Greece other ways of salvation from chaotic repetition were offered in philosophical visions and cultural creations. In India there was a quest for a way of *moksha*, or salvation, from the realm of *maya*, penultimate or profane time and space, to realization of unity with the Ultimately Real, which is "beyond" but also the source of the wheel of *samsara*, driven by the natural/moral law of cause and effect, *karma*. In Hinduism there are many paths to the escape from history. Buddhist enlightenment sees the transitoriness of all that is as the heart of sorrow, and desire or thirst as that which propels beings in transitoriness. That desire, in turn, may be overcome through the Eightfold Path leading to *nirvana*, which is both "blowing-out" and bliss. Again, in Eliade's view, the goal is to overcome "the terrors of history."

With the Hebraic sensibility came a monumental shift: history itself was understood to be the arena of action of the sacred. History was seen as linear, not cyclical, and salvation was to be attained in a community obedient to the divine will "at the end of history"—an ending that is also the goal. Yet eschatology, Eliade suggests, may also be seen as a way of abolishing history. In Christianity the sacred is affirmed to be incarnated in a specific person at a specific time and to reveal its nature decisively through the life, death, and resurrection of that person. Yet in the fulfillment of history expressed in terms of the "Second Coming" of that person, there may also be a form of achieving the "end" of history through an ending of history.

The "valorization" of history as its own savior occurred, Eliade says, in the secularization of the Hebraic and Christian views in various Western philosophies of progress. Now these philosophies have themselves been dissolved in the cataclysms of the twentieth century and in existentialist critiques of all forms of "essentialism." With the industrial revolution and the artificialities of modernity there may be, for the first time in history, the possibility of purely profane existence, without direction or meaning, except that provided by the "false gods" of secularism, whose efficacy is soon belied in the lives of humans who are at least the *descendants* of *homo religiosus*.[20]

Can humans evolve into a nonreligious species, or fall away from that which gave (gives?) meaning to *homo religiosus*? At times Eliade seems to leave the question open. His predominant message, however, seems to be that the sacred cannot disappear, and that humans are by definition "religious" in his sense of the term. He finds many signs of this in the persistence of perennial myths of return to the sacred that are embodied in the art and literature of modernity. These myths and the archetypes they express are also encountered, through dreams and other media, in the "unconscious." Eliade had developed his basic conceptuality before he became fully engaged in dialogue with Jung and his followers, but he found in much of the material of depth psychology a confirmation of this theory of religion. His theory of religion is not, however, a psychology or—I submit—simply a phenomenology of religion. As the key to his understanding of the history of religions it is also—for him,—and implicitly for all descendants or contemporary exemplifications of "religious man"—the key to the achievement of a "new humanism."

It is through his understanding of *symbol* that Eliade most directly relates his work as a historian of religions to his work as a creative artist.[21] Symbols include images and actions of many kinds. Their differentiating distinction from all other modes of articulation lies in their transconceptual dimension. Writing of the role of symbols of *homo religiosus* in archaic cultures, Eliade says

> When we say that symbols [in archaic cultures] succeed in disclosing structures of the real, which much later and in certain cultures has been signified by concepts, we do not intend to homologize symbols with concepts. Their essence and their function are different. Symbols still maintain contact with the deep sources of life; they express, we may say, the "lived" spiritual. This is the reason why symbols have a numinous aura; they disclose that the modalities of the Spirit are at the same time manifestations of Life, and, by consequence, directly engage human existence. Symbols not only disclose a structure of the real or even a dimension of existence, at the same time they carry a significance for human existence. This is why even symbols bearing on ultimate reality conjointly constitute some existential revelations for the man who deciphers their message. Here we can measure the entire distance which separates conceptual language from symbolic language.[22]

Symbols are also "multivalent":

> one characteristic which is specific to a symbol [is] its *multivalence*, which is to say the multiplicity of meanings which it expresses simultaneously. If we retain only one of its significations, in declaring it the only "fundamental" or "first" or "original" signification, we risk not grasping the true message of the symbol. Whatever a symbol strives to show us, it is precisely the unity between the different levels of the real. . . . The cognitive function of the symbol is precisely to disclose to us a perspective from which things [that appear to be] different and very distinct activities are revealed as equivalent and united.[23]

A major form of verbal symbolic expression is myth, in which narrative structure is employed to present fundamental relations, ambiguities, and resolutions in human life. Eliade engaged in extensive analysis of both the myths of religion and those "hidden" myths that operate in many areas of modern culture. He devoted equal attention to rituals, which are understood as enactments of myths. But there are myriad nonverbal images that also perform symbolic functions, and Eliade engaged in extensive description and analysis of a wide range of these images as they function in both "religious" and "secular" cultures. Among other modern visual artists with whom he felt a special affinity are Marc Chagall, Isamu Noguchi, and his fellow Romanian Constantin Brancusi, whose fascination with light and matter Eliade related to the role of light and material in the icons of the Eastern Orthodox Christian tradition. Literary artists to whom he devoted special attention include Marthe Bibescu and Eugene Ionesco,[24] though he also produced arresting critical essays on many other artists working in various media.

Critical appraisals of Eliade's own literary productions have noted the pervasiveness of a sense of mystery and "the magical" in his portrayals of "authenticity." These portrayals, which are consonant with his theory of religion, frequently focus on the search for "centering" in the chaos or "terrors" of history.[25]

Our purpose in this section, again, is not to enter extensively into Eliade's analyses of various art forms from the perspective of his theory of religion, or to present at length varieties of literary criticism of his literary oeuvre. It is instead, as is the case throughout this chapter, to show how aesthetic sensibility and analysis entered into the construction of a theory of religion, and only briefly to illustrate the application of the theory to aesthetic data, as a dimension of the theory itself. In 1967 Eliade published an article on "Cultural Fashions and the History of Religions"[26] in which he analyzed the then-fashionable procedures of structuralism and other critical positions in terms of themes from the history of religions. We may now suggest that, in the light of heightened awareness of cultural pluralism and its significance for theory and method, an appraisal of Eliade's theory might engender another article on "Cultural Fashions in Theories of Religion and the Significance of Cultural Pluralism."

GERARDUS VAN DER LEEUW (1890–1950)

Van der Leeuw, Eliade said in his preface to van der Leeuw's *Sacred and Profane Beauty: The Holy in Art*, was the author of "the only existing large and complete treatise on the phenomenology of religion"[27] At the same time Eliade described van der Leeuw as "one of the outstanding historians of religion in the world"—suggesting, perhaps, an ambiguity in Eliade's own use of the term "historian of religion." Eliade then added that van der Leeuw "was at heart an artist and a religious man."[28] Van der Leeuw and Eliade were thus in many respects kindred spirits. Eliade's art was verbal; van der Leeuw was a musician. Whereas van der Leeuw was much more specific than was Eliade in his description of the *method* that he employed in the study of religion, Eliade was perhaps more explicit with respect to the *theory* that underlay his own, less clearly specific, methodological stance. Both scholars combined aesthetic sensibility with scholarly research in their studies of religion. As was the case in our brief treatment of major themes in Eliade's work, we shall in this section highlight those affinities with aesthetic forms of apprehension and articulation of the real that are exhibited in the work of van der Leeuw.

Like Otto, but unlike Eliade, van der Leeuw was trained in theology as well as in the history of religions. The historical research that complemented his theological studies centered on ancient Egyptian religion. His voluminous writings embraced theological and anthropological topics, but his most lasting influence in the field of religion stems from his *Phänomenologie der Religion*, translated into English as *Religion in Essence and Manifestation*.[29]

What, then, is "the phenomenology of religion?" George Alfred James has written an illuminating account of the origins of this term and has illustrated some common themes in its recent use through analyses of the work of P. D. Chantepie de la Saussaye, William Brede Kristensen, and Gerardus van der Leeuw.[30]

Kant, we recall, distinguished between phenomena, the basic materials of knowledge, and noumena, or "things in themselves." Hegel went on to speak of the unfolding of conceptual reality in the phenomena of mind and culture, in his *Phenomenology of Spirit*, suggesting thereby a distinction between "essences" and their "manifestations," including the essences of art or religion and their manifestations in various historical periods and cultural configurations. Current use of the term phenomenology in philosophical circles, however, is associated primarily with the work of Edmund Husserl, who undertook a "presuppositionless" analysis and description of the forms of pure consciousness and their experienced "intentions" or putative references. Although Husserl's view has been widely appropriated in proposals of a phenomenological approach in many of the human sciences, this is not the approach that is most clearly evident in the work of various practitioners who understand themselves to be engaged in the phenomenology of religion. Although van der Leeuw makes use of a Husserlian notion of epochē or "bracketing" of metaphysical, ontological, psychological, or other factors in the description of phenomena, his references to Heidegger and Jaspers are more numerous than his references to Husserl.

The first use of the term phenomenology occurred in the work of Johann Heinrich Lambert (1728–1771), stemming from Lambert's work in optics. Then John Robinson, in his article on "Philosophy" in the third edition of the *Encyclopaedia Britannica*, used the term to designate the description, arrangement, and reference ("meaning?") of phenomena or events. Chantepie, in his *Manual of the Science of Religion*, employed a similar meaning, to designate "the perspicuous description and arrangement of a subject." It is with this latter usage, George James says, that Chantepie, Kristensen, and van der Leeuw have the greatest affinity. Each of them, James concludes, is ahistorical, systematically descriptive, and nontheological, but at the same time nonreductive, in his employment of a phenomenological method in the study of religion. Yet each draws on the data of anthropological observation and historical research, and each views the results of phenomenological analysis as subject to enrichment or modification by such data.

Van der Leeuw is quite straightforward in describing his understanding of phenomenology:

> Phenomenology seeks the phenomenon as such; the phenomenon, again, is what *appears*. This principle has a threefold application: (1) Something exists. (2) This something "appears." (3) Precisely because it "appears" it is a "phenomenon." But "appearance" refers equally to what appears and to the person to whom it appears; the phenomenon, therefore, is neither pure object, nor *the* object, that is to say, the actual reality, whose essential being is merely concealed by the "appearing" of the appearances. With this a specific metaphysics deals. The term, "phenomenon," still further, does not imply something purely subjective, not a "life" of the subject; so far as is at all possible, a definite branch of psychology is concerned with this. The "phenomenon," therefore, is an object related to a subject, and a subject related to an object; although this does not imply that the subject deals with or modifies the object in any way whatever, nor (conversely) that the object is somehow or other affected by the subject. The phenomenon, still further, is not produced by the subject, and still less substantiated or demonstrated by it; its entire essence is given in its "appearance," and its appearance to "someone." If, finally, this "someone" begins to discuss what "appears," then phenomenology arises.[31]

"Life" and "experience" are, as such, inaccessible to phenomenological analysis; they are givens. All analysis and description is reconstructive. Phenomenological analysis and description begin with "the sketching of an outline within the chaotic maze of so-called 'reality,' this outline being called 'structure.' " (One is reminded of the visual artist sketching an outline of structure in the materials of her or his media.) "Structure," van der Leeuw continues, is *"reality significantly organized."* This is a phrase that will recur in the semiotic "reading" of cultures by the cultural anthropologist Clifford Geertz, to whose views we will turn at the end of this chapter. But structure is not a matter to be arrived at through straightforward inductive inspection; it is not a bloodless classification.

"The understanding of a connection, or of a person or event, *dawns upon us,"* says van der Leeuw. This suggests that something like aesthetic intuition is involved. This analogy gains further credence when van der Leeuw goes on to say, "The appearance . . . subsists as an image. It possesses background and associated planes; it is 'related' to other images that appear, either by similarity, by contrast, or by a hundred *nuances* that can arise here; conditions, peripheral or central position, competition, distance, etc. These relationships, however, are always *perceptible* relationships, 'structural connections'; they are never factual relationships nor causal connections."[32]

One could almost imagine that van der Leeuw is "reading" a painting or explicating a symphony. The result of such reading, in turn, is the perception of a controlling theme, or "ideal type." We shall note his use of this idea in his classification of the types of religion, each of which, in his view, preeminently exemplifies a major theme. Schleiermacher, we recall, said that the various forms of religion are to religion as such as the various forms of music are to music as such. Van der Leeuw the musician provides a thematic analysis of the various types of religion as he "sees" or "hears" them. Like Schleiermacher, however, he goes on to say that the types *exist* only in the living realities that they typify: religion *exists* only in the religions.

Phenomenological discussion proceeds, then, through two operations: "naming" and "interpolation of the phenomenon into our own lives." The naming is simple classification. A mere classification as such, however, may be bloodless and arbitrary. The crucial step for the phenomenologist of religion is the interpolation of the religious phenomena thus classified into her or his own life through what others have termed "empathy." Here again van der Leeuw appropriates language analogous to that employed in "music appreciation": "Only by surrendering oneself, and by submersion in these spiritual traces of vanished time . . . can we train ourselves to recall their feeling; then chords within ourselves, gradually becoming sympathetic, can harmoniously vibrate and sound, and we discover in our own consciousness the strands linking together the old and new."[33] The specifically religious element of such experience is described by van der Leeuw, as by Otto, in terms of "awe," "wonder," "mystery," and "thrill," recalling Kant's description of the sublime. Van der Leeuw, unlike Otto, however, does not ascribe the "sense of the numinous" to a religious *a priori*. It is simply an observed ingredient of certain forms of experience. And, unlike Schleiermacher, he does not identify religion exclusively with a specific kind of experience called "religious experience."

What, then, is religion as a phenomenon? It is rooted in a sense of inadequacy, insufficiency, ambiguity (perhaps "fallenness," in Biblical language), in the experience of life. It entails a quest for soteriological deliverance, or completion, or fulfillment. "The religious significance of things . . . is that on which no wider or deeper meaning can follow. It is the meaning of the whole. It is the last word." But inherent in the phenomenon of religion is the sense that "this meaning is never understood, this last word is never spoken; always they remain superior, the ultimate meaning being a secret which reveals itself repeatedly, but only nevertheless to remain eternally concealed. It implies advance to the farthest boundary, where only one sole fact is understood—that all comprehension is 'beyond'; and thus the ultimate meaning is at the same time the limit of meaning."[34]

The "beyond" is experienced phenomenologically as a vertical axis intersecting the horizontal plane of religion. Phenomenologically it assumes many configurations and designations. But, in van der Leeuw's view, "it-itself," "the Beyond," "the More," is not itself a *phenomenon*; its "traces" appear, but it as such does not. At this point van der Leeuw the theologian employs theological language: "*God*," he says, does not "appear" as a phenomenon; God is *revealed* in the mystery of faith. And the task of theology is not description; it is proclamation. Ninian Smart formulates van der Leeuw's view of the relation of the phenomenon of religion, and therefore of the phenomenology of religion, to divinity in a manner that suggests Paul Tillich's formulation of the relation of philosophy to theology, to which we will turn below. "It is," writes Smart, "as if phenomenology in delineating the existential categories of humankind's religiosity poses questions which ultimately only some form of ultimate theology can answer; for him this was, of course, Christian theology."[35] Van der Leeuw's theology, however, may have more in common on this point with the "high" theology of Karl Barth, in which the radical "otherness" of revelation is affirmed within the context of grace.

In any case, van der Leeuw goes on to say that "Understanding" of these matters "presupposes intellectual restraint. But this is never the attitude of the cold-blooded spectator; it is, on the contrary, the loving gaze of the lover on the beloved object."[36] Elsewhere he speaks of this attitude as a uniquely human possibility, exemplified in Buddhist contemplation and Platonic vision, and perhaps adumbrated in Husserl's phenomenological reduction. "Phenomenology, therefore, is not a method that has been reflectively elaborated, but is man's true vital activity, consisting in losing himself neither in things nor in the *ego*, neither in hovering above objects like a god nor dealing with them like an animal, but in doing what is given to neither animal nor god: standing aside and understanding what appears to view."[37]

From this stance stems both the work of the phenomenologist, who would "understand," "testify," and "discuss," and the work of the artist. Each, for van der Leeuw as for Eliade, may fructify the work of the other, and both are rooted in a distinctive way of "being in the world." Although "the phenomenology of religion is not the poetry of religion," says van der Leeuw, "it should not be forgotten that art is just as much investigation as is science." The phenomenologist, however, "is bound up with the object; he cannot proceed without repeatedly confronting the chaos of the given, and without submitting again and again to correction by the facts; while although the artist certainly sets out from the object, he is not inseparably linked with this. In other words, the poet need know no particular language, nor study the history of the times. . . . In order to interpret a myth he may completely remodel it." The phenomenologist, however, "experiences his own limit, since his path lies always between the unformed chaos of the historical world and its structural endowment with form. All his life he oscillates hither and thither. But *the poet advances*."[38] In a moment we will turn to van der Leeuw's observations on the relation of the arts to the sense of the holy described by the phenomenologist. First let us briefly summarize what van der Leeuw the phenomenologist "saw" and systematically described in the phenomenon of religion.

In keeping with his description of a phenomenon as the appearance of an object to a subject, van der Leeuw addresses first the varieties of forms in which the religious object has appeared. At this point he introduces the concept that most closely approaches a *theoretical* component in his interpretation of religion: the concept of numinous Power. He perhaps derived the concept from its employment in the anthropological work with which he was most familiar, in particular that of Lucien Lévy-Bruhl. By it, of course, he does not mean simple force; its meaning is extended to embrace the referent of the total quest for "empowering" meaning with which he identifies religion. A crucial characteristic of this power is its numinous character—though, as we have noted, he does not make of the numinous a religious *a priori* as Otto did. He then goes on to delineate the varieties of phenomena centering in the "subject" of religion: the "sacred man," the "sacred community," and "the sacred within man" or "the soul."

Since a phenomenon is a subject in relation to an object or vice versa, van der Leeuw next turns to the types of reciprocal relations between subject and object in religious phenomena, in terms of "outward" and "inward" action. Then he describes various understandings of and approaches to the world as the phenomenal context of phenomena in all their relations. This leads to the thematic classification of religions to which we referred above: "Religions of Remoteness and Flight" (e.g., deism); "Religions of Struggle" (e.g., Zoroastrianism); "Religion of Repose"; "Religion of Unrest" (e.g., volitional themes in Judaism, Christianity, and Islam); "The Religion of Strain and Form" (e.g., Dionysian/Apollonian themes in religions); "The Religion of Infinity and Asceticism" (e.g., some forms of Buddhism and Hinduism); "The Religion of Will and of Obedience" (e.g., aspects of Judaism); "The Religion of Majesty and Humility" (e.g., again, aspects of Judaism, Christianity, and Islam); and, finally, "The Religion of Love" (which is, in his view, uniquely Christianity).

Van der Leeuw recognizes the fact that his view of interpretation as a phenomenologist of religion is inextricably bound up with his own religious orientation; the "god's-eye" view is not available to the phenomenologist, nor is it the phenomenologist's aim to attain such a view. Qualified scholars with other religious orientations might appropriately discern other thematic classifications or exemplifications. It seems clear, however, that in van der Leeuw's view a scholar with no personal religious orientation and sensibility would find it difficult if not impossible to engage responsibly in the work of the phenomenology of religion. Similarly, it would be difficult if not impossible for a tone-deaf person to engage in responsible music criticism. Whether there is or could be such a totally areligious person appears at times, for van der Leeuw *as phenomenologist*, as it did for Eliade *as a "historian of religions,"* to be an open or unanswerable question. In the holistic theories of both, however, there would appear to be a perennially indigenous *homo religiosus*.

This observation may be further substantiated in van der Leeuw's analysis of "sacred and profane beauty." In faithfulness to the phenomenological enterprise, van der Leeuw eschews the reduction of art as a phenomenon to religion as a phenomenon, or vice versa, as well as "imperialistic" attempts by art or religion to use the other only as a means to its own ends. There is and has been, he writes, a tension between the two which has sometimes been expressed as rivalry, sometimes as attempted subjugation.

Pious men of strict observance can hardly see in art an obedient maidservant. Artists of *l'art pour l'art* look down on religion with distrust and often with contempt. . . . Thus rivalry begins; first, in rivalry between the religious spirit and the aesthetically . . . oriented man. . . . . Religion is always imperialistic . . . but science, art, and ethics are also imperialistic, each in its own right and in combination with the others . . . and yet, the paths of religion, art, ethics and science not only cross, they also join. [39]

The task of phenomenology, in this matter as in all others, is not to adjudicate the claims made by religion and art, or arbitrarily to set their boundaries.

We limit the question of the relationship between beauty and holiness to the analysis of the relationship between beauty and holiness as man experiences them; that is to say, to the holy act and the beautiful act, or art. . . . Thus we see from our paraphrase of the holy that the relationship can only be grasped by the question, "Can art be a holy act?" The reverse question, "Can religion be art or resolve itself into art?," becomes inadmissible on the general ground of our definition of the holy as "wholly other" and the "absolutely valid."[40]

With these methodological strictures, van der Leeuw engages in analysis and description of how numinous dimensions or ingredients have appeared in various art forms. The first of these forms are forms of motion. He would agree with Suzanne Langer[41] that dance is the primordial art form, and in its origins he sees a unity of dance and religion—a unity that may yield, and indeed in some cultures and historical periods *has* yielded, to estrangement and enmity, but which may point toward an ideal harmony in a religious conception of "the Heavenly Dance." He then turns to "movements and countermovements" in "holy play," tracing a similar unity moving through estrangement or enmity toward a possible ideal harmony. Similar analyses are then made with respect to "beautiful words" and to the pictorial arts. This leads to remarks on religious architecture. Perhaps his most suggestive aesthetic/religious analysis is his analysis of music.

His study of "sacred and profane beauty" concludes, however, with van der Leeuw the theologian's construction of a "theological aesthetics" in which he asks, "What do all the arts have in common, from the theological point of view? What is the midpoint about which everything turns?" The answer, briefly, is as follows: "The dance reflects the movement of God, which also moves us here on earth. The drama presupposes the holy play between God and man. Verbal art is the hymn of praise in which the Eternal and its works are represented.

Architecture reveals to us the lines of the well-built city of God's creation. Music is the echo of the eternal Gloria."[42]

Although it is true that "holiness always comprehends beauty," and "their unity does not have to be discovered, but simply observed," still there is need for discussion. "First," says van der Leeuw,

> let us observe that this truth is not reversible. Beauty is holiness. But holiness is not absolutely, or exclusively, beauty; it is more. "Holy" is the ultimate word, "beautiful" the penultimate. . . . The question is not "How can we make art religious?" Nor is it "When or how does art become religious?". . . . We ask only, when and how is the unity revealed to us which was self-evident to primitive man, but which we perceive only with effort? In other words, there is no particular art which can be designated as religious. Still less is there a religion which we can call aesthetic. There is only a single art, and it is first of all, art. There is only a single religion [i.e., a single phenomenon, "religion"]. But again and again we discern an essential unity between art and religion; again and again holiness and beauty appear to us in the same guise.[43]

Yet, "with an external division between 'Sacred' and 'Profane' one will never achieve an expression of the holy in art. 'Holy' material is never the cause of art, least of all religious art. . . . All music that is absolute music, without additions, without anything counterfeit, is the servant of God; just as pure painting is, whether it treats religious subjects or not; and as true architecture is, apart from the churches it builds."[44]

PAUL TILLICH (1886–1965)

Like Otto and van der Leeuw, Paul Tillich was a theologian as well as a theorist of religion and culture. More explicitly than either Otto or van der Leeuw, however, he understood his primary task to be that of the systematic philosophical theologian, bringing the insights of Christian faith as he understood them to bear on problems posed in an existentialist analysis of modern culture. His understanding of religion and art, therefore, stemmed from a theology of culture. The theology was, in his view, distinctively Protestant in many of its major concepts, including what he called "the Protestant principle" of judgment in cultural analysis. The concept of culture that he employed has an affinity with the classical concept of *paideia* and with the Hegelian concept of culture as the corporate embodiment of Spirit.

Tillich's association with Otto began when they were briefly colleagues at Marburg (1925–1926). He later assumed that his students were familiar with *The Idea of the Holy*, and he drew on Otto's characterization of the dialectic of the numinous as both *mysterium* and *fascinans* in many of his writings, but especially in the first volume of his

Systematic Theology and in popular works like *The Dynamics of Faith*.[45] Unlike Otto and Eliade, however, he had only brief firsthand experience with Oriental culture.[46] Whereas Otto was a colleague in his earlier years, Eliade was a colleague in the last years of Tillich's teaching career, and his seminars with Eliade marked a deepening interest in the history of religions. From the time of his doctoral dissertation through the entire development of his theology of culture, he was deeply influenced by Schelling's reflections on art, and by the role that history of religions played in Schelling's "positive philosophy."

Van der Leeuw, we have seen, could speak of a theological aesthetics. Tillich did not, though he analyzed and employed his own, somewhat idiosyncratic, versions of aesthetic theory and history and philosophy of art in his theology of culture. The arts had a significant influence on Tillich. Like Ludwig Wittgenstein in Vienna, he once aspired to be an architect. "In my early life I wished to become an architect, and only in my late teens the other desire, to become a philosophical theologian, was victorious. I decided to build in concepts and propositions instead of stone, iron, and glass. But building remains my passion, in clay and in thought, and, as the relation of medieval cathedrals to the scholastic systems shows, the two ways of building are not so far from each other. Both express an attitude towards the meaning of life as a whole."[47]

John Paul Clayton, however, has suggested that the art of Tillich's theology is more like the art of the sculptor Rodin, in that he crafted malleable conceptual components that were employed in many related works, refining and relating them to each other in creative ways in an ongoing process of theological composition.[48] But the philosophy of Schelling, a principal source of Tillich's thought, was more like the work of a visual artist, combining forms and values in a succession of visions and re-visions. And it was finally visual artists, along with some literary artists, on whom Tillich focused most intensively in his own reflections on the relation of the holiness of beauty to the beauty of holiness.

In World War I Tillich served as an army chaplain, an experience that made a deep and lasting impression on his life and thought. It was while he was on leave from the trenches that he had his first "revelatory" experience through the medium of a work of art:

> it was the dirt, the horrors, and the ugliness of the First World War . . . which induced me systematically to study the history of art and to collect as many as possible of the cheap reproductions available to me on the battlefields. Then on one of my furloughs I happened to visit the Berlin (Kaiser Friedrich) Museum and stood before a round picture by Botticelli

(*Madonna and Child with Singing Angels*) and had an experience for which I do not know a better name than revelatory ecstasy.[49]

Though this painting is of a style that Tillich would later criticize as lacking authentic religious import, it was for him at the time power-fully expressive of an essential contrast between the "brokenness" of life in the trenches (and, later, of life in postwar Germany) and an anticipated consummation of human tragedy and human comedy in faithful hope. The most powerful symbol of that consummation was, for him, the Christian concept of the Kingdom of God.

It was, however, the *expressiveness* of the painting that was funda-mental for Tillich, and in the immediate postwar period it was in the work of a variety of artists arbitrarily labeled "abstract expressionists" that Tillich found the most religiously significant visual art. We will return to this theme in our brief description of Tillich's aesthetic the-ory below. But first let us summarize the theory of religion that un-derlies Tillich's aesthetic views.

Tillich's definition of religion, which has been widely appropriated by scholars in various disciplines, is that religion is "ultimate concern." The phrase includes both subjective and objective emphases. It ex-presses, for him, the most fundamental and dynamic orientation of personality. To be human is to be concerned. "Concern," as he em-ploys the concept, encompasses any and all human needs and objects of need, all the intentionalities of persons and societies. There are, however, concerns that focus and order all other concerns. There are, in any specific configuration of ordering, the concerns that are "ulti-mate."

Echoing themes of existentialist philosophers, Tillich characterizes the most vital concern of humans *qua* human as the concern for mean-ing. Ultimate concern for meaning, in turn, is concern for the uncon-ditionally meaningful. Humans have sought to find the uncondition-ally meaningful in a host of allegiances to foci of concern that prove to be only conditionally meaningful and therefore, in the language of religion, "demonic" or idolatrous: self, nation, cause, even forms of "religion" as such. Authentic ultimate concern must be concern for that which is truly ultimate. That which is truly ultimate *subjectively* pro-vides productive centering of personality; *objectively* it is concern for that which Tillich at various time calls "the Unconditioned"; "the In-finite"; "being-itself"; "the ground and power of being"; "being as both ground and abyss" (Otto's *mysterium*, Boehme's *ungrund*); or, theologi-cally speaking, "God"—or "the God above or beyond 'God.' " In these locutions Tillich articulates an awareness of that which is "beyond" subjective/objective, finite/infinite polarities.

In the phrase "ultimate concern," therefore, Tillich includes both the psychological ultimacy of the existentialist and the ontological ultimacy of the essentialist renderings of reality. Central to his vision is a sense of the "split" between essence and existence, or of the "estrangement" of finite beings from infinite being—a split or estrangement expressed theologically in the myth and doctrine of the Fall. Estrangement is not, however, total separation. To be, he says, is to "participate" in "the power of being." Here he draws on the long tradition of perceiving forms of being as "participations" in the ultimately Real—a tradition stemming from Neoplatonic-Augustinian thinking that was an important ingredient of Tillich's own sensibilities and his modes of expressing them. In estrangement there is yearning for reunion with that from which (or from whom) one is estranged. Recalcitrant finite being seeks harmoniously dynamic participation in being-itself. Estrangement is exacerbated, and finitude becomes anarchic, when psychological ultimacy is centered on that which is not ontologically or axiologically ultimate.

How may this construal of the matter be best expressed in *theos*-language, or theology? Thomas Aquinas rendered the divine name in Genesis, "I am that I am," or "I will be what I will be," in the philosophical language of "He Who Is," whose "essence" is "existence"—for Aristotle as interpreted by Thomas, *actus purus*. Tillich affirmed that the paradigmatic Biblical expression of "the Unconditioned," "the Infinite," "being-itself," is "Thou shalt have no other gods before me."[50] It is this command, with all of its ontological and cultural implications, that Tillich calls "the prophetic principle" or, later, "the Protestant principle." The latter designation reflects his view of Christian history. Humankind, he said, is driven by its fundamental situation in reality to seek an ultimate referent for its ultimate concerns in autonomy, affirming the self-sufficiency of the finite; in heteronomy, where infinite significance is ascribed to a finite reality, such as nation or Church; and in theonomy, in which all finite goods are both affirmed and qualified as penultimate in relation to the ultimate source of being and meaning. He saw the Protestant Reformation as an attempt to reform the Christian Church in the face of misused heteronomous authority and practice. His primary use of the term Protestant principle is, however, more technical and programmatic. It is with this usage that he speaks of Picasso's *Guernica* as "the most powerful Protestant picture of our time."

Tillich, however, always speaks as a Christian theologian. He saw in the Biblical story of Israel and of Christianity as the New Israel the definitive expression of the human predicament and its resolution. It is normatively in the New Testament "picture of Jesus as the Christ," he believed, that humans may perceive the lineaments of salvation. Although there is an irreducible element of historicity in the composition of that picture, the power of salvation lies in the power of the picture as such. Why? Because in the New Testament picture of Jesus (historical person) as the Christ (transhistorical medium of reconciliation, reunion, beatitude) we see a dynamic portrait of One who was completely open to the Infinite—to the will of One whom he called "Father" in unique accents. Jesus affirmed life but made no claims of autonomous ultimacy. He was completely transparent to the Real (cf. Schleiermacher). The definitive symbol of that transparency is the symbol of the Cross, where acceptance of "God-forsakenness" is affirmed as the most powerful presence of the divine. In the Crucifixion all the contradictions and paradoxes of the human situation are offered up to a Power that becomes the Power of Resurrection—the Power of "the New Being." The Resurrection Power of the New Being sustains the Christian in a faith that undergirds hope, issuing in acts of love. The symbol of the consummation of that hope, as we have noted, is the Kingdom of God, which is both historical and transhistorical.

It is in terms of his version of Christian theology that Tillich's views of culture, and therefore of aesthetics and the arts as ingredients of culture, are to be understood. A "theological theory of religion" is employed by Tillich in both his theological analysis of religion and culture and in his systematic exposition of the major doctrines of Christian faith. In the latter enterprise he followed what he called the "method of correlation," in which existential philosophical analysis is employed to delineate those features of human and nonhuman nature that pose the questions to which the affirmations of Christian faith are addressed: the dilemmas of reason to which the resolutions of revelation are offered.

In accord with the central Christian doctrine of the Trinity, the first volume of the systematics addresses the mystery of God the Father; the second, the mystery of the Son; the third, the mystery of the Spirit. Issues of the relation of the aesthetic to the religious, or of beauty to holiness, are most extensively addressed in the third volume. This is because aesthetic sensibility and artistic creativity are understood as (with Hegel and others) works of *Geist* or Spirit. Spirit is the source and medium of all that is distinctively human in creation. The corporate expression of Spirit is culture. Tillich does not offer a highly nuanced theory of culture. His theory of culture, I have suggested, is in continuity with the classical Greek concept of *paideia*, a concept that provided the context of discussions of culture in the German philosophical milieu from which Tillich drew many of his assumptions. It is in this light that we are to understand his often-quoted formulation of his theology of culture: religion is the soul (or substance) of culture; culture is the form (or expression) of religion. If religion is that ultimate concern which provides the dynamics of the human spirit, then culture is the various forms in which the dynamics have expressed themselves in cultural history: the "forms" and "formings" of ultimate concern. Among the most important of these are those that are analyzed in aesthetic theory and assessed in the philosophy of art. What, in Tillich's view, are the most viable or significant of these forms and theories?

Culture, for Tillich, consists of both theoretical and practical activities. The realm of *theoria* is the realm of apprehension of the real, cognitively and aesthetically. The realm of *praxis* is the realm of technical and artistic transformation of the real. Is aesthetic apprehension, then, a mode of cognition? Yes and no. Cognitive apprehension understood as conceptual knowledge entails a certain cognitive "distance" from that which is "seen."

> The word *theoria*, "theory," is derived from *theoreo*, which means looking at something. . . . Even more characteristic is the derivation of the Greek word *eidenai*, "to know," from *idein*, "to see." The object of knowledge is that which you see in a thing as its essence. Finally we must remember that *aesthetics*, the word itself, is derived from *aisthanomai*, that is, I am aware of something. All of this shows the identity between the cognitive and the aesthetic functions. Both receive reality without changing it as such. They transform it into images, concepts, words, sounds, colors. But they do not transform the object as such. . . . The theoretical transformation of what is given to us does not transform the actual state of the given. It transforms the content of the ordinary encounter into an object of a cognitive or aesthetic perception. . . . On the basis of this identity the difference can be described: *theoria* as cognitive reception and transformation gives us an analysis of what the things are in their relation to each other. *Theoria*, as aesthetic reception and transformation, gives the vision of what the things are for themselves. . . . If knowledge is defined as the aim of the cognitive function . . . art does not mediate knowledge. If knowledge stands for aesthetic awareness of a level of reality, the answer must be that art does mediate knowledge. But one may question whether it is wise to call the aesthetic awareness of what things are, for themselves, knowledge. [51]

Presentations of aesthetic awareness involve (1) content (subject matter); (2) form—by which Tillich means the way in which "meaning" is imparted to subject matter by line, color, words, sounds, and so forth, and (3) what he variously calls "sense" (*sinn*), "substance," or "import." Articulations of form and "sense" or "substance" are, for Tillich, the most significant ingredients of aesthetic judgment, because the ultimate can be transmitted only through finite forms that are judged to have specific import or significance.

"Style" is another feature of aesthetic creations. It is an expression of the artist's creative imagination in relation to the "school," tradition, and cultural situation in which the artist operates. Tillich offered varying typologies of style. Speaking theologically, he could say that what he called "idealistic" art—the art of the "beautiful" or "beautifying"— seeks to express the "dreaming innocence" of humankind's "original" ("essential") situation "before the Fall." Perhaps the Botticelli painting that first moved Tillich imparted something of this sense in the midst of the most horrible experiences of "fallenness." In general, however, Tillich considered most examples of idealistic art to be inferior aesthetically and religiously because they misleadingly express ideal essence apart from the existential estrangement that characterizes the actual human situation. Thus he both appreciated and criticized classical Greek art and the art of the Renaissance as artistically impressive but existentially misleading renderings of the real. Elsewhere he suggests that even the "dreaming innocence" of idealistic art expresses the finite freedom that underlies the possibility of both Fall and Redemption. The experience of the Botticelli painting could therefore be seen as an experience of anticipated resolution.

The style that was most appreciated by Tillich, however, is that which he called "expressionist." Its exemplars, for him, were the postwar German abstract expressionists. In their work he saw a prophetic rendering of both the depths of formlessness and meaninglessness in a shattered culture and a prophetically courageous acceptance of this, drawn from a contrasting and perhaps incipient resolution in the possibilities of new social realities or—ultimately, for Tillich—transhistorical or eschatological salvation. Why did he associate the most powerful art with *expression*? The answer lies perhaps in his sense of a transforming apprehension of the Infinite that is *simultaneously* "intuition" and "expression"—where "intuition *is* expression." This is a view of aesthetic apprehension that is formalized in aesthetic theory by Benedetto Croce and R. G. Collingwood. Furthermore, if for Tillich the truly ultimate focus of ultimate concern is beyond conceptualization or imagination, then only those art forms that seem explicitly to conflate apprehension and expression can point to the ultimately Real.

These art forms, however, can only point to the transcendent. And other forms, like Impressionism as interpreted by Tillich, only dwell lovingly on the varied surfaces of things. Nevertheless, the "realism" that arose in reaction to Impressionism could, Tillich thought, affirm the sense of transcendence in the starkness of the real, if it is judged in terms of what he called "belief-ful realism." Other renderings of the natural, as in some Chinese landscape painting or some Western medieval "naive" realism, might portray what he called an "immanent mysticism." But it was expressionism as such, in whatever forms it might present itself in art history, that was for Tillich the most authentic aesthetic rendering of holiness. Indeed, expressionism became for him a category that is not reducible to works of specific periods, even though in his own time it was seen by him to be most powerfully incorporated in the work of the abstract expressionists. Tillich's theology of culture, however, is of culture as ongoing and dynamic, and he prescinds from fixing the most authentic rendering of the holy in art in one particular historical style. Styles, he thought, like symbols, are born, live, and die; when they have died new forms more adequate to new situations cannot be arbitrarily produced by self-conscious "taking thought" or through programmatic manifestos.

This reflection leads us to note briefly Tillich's view of symbol as such. We have seen the importance of Eliade's concept of symbol for his delineation of the configurations of the sacred in relation to the profane. Tillich makes a basic distinction between symbols and signs. The latter are any items that are understood to point to or stand for any other items. The protocols of their pointing are purely conventional, and there is nothing inherent in any sign that makes it the pointer to another sign. Symbols, however, not only point to but also "participate in," ontologically inhere in, that which they symbolize. Again we note the role of the concept of participation in Tillich's ontology. His examples of signs and symbols include traffic lights, on the one hand, and flags, on the other.

Symbols, through their participation in that which they symbolize, also reveal the "depths" of the symbolized to the "depth" of the percipient. They "unfold" levels of reality. Symbols may take many forms, including those of myth, ritual, and verbal images. Theological language is first and foremost symbolic language. Philosophical language, on the other hand, aspires to be conceptual. Philosophical theology, the enterprise in which Tillich thought of himself as primarily engaged, seeks to render the verbal and other symbols of Christian faith in conceptual interpretation. "God" may thus be understood as "Being-itself"—though given Tillich's "high" doctrine of God, it remains an open question whether "Being-itself" is, theologically speaking, also for him a symbol. Tillich the philosophical theologian was inclined to say that it is not; Tillich the mystic, who spoke of "the abyss" as well as of the "ground" of being, was inclined to say that it is. Religious symbols, in any case, differ from all other symbols in their intrinsic communication of their inadequacy to reveal fully that in which they participate. For Tillich, we have noted, the Cross is for this reason the most powerful symbol of Christian faith—and, he would claim, for the life of faith to which the various "ways of faith" in the religions of the world aspire.

In the light of these reflections we conclude that in the last analysis, Tillich's theory of aesthetics, like his theory of religion, is a theory stemming from a specific theological orientation. Michael Palmer is justified in saying that Tillich would probably find favor with very few art historians. This is not simply because his aesthetics is so largely dependent on a conceptual framework that is rarely informed by any analysis of particular works of art, but also "because he believed that what he called 'import' is an ingredient in an artwork in the same way that content and form are. . . . Invariably we find that an aesthetic judgment can be explained only by reference to theological or philosophical concepts that stand behind it."[52]

Tillich may be appreciated for an impressive theologically shaped view of the relation of the aesthetic to the religious that made a major contribution to the ongoing discussion of the relation of holiness of beauty. At the same time it must be said that though he was a theologian who aspired to a global vision, his theology of culture itself embodies assumptions peculiar to the specific culture of "Christendom" as he experienced it in the twentieth century. In the next section we will look at another theory of culture, and of art and religion, that seeks to be confessionally neutral in addressing questions of cultural pluralism and in "reading" two configurations at the opposite ends of a culture called "Islamic."

CLIFFORD GEERTZ (1929–)

Whereas Tillich's theory of culture has an affinity with the classical concept of *paideia* and with Hegel's view of culture as the corporate embodiment of Spirit, Clifford Geertz draws on a concept of culture that is rooted in the development of the social sciences, beginning in the eighteenth century. The goals of these versions of the *Geisteswissenschaften* combined some of the emphases of Vico's vision of "the new science" with some of those expressed in Francis Bacon's. In France, Emile Durkheim sought to emulate some of the ideals of "positive science" in his pioneering study of *The Elementary Forms of the Religious Life*.[53] Others pursued a search for the "origins" of religion in cultural history.[54] But it was Max Weber (1864–1920) who brought together the formative theses of sociology in relation to religion and art, drawing on both scientific investigation and comparative analysis. His principal interest was in the interplay of religion and culture, especially with respect to the role of economic theory and practice in cultural configurations. He saw each religious tradition as a specific pattern of culture reflecting a broader cultural context. The major function of religions, he thought, was to provide ways of dealing with problems of meaning in human life in the light of contingency, powerlessness, scarcity, and the "breaking points" that threaten morality and morale.[55]

The most influential heir of the Weberian program in the United States was Talcott Parsons of Harvard, who developed powerful concepts of social systems and social action in terms of which religious and other social phenomena might be interpreted. His students included Thomas O'Dea, who also drew explicitly on Tillich's definition of religion in his *Sociology of Religion*;[56] Robert Bellah, who explored both the Tokugawa religion of Japan and the forms of "civil religion" in America and contemporary American "habits of the heart";[57] and Clifford Geertz.

We have chosen to examine Geertz's theory of culture, and of religion and art as cultural phenomena, for several reasons. He has incorporated in his cultural anthropology major themes enunciated by other sociologists and cultural anthropologists. He has done extensive fieldwork in two different configurations of Islamic cultures. And, perhaps more than any other representative of social-scientific theories of religion and art, he has thought deeply and productively not only about the religious and the aesthetic dimensions of culture as such but also about the "art" of ethnographic work itself. Finally, he poses in an arresting way the problems of cultural pluralism, and of methodological self-consciousness in the postmodern age, to which we will turn in Chapter Six.

Writing of the work of Parsons, Geertz says,

> Until Talcott Parsons, carrying forward Weber's double rejection (and double acceptance) of German idealism and Marxist materialism, provided a viable alternative, the dominant concept of culture in American social science identified culture as learned behavior. . . . In place of this near-idea, Parsons, following not only Weber but a line of thought stretching back at least to Vico . . . elaborated a concept of culture as a system of symbols by which man confers signficance upon his own experience. Symbol systems, man-created, shared, conventional, ordered, and indeed learned, provide human beings with a meaningful framework for relating themselves to one another, to the world around them, and to themselves. At once a product and a determinant of social interactions, they are to the processes of social life as a computer program is to its operations, the genic helix to the development of an organism, the blueprint to the construction of a bridge, the score to the performance of the symphony.[58]

Geertz himself would go on to see these "symbolic systems of significance" as not only "models for" (templates) but also "models of" (paradigmatic exemplars of) cultural meaning. And he would draw not only on a Weberian-Parsonian concept of symbols and their roles but also on the "philosophy of symbolic forms" developed by Ernst Cassirer and articulated by Suzanne Langer.[59] In the light of these and other influences he has developed a "semiotic" theory of culture, in which cultures are seen as "texts" to be "read" and interpreted. This suggests to him affinities between the work of the cultural anthropologist and that of the literary critic—an interplay between, as Giles Gunn has put it, the "criticism of culture and the culture of criticism." The literary critic to whom he acknowledges special indebtedness is Kenneth Burke.[60]

Geertz employs many analogies from aesthetics in the exposition of his interpretive theory of culture. The method employed by the ethnographer is that of "participant observation." The cultural anthropologist adopts the difficult but creative stance of one who both "participates in" (recall other senses of "participation" above), "lives-into" or "as a member of," the culture he or she wishes to interpret, and at the same time exercises disciplined habits of "observation." The interpreter places himself or herself in patterns of relationship among the subjects of study and at the same time views these subject phenomena as "objects" of interpretation. Geertz raises the fundamental questions of what sort of object the observers are to the "subjects" of their inquiry—and of what sort of object or subject the observers are to the observers themselves. All these questions resonate with questions about the relations of "author" to "text" in literary production and interpretation. Does the ethnographer/author *de*-scribe or *in*-scribe? By what author-ity?

In any case, cultural anthropologists, according to Geertz, should seek intimate knowledge of carefully delimited "local" configurations of the broader culture they seek to understand. And they should employ the technique of "thick description" in seeking to convey a sense of the matter to be interpreted.

> What the ethnographer . . . is faced with—except when (as, of course, he must do) he is pursuing the more automatized routines of data collection—is a multiplicity of complex conceptual structures, many of them superimposed or knotted into one another, which are strange, irregular, and inexplicit, and which he must contrive first somehow to grasp and then to render. . . . Doing ethnology is like trying to read (in the sense of "constructing a reading of") a manuscript—foreign, faded, full of elipses . . . but written not in conventionalized graphs of sound but in transient examples of shaped behavior.[61]

We may note that visual artists as well as literary artists render interpretations of human and natural locales. Van Gogh employed "thick" brush strokes in rendering his subjects. Geertz recommends "thick description" in rendering his—though his sense of "thick" incorporates also the delicacy of the miniaturist. And Cezanne rendered again and again the particularity of his beloved Mont St. Victoire. Geertz observes that "Once human behavior is seen as symbolic action—action which, like phonation in speech, pigment in painting, or sonance in music, signifies . . . the question as to whether culture is patterned conduct or a frame of mind . . . loses sense.[62] And, as is the case in painting, the distinction between content or subject matter and mode of articulation becomes quite tentative.[63]

In his study of four "authorial" figures in anthropological writing— relating in this concept to the views of Foucault and Roland Barthes on "classics" and "derivatives"—Geertz states that "As the criticism of fiction and poetry grows best out of an imaginative engagement with fiction and poetry themselves, not out of imported notions about what they should be, the criticism of anthropological writing (which is in a strict sense neither, and in a broad one both) ought to grow out of a similar engagement with *it*, not out of our preconceptions of what it must look like to qualify as a science."[64] Anthropological works *are* things *made*, the fruit of *poiesis;* yet they are also a distinctive blend of Bacon's vision and Vico's. Like other scientific works, they must be grounded in observable and reportable behavior, and their aim is not simply delectation or to be a "good read."

Geertz describes Ruth Benedict's approach to her material on Japan as the product of "an aesthetic mind" and says that she had an "aesthetic view of human behavior, surrounded by the trappings of an activist social science." He suggests that her work on cannibalism and other "exotic" human behavior may be compared in its intent with the work of Swift. Although her work and that of others whose approach is similar is to be appreciated for what it is, Geertz cautions against the peril of "sociological aestheticism." I maintain that a good safeguard against aestheticism of all sorts—sociological, religious, or artistic—is a knowledge of philosophical aesthetics. Of sociological aestheticism Geertz says:

> The only defense against it . . . is to look at the symbolic dimensions of social action . . . [in such a way as] not to turn away from the existential dilemmas of life for some empyrean realm of de-emotionalized forms; it is to plunge into the midst of them. The essential vocation of interpretive anthropology is not to answer our deepest questions but to make available to us answers that others . . . have given . . . and thus to include them in the consultable record of what man has said.[65]

What, then, is "culture," what are its "symbolic forms," and what are the specific roles of religion and art as "cultural systems," in Geertz's view? Kenneth R. Rice has traced the development of Geertz's theory of culture from early formulations that stressed functionalist themes to his mature semiotic theory.[66] A succinct formulation of the latter is as follows: "the culture concept to which I adhere . . . denotes an historically transmitted pattern of meanings embodied in symbols, a system of inherited conceptions expressed in symbolic forms by means of which men communicate, perpetuate, and develop their knowledge about and attitudes towards life."[67] Note the emphasis on historical transmission, on "patterns of meaning," and on "symbolic forms." Geertz is acutely aware of constant historical change within cultural continuities. But in these changing configurations he discerns *patterns* of *meaning* expressed in *symbolic forms*.

What, then, is a symbol?

> In some hands [the term] is used for anything that signifies something to someone: dark clouds are symbolic precursors of an on-coming rain. In others it is used only for explicitly conventional signs of one sort or another. [Cf. Tillich's concept of "sign."] In yet others . . . it is used for any object, act, event, quality, or relation that serves as a vehicle for a conception—the conception is the symbol's "meaning"—and that is the approach I shall follow here. The number 6, written, imagined, laid out as a row of stones, or even punched into the program tapes of a computer, is a symbol. But so also is the Cross, talked about, vizualized, shaped worriedly in the air or fondly fingered at the neck, the expanse of painted canvas called "Guernica" [Note the references to two of Tillich's favorite examples.] or the bit of painted stones called a charinga, the word "reality" [Cf. Tillich's "being-itself"?], or even the morpheme "—ing." They are all symbols, or at least symbolic elements, because they are tangible formulations of notions, abstractions from experience fixed in perceptible forms, concrete embodiments of ideas, attitudes, judgments, longings, or beliefs.[68]

Symbol systems provide both "models *for*" and "models *of*" specific cultural behavior. Then what, specifically, are religious symbols? A religion, Geertz says, is "(1) a system of symbols which acts to (2) establish powerful, persuasive, and long-lasting moods and motivations in men by (3) formulating conceptions of a general order of existence and (4) clothing these conceptions with such an aura of factuality that (5) the moods and motivations seem uniquely realistic."[69] Yet the problem today, he says, "is not one of constructing definitions of religion. . . . It is a matter of discovering just what sorts of belief and practices support what sorts of faith under what sorts of conditions.

Our problem, and it grows worse day by day, is not to define religion, but to find it."[70]

Whereas faith may be defined as "steadfast attachment to some transtemporal conception of reality,"[71] the specific function of religious symbols is so to articulate "a general conception of the order of things" and, simultaneously, a set of attitudes and motivations for a specific "way of life," that each of these components appears to validate the other—to be the obverse of one face on a coin. A specific way of life, with its distinctive "moods and motivations," is believed to be grounded in a specific view of the world; and the view of the world is seen to be validated in the way of life that it entails. "This way of life is authorized by this view of the world"; "this view of the world is validated in the practice of this way of life." "By their fruits you shall know them; and the distinction between good and bad fruit is grounded in the 'true world-tree.'" Locutions like these would, I suggest, express Geertz's view that religious symbols articulate worldviews and ethos in such a way that each seems to authenticate the other. This circularity seems, indeed, to characterize the phenomenological reality of religious traditions, or the philosophical thrust of a view of religion as ultimate concern—though one would add to the latter, following Clement Webb, the adjective "intimate." (Webb said that "intimacy and ultimacy are the hallmarks of religion.")[72]

Following Weber, Geertz goes on to say that religious symbols provide foci of order in chaos (cf. Eliade's sacred space and sacred time) and address especially questions of meaning in the face of contingency, suffering, and guilt. Religious symbols, he affirms, are generated in ritual, and ritual is the enactment of narrative orderings of symbols.

It is in the light of this understanding of religion and religious symbols that Geertz has sought to discover the meaning (*conceptual* rendering) of a specific religious tradition in specific places and times. In "observing" Islam in Morocco and Indonesia he assumes as a common ingredient of both cultures the universally shared "Pillars of Islamic Faith."[73] His technique is to focus first on two classical figures who would seem to embody the distinctive character of Islam in the desert country of the Berbers, on the one hand, and in a more complex and highly nuanced Indic culture into which Islam came, on the other. He then traces the fortunes of the faith in the two cultures, the one dominated by the ideals of the Marabout and Sheik, the other by a model of the "theater state." He is especially interested in the impact of "modernity" on the two cultures—and, significantly, he does not equate modernity with "Westernization." He suggests, rather, that there are strategies of "internal conversion" in religious traditions that enable them to incorporate change within an ongoing identity. Of special contemporary interest is the role of what he calls "the scripturalist interlude" in both cultures, in which the seeds of what is now called "fundamentalism" may be found. He concludes his study with sketches of two contemporary exemplary figures: a Muslim student from Morocco en route by air to study in the United States, clutching the Koran in one hand and a glass of Scotch in the other; and a mystical theoretical physicist in Indonesia who spends his spare time elaborating an esoteric metaphysic. The sketches of these figures bespeak Geertz's interest in the problems of modernization, cultural pluralism, and methodological self-consciousness, to which we will return in Chapter Six.

What is the role of art in relation to religion, in Geertz's view? Art, like religion, he asserts, may be seen as a "cultural system." This means that abstract aesthetic theories that place distinguishing characteristics of artworks in specific ingredients like form or content—or in theories of uniquely aesthetic apprehension and articulation of the real—may be misleading if not distorting. He expresses appreciation for Michael Baxendall's *Painting and Experience in Fifteenth-Century Italy*,[74] in which Baxendall stresses the importance of what he calls "the Period Eye" in assessing a work of art. This means "the equipment that a fifteenth-century painter's public—(that is, other painters and the 'patronage classes')—brought to complex visual stimulations like pictures."[75] These public factors include the painterly techniques available at a given time, "and, in this case . . . living a quattrocentro life and seeing things in a quattrocentro way." This means, of course, an awareness of how and in what sense most of these paintings were "religious" paintings—and that means knowledge of both the theoretical and the practical components of the religious orientation of the time, in the light of which the beholder "completed" the beholder's highly personal experience of the picture.

Any responsibly informed assessment of either art or religion, and of their relations, is, I maintain, inherently *culturally relative*, and it entails sensitivity to the complexities of the broader cultures in which particular religious and aesthetic systems of culture occur. It is the absence of this sensitivity that vitiates Tillich's broad use of the concept of expressionism and his idiosyncratic application of it to arbitrarily selected works in various periods. Geertz exemplifies the goals of another approach when he presents an intriguing analysis of the vocation of the poet in Moroccan Islamic culture (a vocation that is also honored in many other Muslim cultures) and of the relation of Koranic authority to poetic inspiration and performance in the figures on which he focuses. And, with respect to the usefulness of a proffered distinctively aesthetic category such as beauty, he writes,

> It is, after all, not just statues (or paintings, or poems) that we have to do with, but the factors that cause these things to seem important—that is affected with *import* [italics added—cf. Tillich's use of this concept, above]—to those who make or possess them, and these are as various as life itself. If there is any commonality among all the arts in all the places that one finds them (in Bali they make statues out of coins, in Australia drawings out of dirt), that justifies including them under a single, Western-made, rubric, it is not that they appeal to some universal sense of beauty. That may or may not exist, but it does not seem, in my experience, to enable people to respond to exotic arts with more than an ethnocentric sentimentalism in the absence of a knowledge of what those arts are about or an understanding of the culture out of which they come. (The Western use of "primitive" motifs, its undoubted value in its own terms aside, has mainly accentuated this; most people, I am convinced, see African sculpture as bush Picasso and Javanese music as noisy Debussy.) The variety of artistic expression stems from the variety of conceptions men have about the way things are, and is indeed the same variety.[76]

It is from the ever-increasing awareness of this variety, and of the problems involved in assessing it, that the major challenge to responsible reflection on the relations of beauty to holiness in the postmodern world stems. In Chapter Seven I will propose some ways in which this challenge may be met. First we will examine the conceptions of these relations exemplified in some modern philosophical theories of aesthetics and religion and in Eastern thought. Then we will see how the issues posed by these varying theories have led some thinkers to conclude that the concepts of art and religion, and of beauty and holiness, may no longer be viable.

CHAPTER FOUR

Aesthetics and Religion in Twentieth-Century Philosophy

*I*T IS sometimes said that modern philosophy began with Descartes' turn to subjectivity and to mathematical clarity as the model of truth. It is also said that modern philosophy began with Kant's critique of traditional metaphysics and his critical amalgam of empirical and rationalistic factors in his epistemology as a "prolegomenon to any future metaphysics." We have seen that, in any event, it was in the eighteenth and nineteenth centuries that conceptual specification of aesthetics and of religion emerged, as an aspect of the new critical philosophy and the enlarged senses of history and culture engendered by the Enlightenment.

Twentieth-century philosophy has addressed, in various ways, some of the excesses and discontinuities that characterized representative nineteenth-century philosophies. A common aim is to "get behind Kant" and the radical distinctions between subject and object, between experience and reality, and between cognitive and other forms of experience, that characterized his enterprise. In this chapter we will examine some representative examples of the critical recovery of some pre-Kantian sensibilities.

We begin with two representatives of American naturalistic humanism, George Santayana and John Dewey. We continue with an exposition of some relevant features of the philosophy of Alfred North Whitehead, who shared many goals with the humanistic naturalists but pursued them in a subtler revision of basic categories of thought and reality. Then we turn to the thought of Martin Heidegger, who viewed the entire enterprise of classical and modern Western philosophy as a betrayal of a sense of Being and its forms that had been richly articulated by the pre-Socratic Greek philosophers. Finally we note features of what Richard Rorty has called "the linguistic turn" in twentieth-century Anglo-American and continental philosophical developments. Anglo-American linguistic philosophy moved from an analysis of what were believed to be foundational linguistic expressions of concepts articulating fundamental "posits" of knowledge, in logical positivism; to Ludwig Wittgenstein's later analysis of the multiple forms of language use incorporated in "language games" indigenous to various "forms of life"; and to the analysis of "ordinary language" as a way of resolving philosophical dilemmas. In continental thought Martin Heidegger moved from the affirmation that language is "the dwelling place of Being" to an analysis of the various forms of Being's expression. All these developments in the "lingustic turn" in philosophy, along with a reappraisal of the philosophy of Nietzsche, contributed to various forms of criticism related to the postmodern sensibility that we will examine in Chapter Six.

This exposition must again, perforce, be summary and selective. In each instance we will focus on those features of the thought of the philosophers considered that are most relevant to their understandings of the relation of aesthetics to religion. I have chosen to deal with these thinkers, among others we might have considered, because I believe that each offers uniquely important insights into the subject matter of this inquiry.

GEORGE SANTAYANA (1863–1952)

The first we shall consider, George Santayana, was less interested in the character and implications of scientific inquiry than were the others, and he did not give to the experimental character of such inquiry the central role in understanding all forms of experience that was assigned to it by others. An American who was the bearer of a Spanish Catholic heritage, he responded critically to the understanding of experimental empiricism that motivated the work of colleagues such as William James during his years at Harvard. He was more catholic in taste and more classical in orientation than were many of his American peers. He was a poet, essayist, and novelist as well as a professional philosopher, and his philosophy is strongly imbued with a sense of the aesthetic as a controlling aim and organizing principle.

The basic component of existence, Santayana believed, is matter. In ontology, he always insisted, he was a materialist. Matter, for him, is that which it is understood to be in physical science—the material component and locus of all that exists. To matter, as existence, belongs ultimate power. If power is understood as force, or as that which determines existence and nonexistence, it is matter that has the last word. And, if matter is that which physical science understands it to be, there is no warrant for assigning to matter any properties of intentionality or purpose. Santayana was quite content with the Democritean vision of atoms falling in the void that inspired the philosophical counsels of Lucretius, one of his favorite "philosophical poets." Or, if the formal aspects of matter are highlighted in a vision of the world, Santayana's affinities were, with some qualifications, with Spinoza. In any case, the ultimate power of existence belongs to a nonsentient, nonpurposeful, "realm of being" that he once called "that great engine of mud and fire." To forget, or to attempt to gloss over, this basic fact, said Santayana, is to fall into one of the many illusions by which humankind has tried to assure itself that its ideals have the ontological power and permanence of material existence. Superstitious religion has provided many of the most beguiling of these illusions.

Material existence, however, is not the only form of being. Matter has come into arrangements that are life and sentience. Human life, when it appears, is grounded in instinct and impulse in its traffic with the world. Impulse may become disciplined by experience, however, and the human capacity for memory and foresight may transmute impulse into imagination. For Santayana, as for many others whose thought we have considered, it is imagination that provides the basic medium of human apprehension of all that may be apprehended. When the mind is stimulated through the senses, said Santayana—principally the senses of hearing and sight, with sight being the dominant factor—the imagination engages in acts of synthesis, abstraction, reproduction, and invention that become the ingredients of understanding. Concepts that, having arisen spontaneously in the imagination, prove to be serviceable in practice and capable of verification in further sensory perception are termed concepts of the understanding. It is imagination doing the work of understanding that gives us knowledge and a degree of control over our world.

In addition to understanding, however, imagination has the power of free play and of envisionment of ideals—of apprehension of what might be in addition to what is, or of what might never be, as existence, but is nevertheless valuable. What Santayana called a "realm of essence" is among the realms of being, along with the realm of existence. In its ideal dimensions this realm borders on the realm of spirit. It should be pointed out that for Santayana the realm of spirit is not independent of the realm of matter, or of body. Spirit is the body's capacity for attention, for consciousness, and for synoptic vision. Spirit has no power basically or permanently to rearrange the powers of existence or to eliminate the exigencies of life. But spirit may enable persons to witness the exigencies of life as necessities of that particular confluence of natural powers that has eventuated in a life, a culture, or an epoch. Spinoza spoke of "the intellectual love of God"; Santayana could speak of a spiritual transmutation of the ills and the felicities of life, "under the aspect of eternity." The gifts of the spirit entail more, however, than passive acquiescence in fortune or an affirmation of the blessedness of the given. Through spirit, imagination may envision and affirm that which would be a source of endless delight and fulfillment, even though—or perhaps because—it may never be fully incarnate in the realm of existence. In the realm of spirit are those ideal values that are goals of the highest human aspiration and that are the source of deepest human beatitude. The chief of these values is, for Santayana, revealed in the sense of beauty.

Plato, we noted, held that beauty is the principal lure to the good. For Santayana, beauty itself exemplifies that harmony which is the good. The sense of beauty pervades all of Santayana's reflections on the realms of being and their relation to human good.[1] The ideal world is a world of perfect harmony—not a static harmony, or a harmony of standardized components, but a harmony of all the forces, aspirations, struggles, and delights of human life in its heights and its depths. Dante portrayed such a harmony in his description of the Beatific Vision. Others have portrayed it in the idioms of various philosophical and religious traditions. The most powerful presentations or revelations of that harmony, Santayana thought, are in works of art.

"If happiness is the ultimate sanction of art," said Santayana,

> art in turn is the best instrument of happiness. In art more directly than in other activities man's self-expression is cumulative and finds an immediate reward; for it alters the material conditions of sentience so that sentience becomes at once more delightful and more significant. . . . But in art [man] is at once competent and free: he is creative. He is not troubled by his materials, because he has assimilated them and may take them for granted; nor is he concerned with the chance complexion of things in the actual world, because he is making the world over, not merely considering how it grew or may consent to grow in the future. . . . If the various formative impulses afoot in the world never opposed stress to stress and made no havoc with one another, nature might be called an unconscious artist. In fact, just where such a formative impulse finds support from the environment, a consciousness supervenes. If that consciousness is adequate enough to be prophetic, an art arises. Thus the emergence of arts out of instincts is the token and exact measure of nature's success and of mortal happiness.[2]

Among the arts, the art of poetry is best fitted to articulate the life of the spirit. In content poetry may express not only what is but also what is desired and desirable—not only what is at hand but also what is longed for. It can articulate not only the obvious but also that which seems obvious only after the poet has effected the "shock of recognition." Through its images it may seek to reflect "the light that never was on land or sea." In form, the poem is its own world. The poetic universe is a universe that contains only those features of "reality"

which are selected by poetic imagination and crafted by poetic making. Poetry provides other worlds in which the human spirit may
live—but so does religion.

Do poetry and religion, then, have identical functions? In important respects they are, for Santayana, identical in much of their substance. Both are products of the imagination in its freest forms and
highest powers. Myth, and the enactment of myth in ritual, are the
chief media of meaning and sustenance in religion. Literalness is the
chief enemy of the religious spirit. In Santayana's scale of criticism,
the greatest poetry is that which undertakes to express and celebrate
those cosmic themes that have been the preoccupation of religions.
What, then, is the difference in function of religion and poetry, if
there is any? When poetry becomes the guide of life, it is religion;
when religion "merely supervenes" upon life, it is poetry. Religion is
poetry believed and lived by; poetry is religion valued merely for the
substance and structure of its expression of life. Whereas poetry may
express the highest ideals and most pervasive ambiguities of life, religion may articulate an attitude toward life in the language of prayer.
"At their point of union both reach their utmost purity and benefi-
cence, for then poetry loses its frivolity and ceases to demoralize,
while religion surrenders its illusion and ceases to deceive."[3]

Both poetry and religion are in certain respects ends in themselves
and in other respects means to other human ends. For Santayana, neither poetry nor religion is completely "otherworldly" in the sense that
they possess no efficacy for the realm of existence—for the realm of
natural and social powers. "Aesthetic and other interests are not sepa-
rable units to be compared externally; they are rather strands inter-
woven in the texture of everything," writes Santayana. "Aesthetic sensibility colors every thought, qualifies every allegiance, and modifies
every product of human labor. Consequently the love of beauty has
to justify itself not merely intrinsically or as a constituent part of life
more or less to be insisted upon; it has to justify itself as an influence."[4]
This it does when its apprehension of harmonious form is translated
into social action in behalf of that moral ideal of harmony that is justice.

Religion, too, has its roots in that which is pervasive of all experience and that is a good in itself—so that "whether one live or die, it
is unto the Lord." These roots are nourished in piety—that "natural
piety" that acknowledges the natural sources of our being. It is "rever-
ent attachment to the sources of our being, and the steadying of life
by that attachment." What are the sources of our being? Our parents,
most obviously, and beyond our parents, our ancestors—those ancestral roots of whose importance many members of cultures in which life

seems rootless are becoming freshly aware. Filial and ancestral piety are natural components of religions in numerous cultures. In addition to ancestors there are those national and cultural milieux that have shaped our being and given it meaning. Patriotism is, Santayana believes, an appropriate expression of piety. Piety, in any case, cannot be exercised without locale. It must be expressed through specific traditions. There is a sense, of course, in which it is appropriate to extend pious loyalty to humanity as a whole. An ideal humanity of harmonious fulfillment, were it to exist, could be the object of a higher form of piety. Piety toward humanity as it actually is, however, "must be three-fourths pity." Finally, there is a sense in which the cosmos as a whole is an appropriate object of piety. From its material configurations we have sprung, and to its material destiny we will return. We may acknowledge it as the ultimate source of our being. If we do so, however, we should not imagine that it is purposeful or that it had us in mind in the course of those collocations of matter from which we have sprung, or that the ideal goods that give meaning to our lives receive permanent embodiment in the material world.

To stake loyalty to the ideal on a conviction of its prior or eventual existence, in Santayana's understanding of existence, is to trade truth for illusion and to predicate moral effort on a guaranteed outcome. This is the way of superstition and of traditional supernaturalism. The ideal authenticates itself *as* ideal. And, if the ideal value of chief importance is beauty, then the harmony of beauty must be exemplified in what is, for Santayana, the second component of religion: charity. Charity extends to others an affirmative recognition of their piety— their loyalties to the sources of their being. The sense of charity is the sense of fellow-creaturehood, of complementary aspirations in a common humanity. For Santayana it is perhaps less outgoing and sacrificial than the *agape* of the Christian tradition (cf. Edwards's "Being's gracious consent to being") and perhaps closer to the *jen* of the Confucian tradition. It is, in any case, a natural reflection in human life of commitment to the good as beautiful. It is the social expression of spirituality, which is the third component of religion, in Santayana's view. Spirituality is life in the spirit, and life in the spirit is life in the presence of the ideal. Spiritual effort is effort to pursue life always and everywhere in the presence of the ideal—in the presence of perfection. It is, to translate St. Paul's phrase into Santayana's idiom, so to live that "whether one live or die it is unto the ideal." Such life is eternal, because the ideals that constitute its essence are eternal. They are not everlasting; they are timeless. They may, to some extent, be "made flesh" in aesthetic creation and vivified in the religious life. [5]

JOHN DEWEY (1859–1952)

The background of John Dewey was quite different from that of George Santayana. He was the heir of Calvinistic New England piety, tempered by New England Transcendentalism. But from the time when he began first to reflect critically on religious faith in the context of the realities of his own life, he was aware of a deep-seated sense of alienation, of dichotomies and discontinuities between the real and the ideal self, and between self and society and nature. It was Coleridge's *Aids to Reflection* that planted the seeds of a later philosophy in which the ideal and the actual could receive unification through imaginative devotion to intelligent inquiry and action—a unification best exemplified in aesthetic experience, and best inculcated through a humane and generous religious faith.[6]

In the classroom of George Sylvester Morris at Johns Hopkins University Dewey found a liberating philosophical vision in Morris's version of Neo-Hegelianism. Dewey remained Neo-Hegelian in his basic outlook through his subsequent career at the University of Michigan. By the time he accepted an invitation to come to the University of Chicago as Professor of Philosophy and mentor of its Experimental School, however, his views of educational philosophy as informed by his changing views of the character and importance of natural science were leading to that form of naturalistic humanism with which his work is principally identified. These views are to some extent grounded in the philosophical movement called "pragmatism," which originated in the work of Charles Sanders Peirce (1839–1914) and whose most extensive classical formulation is found in the works of William James. Both Peirce and James could well be included in a consideration of the importance of aesthetics for understanding religion in the American naturalistic tradition. William Clebsch correctly places Dewey in a strand of American religious thought that he calls "esthetic," and which includes Edwards, Emerson, James, and Dewey.[7] When Peirce directed his attention to matters religious, he was likely to speak of them as falling in the domain of the "instinctual" and practical, and he did not develop a systematic view of religion—or perhaps of anything else. It is interesting, however, to note that when Peirce did, on one occasion, reflect on the bases of belief in God, he described the sort of reflection appropriate to such a subject as "musement," akin to the sort of thing that poets do; and one of the attractions of the notion of God to which musement may lead, he said, is its beauty.[8] James's views of religion place heavier emphasis on psychological and moral factors, though there is a sense in which at least some of his views reflect the goal of harmony and wholeness that is akin to an aesthetic ideal.[9]

It is significant that Dewey's basic term for valid human attempts to apprehend the world is "inquiry." The term itself indicates the active and purposeful character of the enterprise. "Inquiry," he says, "is the controlled or directed transformation of an indeterminate situation into one that is so determinate in its constituent distinctions and relations as to convert the elements of the original situation into a unified whole."[10] If the "indeterminate situation" is a cognitive puzzle—a situation of not knowing that which we need to know in order to "understand" and to get on with matters in a clarified situation—then a hypothetical solution is tested with respect to efficacy and "fit." The procedure is informed by carefully stipulated rules ("logical"), and it is consummated in an act of judgment. Judgment is the closure, the "cutting off," of those indefinite possibilities that are candidates for verity in that cognitive situation, in favor of the one that is held to be "verified" by its organizing and facilitating efficacy. Verity occurs in the act of verification. Verification, in turn, must be socially accessible. Private "conclusions" are of value only when socially corroborated. The verifications must harmonize with those previously reached, which are constitutive of the "unproblematic" aspects of the problematic situation. When this occurs we are warranted in saying, in traditional language, that we have knowledge of what is the case in that situation. Cognitive doubt is resolved in warranted cognitive assertion. An indeterminate situation has been transformed into a determinate one through that "controlled or directed transformation" which is knowing.

The patterns of inquiry are not, however, restricted to cognitively problematic situations—situations in which we "do not know what to think." They are also exhibited in morally problematic situations—situations in which we "do not know what to do." Our actions are impelled by needs and desires. Moral dilemmas occur when needs and desires are in conflict. Moral judgment entails careful discrimination between the desire*d* and the desi*rable*. By what criterion are we to decide what is desirable in a conflict of desires? In general, Dewey holds, we are justified in choosing those fulfillments that do not narrow the range of possible fulfillments—those goods that enhance rather than stultify the possibility of a maximum number of goods. A biological term for moral advancement is "growth"; the moral life is that life which is "healthy" in the concurrent functioning of the broadest and richest variety of human goods. Translated into political philosophy, this means a moral preference for democracy, as a system that, ideally, safeguards and supports the maximum achievement of individual potentiality and worth by each member of society.

Is there an analogous exhibition of the patterns of inquiry in aesthetic judgment? Before we attempt to answer that question, let us turn to Dewey's characterization of experience and nature as the locale of all judgment.

In some respects Dewey's theory of experience is quite simple, but in other respects, as contrasted with some of its rivals, it appears to be complex. Experience is, simply put, all our doings and sufferings—all that we do and all that we undergo, in relation to all with which we have to do. This means that experience is no more basically cognitive—a matter of knowing or not knowing—than it is moral—a matter of doing or not doing in a context of moral conflict. It is no more basically sensory than it is nonsensory. In this respect Dewey parts company with the British empiricists, who place a premium on sense experience and presumably primitive "sense data," as well as with Kant, to the extent that Kant adopted some of the assumptions of British empiricism in his attempt to reconstruct the ground and character of knowledge. Experience is a matter of *feeling* just as truly as it is a matter of sensing, but it is not preeminently a matter of feeling, either. It is, simply, what it shows itself to be. It is the matrix and, ultimately, the tribunal of discriminations in our doings and undergoings. For those whose theory of experience places the sensory or the nonsensory, the cognitive or the volitional or the affective, in a controlling position, therefore, Dewey's theory seems either complex or evasive. To others it appears sufficiently rich to do justice to life "as we experience it." We will return to a restatement of it in Chapter Seven.

What, then, is nature? Nature is the matrix and context of experience. Nature *is* what nature is experienced *to be*. Experience is *in* and *of* nature. Experience *is* nature under certain conditions, when within nature there appear organisms capable of experienc*ing*. Experience is *of* nature in the sense that all that is experienced is natural. Nature is not other than what nature is experienced to be; experience is not other than that which occurs in experiencing. For Dewey there are no dichotomies between experience and nature, or between experience as cognitive and experience as moral or aesthetic or religious. The hermeneutical tradition that stems from Kant, and that predicates basic distinctions between the world of "life" and the world of "texts" or "art," and claims a special faculty of divination or empathetic insight for discernment of the latter, is rejected. In its place is a view in which all acts of interpretation, including the interpretations of religion and of art, are seen as exhibiting the same basic pattern of inquiry, in the context of a catholic theory of experience and nature. [11]

What, in the light of this theory, are the aesthetic and the religious in experience, and how are they related? Briefly, the aesthetic in experience is that in experience which makes any experience *an* experience. Cognitive experience moves from problematic situation to cognitive closure in an "act of knowing" that brings what Moritz Schlick has called "the joy of cognition."[12] Moral experience moves from a morally problematic situation to a resolution through moral choice that is "fitting" and "right." In experience as aesthetic, exemplified in those experiential achievements that we call "works of art," the continuity of "form" and "matter," and of creative initiation and artistic consummation, are directly exemplified. "In an intellectual experience," writes Dewey,

> the conclusion has value on its own account. It can be extracted as a formula or "truth" and can be used as an independent entirety as a factor and guide in other inquiries. In a work of art there is no single self-sufficient deposit. The end, the terminus, is significant by itself and by the integration of its parts. It has no other existence. A drama or a novel is not the final sentence. . . . In a distinctively aesthetic experience, characteristics that are subordinate are controlling—namely, the characteristics in virtue of which the experience is an integrated complete experience in its own right. [13]

Experience as aesthetic is consummatory. It is wholly had and wholly enjoyed. Experience as cognitive has its consummations, but these lead to the discernment of new problems and to further inquiry. Experience as moral achieves moral resolutions, but the moral life presents fresh ambiguities. The specifically aesthetic in experience highlights those consummations that give integrity to all forms of experience, by being in and of itself directly consummatory and enjoyable. "That which distinguishes an experience as esthetic is a conversion of resistance and tensions . . . into a movement towards an inclusive and fulfilling close."[14] Yet consummation in experience as aesthetic does not entail elimination of other aspects of ongoing experience. Consummation yields enrichment of perspective. "If we dawdle too long after having extracted a net value, experience perishes of inanation."[15] The aesthetic refreshes and steadies precisely because "an object is peculiarly and dominantly esthetic . . . when the factors which determine anything which could be called an experience are lifted high above the threshold of perception and are made manifest, for their own sake."[16] In the creation and enjoyment of a work of art, as one expositor of Dewey's view has put it, "we are carried to a refreshed attitude towards the circumstances of ordinary experience," and "its efficacy continues indirectly in that we carry back to ordinary experience an enduring serenity, refreshment, and re-education of vision."[17]

Art performs both unifying and communicative functions. "Art," Dewey says, "is the most universal and freest form of communication."[18] "In the end, works of art are the only media of complete and unhindered communication between man and man that can occur in a world full of gulfs and walls that limit community of experience."[19] The sense of communion generated by a work of art, therefore, "may take on a definitively religious quality."[20] In a time when traditional religious expressions and celebrations of the major stages and occasions of human life are of limited accessibility or meaning, authentic and widely shared artistic creation and enjoyment may become the media of a more universal humanism. In any event, Dewey the naturalistic humanist can affirm that the idea of art "is the greatest intellectual achievement in the history of humanity,"[21] and that "art—the mode of activity that is charged with meanings capable of immediately enjoyed possession—is the complete culmination of nature."[22] How, then, is the aesthetic in experience related to the religious in experience, in Dewey's view?

It was only relatively late in his career that Dewey attempted to set forth his characterization of the religious in experience in the Terry Lectures at Yale published under the title *A Common Faith*. This brief statement must be read and understood in the context of his views of the aesthetic in experience, and of the broader reaches of experience and nature, expressed elsewhere. A chief aim of *A Common Faith* is, he said, to liberate "the religious" from "religion"—that is, to identify those factors in experience that, in Dewey's view, are distinctively religious, and to show that these are not inseparably related to traditional forms of belief and institutional expression. Traditional supernaturalism, he believed, has stultified rather than fructified religious commitment and expression, because it has placed emphasis on intellectual assent to a conviction that ideal values have antecedent reality in some "other" world. Institutional expressions of religion that are limited to organizations like churches too easily become associated with limited social aims and assurances. What, then, is the religious in experience that, Dewey hoped, might be freshly appreciated and more widely and effectively celebrated?

In describing it he employs the biological idiom of "adaptation" and "accommodation" or adjustment. We adapt some things in experience and nature to our purposes—such as a piece of property, or a play in another language. Other things we cannot adapt, so we accommodate ourselves to them, such as uncontrollable aspects of weather, or death. The broadest and deepest accommodation of our lives has to do with the principal exigencies of life. It relates not to this or that "problem" but to the underlying character and fact of life itself. In this "accommodation" there occurs a fundamental orientation, in relation to which the major uncertainties and imponderables are "settled." It is the source of basic confidence and trust. It need not be mere stoic resignation. It may, says Dewey, be "more outgoing and glad" than that. It provides the foundation for outgoing and ongoing "adaptations" of those matters that can be changed. "There is," says Dewey, "a composing and harmonizing of the various elements of our being such that, in spite of changes in the special conditions that surround us, these conditions are also arranged, settled, in relation to us."[23] It has been the claim of traditional religions that they are the agents of such orienting faith. Wherever there is such an orientation, says Dewey, there is the religious in human experience—and it need not be limited to traditional religions, which so often distort or stultify it.

This sense of basic orientation that is the religious in experience has its roots in the natural and social contexts of life, and it is apprehended and expressed through the work of imagination. There has been, says Dewey, an inadequate appreciation of the significant role of imagination in religious faith and in all forms of inquiry. There has been a tendency to assume that imagined unities and ideals are somehow less "real" than the familiar "facts" of the everyday world. Imagination, however, is as truly rooted in and constitutive of nature as is any other form of activity in it. Imagined ideals are not rootless; imagined unities are not "mere figments" of a faculty that is other than natural. Through imagination, therefore, we may seek to articulate more fully and richly the character and consequences of that fundamental locus of orientation which is the religious in experience.

One form that this articulation may take is in the sense of a "universe," and of the universe as "an enveloping whole." Through the religious in experience we may perceive ourselves to be rooted in and sustained by such a whole. "The religious experience is a reality in so far as in the midst of effort to foresee and regulate future objects we are sustained and expanded in feebleness and failure by the sense of an enveloping whole."[24] The pervasiveness of such a sense may account for a lack of specific or detailed comment upon it in Dewey's major writings, which have sometimes been alleged to portray an innocent optimism. It may be the case that the religious has to do with those things that are taken for granted, or as granted, and therefore require no extensive comment. Extensive comment, indeed, may betray a certain insensitivity or anxiety with respect to the matters taken as granted.

That Dewey did have a sense of things "as granted" is evident. Both supernaturalism and militant atheism pass over too lightly, he said, "the ties binding man to nature that poets have always celebrated,"[25] echoing a sense of Santayana's "natural piety." A truly religious attitude senses "the connection of man, in the way of both dependence and support, with the enveloping world which imagination feels is a universe." Dewey's natural piety is, however, more affirmative in its appreciation of the nonhuman sources of human life than is Santayana's. But the view that he expressed should not be translated theistically as "pantheism." There are multiple factors in that which imagination perceives as unified in a sustaining whole.

There is a sense in which nature as such is, for Dewey, social: it is a congeries of actions and transactions. Certainly human life is intrinsically social. We are literally "a part of all we have met," and they, of us. Our social ties and dependencies extend, moreover, to indefinite ranges of contemporary society, and to indefinite ranges of past human history. The labors and achievements of those in our past and present who make our lives possible and meaningful are, for Dewey, channels of a sort of "secular grace." The sense of settledness in a sustaining whole is, therefore, related to the social gifts of nature, human and nonhuman.

The religious in experience is not, moreover, simply the medium of confidence and gratitude. Nature in society generates ideals as well as actualities achieved. Imagination may seize upon these ideals as providing impetus for human aspiration and effort. Nature is intrinsically ongoing; to humanity is given the opportunity to shape its ongoingness in the direction of more intensely perceived and widely shared values. The individual self may receive a sense of its unity, not only from its relation to a unifying whole, but also from a commitment to values unified through idealizing imagination. We may be unified by our social "causes" as well as by ontological causes. Indeed, there are those who understand Dewey to be principally an "activist" who sees the possibility of unification for self and society only in unified ideals, in a form of ethical idealism. His natural piety is much deeper and broader. It does entail, however, devotion to one good that is of central importance, and this is "shared experience." "Communication," he says, "is consummatory as well as instrumental. . . . Shared experience is the greatest of human goods."[26] And, "when the emotional force, the mystic force, one might say, of communication, the miracle of shared life and shared experience is felt, the hardness and crudeness of contemporary life will be bathed in the light that never was on land or sea."[27]

Why does the notion of "shared experience" evoke this uncharacteristically poetic statement by Dewey? It is because in shared experience there is an indefinite enrichment of quality in the life of self and society. It is, furthermore, through those forms of shared experience that are cooperative inquiry and social action that there may be an indefinite increase in the number of imagined goods made concrete in human life. The process of concretizing ideals is never ended. Goods achieved open up the possibilities of previously unimagined or unattainable goods—and new factors of precariousness for goods achieved. But the thrust of the imagination to envision both ends and means, and of human effort to implement the means to the achievement of ideal ends, is the activity of central importance for human well-being. We shall note the relevance of this view to the contemporary fact of cultural pluralism in Chapter Seven.

The close analogy of the aesthetic to the religious in Dewey's thought must now be apparent. "Composing and harmonizing" are functions of both the aesthetic and the religious in experience. Enactment of orientation is the work of each. Both forms of experience are consummatory—are enjoyed as ends in themselves—and both provide fresh insight and impetus to further enactments. The sense of belonging to a whole, Dewey says, is "the explanation of that feeling of exquisite intelligibility and clarity which we have in the presence of an object which is experienced with esthetic intensity . . . it explains the religious feeling that accompanies intense esthetic perception. We are, as it were, introduced into a world beyond this world which is nevertheless the deeper reality of the world in which we live in our ordinary experiences. We are carried beyond ourselves to find ourselves."[28] As we find ourselves in experience as religious, we find ourselves in basic accommodation to life as given, as we find ourselves in the presence of commanding ethical and social ideals. These, unified in imagination, become the impetus to social and political action aimed at the realization of these ideals in the social fabric of life. Religious orientation is expressed in life-style and life commitment. Both the aesthetic and the religious are in a sense ends in themselves and in a sense means to further ends. Both are foci of orientation and catalysts of further experience emerging from that orientation. Clifford Geertz, we may recall, identifies the religious with the confluence of orientation, or worldview, and life-style in action, or ethos. For Dewey the consummatory, orienting, and engendering character of the aesthetic in experience provides the most illuminating insight into the nature of the religious in experience.

ALFRED NORTH WHITEHEAD (1861–1947)

If some would see the centrality of the aesthetic in Dewey's thought to be implicit rather than explicit, for Whitehead aesthetic concepts and functions are clearly at the center of the metaphysical/cosmological vision that he believed to be most satisfactory "for our cosmic epoch." The role of philosophy in establishing this synoptic view, he believed, is to engage in an unrelenting critique of the abstractions that are involved in the analysis of the multifarious forms of experience, and especially to abjure the "fallacy of misplaced concreteness"—that is, to treat as metaphysically ultimate those abstractions that emerge through various routes from the full concreteness of the basic ingredients of reality. Whitehead called these ingredients "actual occasions," "actual entities," "events," and "droplets of experience." Each of these designations bespeaks the primacy of ongoing relatedness in the process of reality. Reality *is*, he believed, processive, incorporating in each occasion a funding from the past and an "ingression" from the future. Novelty is a feature of all actual entities, and freedom is a category. [29]

Thus Whitehead spoke characteristically of "the *adventure* of ideas" and of all concretions in actual occasions as "adventures." Whereas the past, along with present circumstance, may set parameters of experience, the future provides ever-present "lures." We have seen that Dewey's empiricism was both experiential and experimental. It is perhaps ironic that Whitehead, in commenting on Dewey's views, said that "the emphasis in his thought is on security. But the vitality of man's mind is in adventure." [30] It is true that Dewey spoke of the consummatory character of aesthetic experience as emblematic of that which makes any experience *an* experience—and we shall see Whitehead also emphasizing this. But both Dewey and Whitehead stressed the openness and experimental "adventuresomeness" of experience in all its forms.

Fundamental to Whitehead's view of the sources of that ongoing process which is reality is his placing of Creativity among the three "formative elements" of Ultimacy in his cosmology, along with "God" and "eternal objects." Creativity is a "given." Creativity, in his view, is not the work of a Creator or other engendering substance or individual. It is the dynamic source of the limited incorporation of infinite possibilities ("eternal objects") in actual occasions. God, in the "primordial" divine nature, posits the time*less* realm of "unfettered" possibilities (cf. Santayana). For Whitehead some logical possibilities are also ontological potentialities. God therefore provides both "lure" and "companionship." The "consequent" divine nature is the result of the enactment of specific possibilities in reality through the agency of Creativity in relating past actualizations to present situations, to produce novel individualizations. The relatedness of each concrete occasion is not only to its neighbors in space/time, but also ultimately to all *relata* in all of that environment which is the cosmos.

Whitehead sometimes calls concretions of actuality "cells" and speaks of his philosophy as "the philosophy of organism." The biological idiom (cf. Dewey), however, should not suggest an actual primacy of biological thought in the scientific sources of his view. He was first of all a mathematician, and he could speak of "vectors" and "nexūs" perhaps more appropriately than of cells. The basic problem addressed in his cosmology, in any case, is the age-old problem of "the one and the many." William James, in his metaphysical pluralism, said that "the world is one—in more ways than one." Whitehead maintained that in each instance of real-ization the world is "one-ed"—and "increases by one."

Turning to features of Whitehead's epistemology that are relevant to our subject, we note that Whitehead employs as a generic term for modes of apprehension as well as modes of that which is apprehended a word classically associated with distinctively aesthetic apprehension: *feeling*. Obviously his use of this term is not intended to connote an exclusively affective function. The dynamics of "affection" are extended to all the dynamics of bringing-together in the processional reality of experience and cosmos. Through feeling in one of its forms ingredients of the real *prehend* other ingredients; through feeling in another of its forms entities *ap*-prehend the prehensions of relevant reality. There are "physical feelings" of objects from the past, prehended as "initial datum" (object as contrasted with subject) and as "objective datum" (aspects of the object selected in accordance with the "subjective aim" of the actualizing occasion). In cognitive and other forms of apprehension there are "conceptual feelings" of those possibilities that are "eternal objects," or potential forms of definiteness, which act as "lures" in the coming-to-be of an actual object. Both physical feelings and conceptual feelings are unconscious. Consciousness arises in "the felt contrast between fact and possibility." Conscious actual entities are capable of perception, which occurs in two "modes."

The "mode of causal efficacy" is

> vague, not to be controlled, heavy with emotion: it produces the sense of derivation from an immediate past, and of passage to an immediate future; a sense of emotional feeling, belonging to oneself in the past, passing into oneself in the present, and passing from oneself in the present towards oneself in the future; a sense of influx from other vague pres-

ences in the past, localized and yet evading local definition, such influences modifying, enhancing, inhibiting, diverting, the stream of feeling which we are receiving, unifying, enjoying, and transmitting. This is our general sense of existence, as one item among others, in an efficacious actual world.[31]

Percepta in the "mode of presentational immediacy," on the other hand, are, by comparison, "distinct, definite, controllable, apt for immediate enjoyment, and with the minimum of reference to past, or to future. We are subject to our percepta in the mode of efficacy, we adjust our percepta in the mode of immediacy."[32] (Cf. Dewey on "accommodation" and "adaptation.")

These two modes are integrated in "propositional feelings." For Whitehead propositions are not solely "logical" propositions. Propositions are, for him, literally *pro*-positions or pro-*positional*, "tales that might be told about particular actualities."[33] Their synthesizing process comes to closure in *decisions*, including but not limited to those decisions we call logical "judgments." They are projected into contemporaneous societies of actual entities through "transmutation." And, says Whitehead, "in the real world it is more important that a proposition be interesting than that it be true. The importance of truth is, that it adds to the interest."[34]

Whitehead never wrote a book on aesthetics—perhaps, as F. S. C. Northrop suggests, because he felt (!) that he was writing one in most of what he wrote.[35] In any case, Donald W. Sherburne, in his *A Whiteheadian Aesthetic*, indicates that, for Whitehead, aesthetic *objects* have the categorical status of *propositions*, in the sense in which Whitehead employs this term. To understand them in this way is to understand the unique confluence of "generalness" and "specificity" that characterizes works of art.[36]

Aesthetic *experience*, in turn, may be interpreted as aesthetic *re*-creation. "It is my contention that an experience is aesthetic when it is an experience of an objectified proposition [artwork?] which lures the subjective *aim* of that occasion of experience into recreating in its own process of self-creation the proposition objectified in the prehended performance [understanding "performance" to include both that which *is* performed and its "performance," in the case of "the performing arts"]."[37] In this sense the proposition that is the artwork is literally "propositionally" incorporated into the experience of one who apprehends the work aesthetically. "I am suggesting that in aesthetic experience the normal goals of everyday living are suspended; in grasping the subjective aim the art object insists that it be experienced as an end in itself. It temporarily short-circuits the long-range, overarching subjective aims that shape life-patterns or dominate ordinary living."[38] (Cf. Dewey's description of aesthetic experience as "consummatory.")

Aesthetic experience, as many have noted, involves a specific form of attention, but the form of attention is not, as such, for Whitehead, solely constitutive of the experience; the "matter" of the artwork is an essential ingredient of the experience. So is the specifically aesthetic category "beauty." Beauty, in Whitehead's view, is neither simply an objective feature of the artwork nor simply a feature of subjective consciousness—neither merely in "that which is beheld" nor merely "in the eye of the beholder." It is "the mutual adaptation of the several factors in an occasion of experience"—"perfection of harmony in terms of subjective form."[39] And beauty is the one self-justifying aim: "In itself, and apart from all other factors, there seems to be no special importance about the truth-relation. A truth-relation is not necessarily beautiful. It may not even be neutral. It may be evil. Thus Beauty is left as the one aim which by its very nature is self-justifying."[40] (Cf. Santayana.)

Aesthetic experience is not, however, merely consummatory or "arresting," and it is not merely representational of that which already is. Creativity, an ingredient of all reality, is uniquely operative in the work of artistic creation. In Whiteheadian terms, this entails not only that "vertical" transmutation which effects concrescence in all its forms; it is also what Sherburne proposes to call "horizontal" transmutation into all the possibilities opened up by the aesthetic experience. The poet provides not only "the shock of recognition" but also a glimpse of "the light that never was, on sea or land" but *might* be refracted in some new, only dimly imagined, way. The artist not only brings to light what others *could* see, and may be led to see through the aesthetic experience; the artist may also "see" that which has never been seen before. The artist, in other words, is not only an enhancer of the known; the artist is, or may be, also a *discoverer*. In religious parlance, the artist is not only priest; she or he is also prophet. This latter function, we shall note in Chapter Six, has been especially emphasized by Thomas Martland.

How, then, does the aesthetic relate to the religious in Whitehead's view? In his "Whiteheadian" interpretation of aesthetic experience Sherburne suggests that the religious dimension of aesthetic experience is that dimension which is most strongly evocative of the richness and wonder of "causal efficacy" as described above. Yet clearly there is also a unique "definiteness" of "presentational immediacy" in specifically aesthetic experience. Thus the aesthetic in experience uniquely exemplifies the issue that is central to both religion and metaphysics—the issue of "the one and the many."

Whitehead's often-quoted statement that "religion is what the individual does with his own solitariness"[41] is frequently misunderstood to connote a radically existential subjective individualism. Nothing could be farther from the Whiteheadian vision. For Whitehead all individuals are *individualizations* of a reality that is inherently social—and inherently transient or "in the making." It is appropriate, therefore, that he called his principal work on religion *Religion in the Making*. Religion, like all else, is "in the making"—and it *is* (has its actuality) in that *making* which is the world. The religious problem is how the one (individualization) relates to the many (indefinitely extensive society of individualizations), and how the transiency of all "making" relates to whatever may be either timeless or everlasting. Reflection on the latter issue has provided ground for dialogue among "process" philosophers, Christian theologians, and Buddhist thinkers. Reflection on both issues has provided some Christian theologians with what they believe to be the most felicitous philosophical framework for theological thought.[42]

In any event, it seems clear that Whitehead was not himself a theist in the classical Christian sense. Some, indeed, have debated the indispensability of the concept of God in his cosmological vision. As it stands, however, Whitehead can say that "the artist does not create *ex nihilo* . . . yet his vision is productive of the 'light that never was, on sea or land.'"[43] Or as Sherburne puts it, "the artist is not God, and his creative novelty presupposes God in the same sense that all advance into novelty presupposes God. From the standpoint of 'sea and land,' from the point of view of actuality, the artist is a discoverer."[44]

Since God in the "primordial" divine nature posits the timeless realm of unfettered possibilities, and God as source of "principle of concretion" actualizes the given of Creativity in actual occasions, Whitehead can say: "Apart from the intervention of God, there could be nothing new in the world, and no order in the world. The course of creation would be a dead level of ineffectiveness, with all balance and intensity progressively excluded by the cross-currents of incompatibility."[45] And, in *Religion in the Making* he can say: "The metaphysical doctrine, here expounded, finds the foundation of the world in the aesthetic experience rather than—as with Kant—in the cognitive and conceptual experience. All order is therefore aesthetic order, and the moral is merely certain aspects of aesthetic order. The actual world is the outcome of aesthetic order, and the aesthetic order is derived from the immanence of God."[46] Here we have indeed "gotten behind Kant" to a view of the relation of the aesthetic to the religious that many find uniquely compatible with the demands of modern thought.

MARTIN HEIDEGGER (1889–1976)

Heidegger was arguably the most influential Continental philosopher of the first seven decades of the twentieth century. The impact of his thought, not only on formal philosophy but also on literary criticism, theology, and other fields, has been of singular importance.[47] His goal was nothing less than a basic reorientation of Western thought.[48]

Heidegger's mentor Husserl called his philosophical program "phenomenology." The aim was to lay bare the basic structures of consciousness and their intentional references through rigorous logical analysis. Heidegger shared the Husserlian goal of thoroughly explicating the realm of phenomena, but he came to believe that Husserl's view of what phenomena are, and how they may best be explicated, was distortingly narrow. Phenomena, he believed, are whatever they appear to be, in all their diversity, complexity, and richness (cf. Dewey: nature is whatever nature is experienced *as*, in all the forms of experience). Furthermore, Heidegger said, there is no "thing-in-itself" or noumenon, of which phenomena are "appearances." Phenomena *are* simply what they are. All apprehension of phenomena, however, is interpretative. Therefore Heidegger's philosophy is sometimes called "hermeneutic phenomenology." But the basic modes of phenomenal appearance and interpretation incorporate those *existentialia* of human being-in-the-world to which philosophers called existentialists draw attention. Therefore Heidegger's philosophy is also sometimes called "existential phenomenology."

In any case, like Whitehead Heidegger found that the articulation of an original philosophical vision necessitated the use of a distinctive vocabulary, drawn in part from Greek and Latin roots and in part from peculiarly German locutions revised to meet Heidegger's needs. Central to the entire enterprise is what he believed to be a recovery of a fundamental sense of primordial Being that had been articulated in pre-Socratic Greek thought but lost in subsequent Western approaches to Being. Being (*sein*) *is* what "appears"—or, in Heidegger's preferred terminology, "comes to light" or is "unconcealed"—in that form of Being which is *Da*-Sein, "*there*-Being." *Dasein* is that form of be-ing which can question itself about its own being. It is *human* being. In this questioning, Being comes-to-light. Authentic openness to Being, however, involves not only questioning but also transparency to all modes of unconcealing of Being—or, as Heidegger would more frequently say in his later writings, patient "listening" to Being.

Basic apprehension of Being in and through *Dasein* is not the apprehension of the "object," Being, by a "subject," human being; it is rather the unfolding of Being through objectifying and subjectifying modes of unconcealment. There are three "equiprimordial" elements in this basic unfolding. The first, which is of special importance for the subject matter of our inquiry, is "moodness" (*Befindlichkeit*). Whitehead had extended the concept of "feeling" to embrace both basic apprehension and the basic source of concretion in that which is apprehended (prehension). Heidegger affirmed that a pervasive component of all coming-to-light of Being in *Dasein* is an element that has affective resonance—overtones of that mode of apprehension which had traditionally been associated with *aesthetic* apprehension. For Heidegger the deepest "sense" of this primordial moodness is that of "thrownness"—of facticity and historicity. *Dasein* experiences itself as ec-sisting, "standing-" or "thrown-" "out" from Being. This characterizes *Dasein's* being as existential.

The second component of Being's coming-to-light in the being of *Dasein* is "understanding"—"standing-under" or "within" that which comes to light. And *all* understanding is *interpretation*. There is no "bare," uninterpreted engagement with Being. Interpretation, however, is not merely an act of *Dasein* as subjective. The ingredients of Being that come-to-light are in themselves interpretations. It is interpretations that come-to-light. There is thus, in Heidegger's view, a primordial "hermeneutical circle."

The third ingredient of unconcealment of being in *Dasein* is "logos"—log-ic and its structures, employed in "discursive" reasoning (reasoning in which Being is "explicated" in *assertions*)—but also, in Heidegger's later philosophy, language as such, as the "dwelling house of Being." What brings these elements of unconcealment of Being together in an ongoing unity? It is "concern" (cf. Tillich), or "care" (*Sorge*). *Dasein* is primordially care-ing Being.

In the unconcealment of Being in *Dasein*, *Dasein* is being-in-the-world and being-with-others. Being-in-the-world is first of all being-in-the-world*hood* of "things." "World" is not the "Whole" of all "parts"; it is the contextual feature of basic unconcealment of Being. The "thinghood" of things-in-the-world is first of all the "thinghood" of "equipment"—things-at-hand-for-use. But use-relations become, through abstraction, *theoretical* relations. *Dasein* abstracts "common properties" and envisions a world of pure components of *theoria* (synoptic vision). In Western thought this turn to theoretical understanding as the definitive medium of understanding, and thus the means of *domination*, of Being-as-object set the agenda for Western philosophy and Western science. It is true that Being is, among other things, that which "comes-to-light" in theoretical knowledge. But Heidegger, like Whitehead, would abjure the "fallacy of misplaced concreteness." Heidegger said that understanding Being principally in this light has led to the course of Western "onto-theology" whose end was announced by Nietzsche.

Dasein is also being-with-others. Heidegger abjured the radical individualism espoused by some existentialists. Like Dewey and Whitehead, he saw human being as inherently social. But for him the question of "authentic" as contrasted with "inauthentic" being-in-the-world and being-with-others is the question of how the "others" are taken to be "other." Certainly not as "things," as Kant had pointed out. Indeed, for Heidegger the others are not to be *"taken*-to-be"; one is to *let* the other "be." Letting-the-other-be is affirming and celebrating the otherness of the other in its integrity. And the authentic relation of the self to the other is that relation which other thinkers have prized as "dialogue." (Cf. especially Bakhtin, whose thought we will examine in Chapter Six.)

The essentially social character of *Dasein* for Heidegger has sometimes been called into question because of Heidegger's further analysis of the character of authentic self-being. This analysis begins with Heidegger's affirmation of the essential *temporality* of Being ("being *and* time") (cf. Whitehead). Temporality for Heidegger, however, is not simply the Aristotelian-scientific understanding of time as "the measure of motion with respect to before and after, expressed in number," in which "pasts" are "nows" that were and "thens" are "nows" that will be, each appropriately placed on the serial continuum of time. Time for *Dasein* is *temporalizing*: bringing Being to "presence" in "the present." And the present is the "opening" of the past as "having-been" to the future as anticipated "may-be."

What is the ultimate future of humans as *Dasein*? It is death. So human living is living-unto-death. Inauthentic living-unto-death views death as a final "moment" in serial time, or fears death as the meaning-destroying end (*finis*) of *Dasein*'s being-in-the-world. Authentic living-unto-death courageously affirms death-as-end (*finis*) as also death-as-goal (*telos*)—not in the sense that "one lives in order to die," but in the sense that one *affirms* one's end (*finis*) as the completion of one's being-in-finitude. (So that "whether one live or die," it is " 'unto' Being-as-affirmed.") In this authentic living "thinking" is "thanking."

What, in the light of this analysis of *Dasein*'s being, and of Being thus come-to-light, is that mode of being which is a work of art? It is, at one level, the thing-being of "equipment," the being-at-hand as an item among beings-in-the-world. *Conservation* is an essential element of its thing-being. It may also *portray* this form of being-at-hand. This point was at the center of a discussion with the art historian and critic Morris Shapiro[49] regarding the interpretation of Van Gogh's portrayal of a pair of farmer's shoes. The "thing" that is an artwork is also, however, an artwork: a *working* of Being in a special mode of *Dasein*. And what is the distinctive character of that working which has been called "artistic creation"? It is, says Heidegger, the character of *poiesis*. The working of the artist, in all media, is "poetizing," *poiein*. Here we are drawn by Heidegger back to a Greek sensibility that we examined in Chapter One—a sensibility that, Heidegger felt, has been obscured in modern intellectualizing or sentimentalizing aesthetic theory. It is through the working of "poetizing" that the "things" that are artworks achieve the distinctive character of being that is art. In this lies their significance and their truth.

What is the "truth" of a work of art? This question becomes intractable if we think of the "true" unfolding of Being in *Dasein* as restricted to that "conformity of intellect with the real" that has furnished the dominant conception of truth in Western philosophy. The supplement to this conception of truth that is needed to fix the "truth" of a work of art is not, however, for Heidegger, something that can be uniquely expressed in an aesthetic judgment of *taste*, à la Hume, Kant, and others. The truth of a work of art is the truth of *Being* "brought to light" in that distinctive mode of Being's "truth-ing" or "uncovering" (*alētheia*).

Modern sensibility associates poetizing preeminently with one art form, poetry, and poetry is a verbal art. We have seen that in the primordial coming-to-light of Being as *Dasein* language plays an essential role. In his earlier analysis of this process (as in *Being and Time*) Heidegger associates linguisticality primarily with the *discursive* work of *logos*, suggesting thereby that it is primarily in logical "picturing" (cf. Wittgenstein, below) or scientific description, explication, and explanation that Being dwells linguistically. In his later work, however, Heidegger increasingly stressed the primacy of that form of verbal art that is called poetry in the pristine unfolding of Being—echoing, we may suggest, some of Vico's sensibility described in Chapter Two.

It is in an essay on "Hölderlin and the Essence of Poetry" that Heidegger adduces the quotation "Full of merit, and yet poetically, dwells Man on this earth."[50] Because poetizing is most readily associated with poetry as a verbal art, it is principally through analysis of this art form that Heidegger seeks to affirm the linguisticality of both Being and poetry as that form of language through which Being "comes to light" in an exemplary manner—or, in the preferred idiom of his later work, in which the chords of being may be most "truly" heard. In poetry there is the most "open" "clearing" of Being. Heidegger might affirm the appropriateness of Robert Frost's selection of a title for his last collection of poems: *In the Clearing*.[51] We should note carefully, however, that Heidegger did not think of poetizing as restricted to that art form called poetry. All art is poetizing—and Being may be "poetically" seen or heard in whatever form, verbal or nonverbal, in which Being unfolds itself poetically.

Does art as poetry, then, have distinctively religious significance for Heidegger? To answer this question we must first ask whether or in what sense there is a "religious" sensibility inherent in *Dasein*. If the religious is associated with a sense of transcendence, then it could be said that, in a sense, "others" transcend self, and Being "transcends" beings-in-the-world of *Dasein*. And Heidegger does speak of Being as that which gives the "power of being" to beings (cf. Tillich). Being, however, is not for Heidegger "the Transcendent"—not even Being understood as "Being-itself." The basic error of Western "onto-theology" or "theo-ontology," he thought, was the theoretical objectification of Being and the designation of the transcendent as Supreme Being. Tillich said that God is not a being among others; neither, said Heidegger, is God transcendent "Being-itself" or a degree of being, "Higher" or otherwise.

Indeed, said Heidegger, the "God" of classical Western thought is, as Nietzsche affirmed, "dead." God "died" with the transmutation of thought into technological mastery of the world and the emergent technocratic civilization. God "died" with the unfaithfulness to Being of theoretical-cognitive rendering of the free and multiple forms of Being's unfoldment, epitomized poignantly in the existential reality of *Dasein* as "human, all too human." Yet, as Heidegger points out, Nietzsche's Madman who proclaimed the "death of God" also proclaimed the "need for God" and called himself a "seeker after God." Heidegger could also say "Only a god can save us."

God is not to be identified with Being, "supreme," "-itself," or otherwise. Yet, if there is God, God "needs" Being as a medium of manifestation. At one time Heidegger seemed to say that such manifestation might occur, unpredictably and uncontrollably, at junctures in history. Such manifestation, however, may not be conformable to classic Christian teleology grounded in concepts of Creation—Fall (though Heidegger speaks of the "fallenness" of *Dasein* in inauthenticity), Incarnation, Redemption. It may be, as Joseph J. Kockelmans puts it, that

> A thinking which becomes free for this happening can no longer attribute the right and wrong way, nearness and distance of the divine to good and bad times or to human good and bad fortune. For this thinking continues to stand under the word of Sophocles, i.e. the last word of the last poetic work of the last poet of original Greece, namely: for everywhere and in every direction, that which has come-to-pass keeps secure a decision concerning its own completion, *pantos gar echei tade kuros.*[52]

Some Christian theologians, nevertheless, have found that Heidegger's basic analyses of human-being-in-the-world provide media of felicitous philosophical expression of Christian revelation. [53]

In expressing his own sense of "the Other," beyond or other than the God of classical theism, Heidegger made increasing use of the concepts of the "mystery" of Being and of "the holy." From the beginning of his creative work he spoke of the "mystery of *Being*"; increasingly the accent seemed to fall on the "*mystery* of Being": the wonder-evoking mystery of the "beingness" of Being, and of the "presencing" of Being in *Dasein's* "language." Sometimes there is talk of the "abyss." This origin-al mystery is articulated, he suggests, in the sense of the holy. But the holy cannot be "thought." In poetry it may be "named."

> Obedient to the voice of Being, thought seeks the Word through which the truth of Being may be expressed. Only when the language of historical man is born of the Word does it ring true. But if it does ring true, then the testimony of the soundless voice of hidden springs lures it ever on. The thought of Being guards the Word and fulfills its function in such guardianship, namely care for the use of language. Out of long-guarded speechlessness and the careful clarification of the field thus cleared, comes the utterance of the thinker. Of like origin is the naming of the poet. But since like is only like insofar as difference allows, and since poetry and thinking are most purely alike in their care of the word, the two things are at the same time at opposite poles in their essence. The thinker utters Being. The poet names what is holy. [54]

If beauty is the form of the "truth" of art, then the holiness of beauty lies in its naming the holy.

•

In a volume published in 1966, that traced "the linguistic turn" in British analytical philosophy and the response to it of people interested in the nature of religious language, I noted that "Many who have learned from Heidegger are asking questions close to those asked by many who have learned from Wittgenstein, Wisdom, Austin, and Ryle." [55] I concluded that

> it is to be expected and hoped that there will . . . be a convergence of interests and activity between those who have philosophized primarily from . . . an "existentialist" orientation, and those who have begun with British empirical-analytical assumptions. As analysts of such traditional concepts as "being" and "existence" proceed along lines opened up by such reconsiderations of the metaphysical enterprise as we have noted; and particularly the analysis of self-knowledge . . . there may be a fruitful confrontation with those whose thinking about being has from the start begun with the significance of the being of the self, and of being perceived from within the depths of self-awareness in its various forms. [56]

This convergence of interests has occurred, and the result is a ferment of activity in contemporary philosophical thought. On the continent the Heideggerian legacy has been especially prominent in hermeneutics, notably as developed by Hans-Georg Gadamer, who places aesthetic idioms and models at the center of his enterprise, and, on both the continent and in America, by Paul Ricoeur.[57] Interest in links with the Anglo-American developments is typified in the request for a German translation of my volume mentioned above.[58]

On the British side, linguistic analysis turned first to analysis of cognitive language. Bertrand Russell, who had worked with Whitehead on the *Principia Mathematica*, sought an "ideal language" incorporating a "logical atomism" in "logical realism." A similar interest led A. J. Ayer to join the "Vienna Circle" of philosophers of science who were working toward a unification of science based on incorrigible cognitive foundations. The search for the latter, in turn, led to incorporation of observational techniques in an account of scientifically warrantable assertions. This led to a search for criteria of verification and falsification. Ayer, who represented a philosophical tradition that had honored Humean empiricism, concluded that the meaning of sentences is equivalent to the protocols of verification or falsification that can be adduced in their support. Although these seemed feasible in the case of cognitive assertions, other forms of utterance could, on these criteria, only be deemed to be "meaningless." Such utterances might express emotions or preferences, but they were literally "without meaning."

Other British philosophers concluded that the program of the "logical positivists" was too narrow to address responsibly the complexities of language use. G. E. Moore sought a more subtle analysis of basic locutions and of the character of certainty and meaning. Gilbert Ryle pursued a form of "conceptual" or "functional" analysis that, he hoped, would lead to the avoidance of "category mistakes" and help to resolve linguistically generated, artificial philosophical "dilemmas." John Austin engaged in more finely tuned analysis of the grammatical forms and word uses of "ordinary language."[59] Among other forms of language use examined by these and like-minded philosophers were aesthetic and religious uses.[60]

All these developments were in a sense exemplified in the work of Ludwig Wittgenstein. We shall, therefore, concentrate in the remainder of this brief exposition on the relevant developments of Wittgenstein's thought, on some of his views on aesthetics and religion, and on the "family resemblances" that may be exhibited through analysis of their linguistic structures and expressions.

LUDWIG WITTGENSTEIN (1889–1951)

Wittgenstein's first major work was dedicated to rigorously clear analysis of descriptive-cognitive language and the "world" that such language reveals. The world, he said in the *Tractatus Logico-Philosophicus*,[61] is "what is the case." "What is the *case*" is those logical basics that are "atomic facts," incorporating and expressing "objects." From these one builds, rigorously and systematically, an account of "what can be said." What can be said on this basis is what can be said in natural science. Philosophical "problems" that emerge in the dilemmas of other kinds of pseudo-sayings are revealed, on close analysis in the light of what can be clearly (scientifically) "said," to be pseudo-problems. And where there are no "answers" to such problems the "questions" disappear.

But how do atomic facts express the ingredients of the world? They "picture" them. In atomic facts there is an isomorphism of expression and expressed. Note that in appealing to the concept of picturing, Wittgenstein opens up the complex domain of types and forms of "images," a domain that has been central in aesthetic and religious thought.[62] Wittgenstein must therefore answer the question "how do pictures picture," or "how do images image." Wittgenstein, in the *Tractatus*, says that the answer to such a question cannot be "said." One cannot picture picturing or image imaging. Pictures "show themselves" and in the showing depict that which they picture. "What can be shown," said Wittgenstein, "cannot be said."

Some have interpreted this remark as providing a basis for a general distinction between verbal and nonverbal expressions of the real. This, I believe, is not Wittgenstein's intent in the *Tractatus*. There he is simply saying what can and cannot be said about *how* those pictures that are cognitively foundational "picture."

Given the nature of the world of the *Tractatus*—the world of "facts"—what can be said about nonfactual (in the sense prescribed by the *Tractatus*) domains such as ethics and aesthetics? They are "transcendental" of this world. As Allan Janik and Stephen Toulmin remark,

Perhaps the most important prerequisite for understanding the *Tractatus* is a distinction between the *philosophy* it contains—the model theory, the critique of Frege and Russell, and so on—and the *world-view* which is expounded in it. [Wittgenstein's] philosophy aims at solving the problem of the nature and limits of description. His world-view expressed the belief that what can only be *shown* must be protected from those who try to *say* it. The philosophy of the *Tractatus* is an attempt to show, from the very nature of propositions, that poetry does not consist of propositions. In this world-view, poetry is the sphere in which the sense of life is expressed, a sphere which therefore cannot be described in *factual* terms. [Cf. Heidegger.] It is the will, rather than reason, that introduces value into the world. The world—the totality of facts—relates to the will . . . in very much the same manner as Schopenhauer's world as representation relates to the world as will, as husk to kernel, as *phenomenon* to *"noumenon."*[63]

"There are, indeed," said Wittgenstein, "things that cannot be put into words. They *make themselves manifest*. They are what is mystical."[64] As for the propositions of the *Tractatus* itself, "My propositions serve as elucidations in the following way: anyone who understands me eventually recognizes them as nonsensical, when he has used them—as steps—to climb up beyond them. (He must, so to speak, throw away the ladder after he has climbed up on it.) He must transcend these propositions, and then he will see the world aright. What we cannot speak about we must pass over in silence."[65] Some have seized upon these remarks to count Wittgenstein among the mystics. Others have attempted to delineate more carefully the role of "silence" in the analyses of both Wittgenstein and Heidegger.[66]

In the later *Philosophical Investigations* Wittgenstein confessed that in the *Tractatus* he had in a sense been "bewitched" by certain grammatical forms in giving the cognitive language he so carefully analyzed the dominant role in characterizing "the world." Fact-stating use is one form of language use. Now, however, he proceeded to an analysis of whatever forms of language use there are, leaving open the question of how many there may be, and without prejudice with respect to the primacy of various uses for various purposes.

The uses exhibit themselves in formally or informally rule-regulated "language games." But there is no "essence" of language in the sense of what all the "games" have in common, if there is anything other than the varying patterns of rule establishment and rule use. In any case, in the interrogation of language one should not ask for "meaning" only in the specific sense entailed in cognitive use; rather, one must seek to discern the specific use among the various forms of language use that is exhibited in the specific linguistic reality to be analyzed. The resultant program, as this is carried out in the *Investigations*, conveys an aura of wonder at the ways of language that reminds one of Heidegger's sense of the mystery of language as the "dwelling house of being." But there is no talk of an extra-linguistic "world." There are many worlds of many forms of engagement expressed in differing language games. Among them are the worlds of the aesthetic and the religious—and a world of resemblances between these two worlds.

Language games may not only be construed as expressive of worlds in the sense of horizons relevant to a particular linguistic standpoint. They are also, says Wittgenstein, expressive of "forms of life." And forms of life are forms of what others call "culture."[67] "What belongs to a language game," says Wittgenstein, "is a whole culture."[68] How, then, may one seek clarity with respect to that family of language games that might be called "aesthetic"? "In order to get clear about aesthetic words you have to describe ways of living. We think we have to talk about aesthetic judgments like 'this is beautiful,' but we find that if we have to talk about aesthetic judgments we don't find these words at all, but a word used something like a gesture, accompanying a complicated activity."[69]

One will not find a "theory" of aesthetics or of aesthetic judgment in Wittgenstein—or a theory of religion, for that matter. His approach, indeed, is congruent with that cited in Chapter Three, in the book called *Against Theory*, edited by W.J.T. Mitchell. "I draw your attention to differences and say: 'Look how different these differences are!' 'Look what is common to the difference cases.' 'Look what is common to Aesthetic judgments.' An immensely complicated family of cases is left, with the highlight—the expression of admiration, a smile or a gesture, etc."[70]

There is no doubt that Wittgenstein was a person with deep aesthetic sensibilities, sensibilities that he shared with Viennese culture of the early decades of the twentieth century. He had a passion for music and once thought of being an architect, gaining some proficiency in that art. (Cf. Tillich, and Tillich's remarks on the architectural character of some forms of philosophy.) Throughout his life his aesthetic sensibility remained acute. To talk about this sensibility, however, he found that he had to talk about specific locutions or "gestures" used by persons in specific circumstances of aesthetic enjoyment of specific forms of art—*this* comment on, or reaction to, *this* musical performance, or painting, or poem. "It is not only difficult to describe what appreciation consists in, but impossible. To describe what it consists in we would have to describe the whole environment."[71]

Thus "If a man goes through an endless number of patterns in a tailor's [and] says 'No. This is slightly too dark. This is slightly too loud,' etc. he is what we call an appreciator of material. That he is an appreciator is not shown by the interjections he uses, but by the way he chooses, selects, etc. Similarly in music: 'Does this harmonize. No. The bass is not quite loud enough. Here I want just something different. . . .' This is what we call appreciation."[72] "We talked of correctness. A good cutter won't use any words except words like 'Too long,' 'All right.' When we talk of a symphony of Beethoven we don't talk of correctness. Entirely different things enter. One wouldn't talk of appreciating the *tremendous* things in Art. In certain styles in Architecture a door is correct, and the thing is you appreciate it. But in the case of a Gothic cathedral what we do is not at all to find it correct—it plays an entirely different role with us. The entire *game* is different."[73]

One will not find in Wittgenstein, therefore, "theories" of various art forms. One may at times find some more general remarks (and is not philosophy a series of general remarks?) that suggest elements of what others discuss more pretentiously in the guise of general aesthetic theory. A sample is the following: "Aesthetic questions have nothing to do with psychological experiments, but are answered in an entirely different way."[74] (Cf. a whole literature about the psychology of aesthetic judgment.) "The criterion for it being the one that was in your mind is that when I tell you, you agree."[75] (Cf. convoluted discussions about the communication of aesthetic agreement.) "You could say: 'An aesthetic explanation is not a causal explanation.'"[76] (Other remarks bring out the differences between motives and causes.) "If you are led by psychoanalysis to say that really you thought so and so or really that your motive was so and so, this is not a matter of discovery, but of persuasion."[77] "Much of what we are doing is changing our style of thinking."[78] "In art it is hard to say anything as good as: saying nothing."[79]

Then what about "the religious" in language games? First we must affirm that, for Wittgenstein, just as there is not one game that is aesthetic-in-general, so there is not a single game that is *the* religious language game, though many theologians and others have assumed that there is. Indeed, one commentator held that "the religious language game" is like the Olympic games in relation to all games![80] There is no self-enclosed or self-justifying language game of any kind, though again some theologians and philosophers of religion have appealed to such a notion in a view of *the* religious language game that is sometimes called "Wittgensteinian fideism."

At the beginning of the *Investigations* Wittgenstein adds to the end of a list of various types of language games the following words: asking, thanking, cursing, greeting, praying.[81] These do not constitute *a* "language game," and "praying" has a space of its own. They are a cluster of activities whose linguistic expression may exhibit some "family resemblances." Henry L. Finch suggests that "ritual" may be an appropriate designation for the general form of activity named in such a cluster.[82] A sense of the integrity of such a form underlies Wittgenstein's scathing critique of Frazer's *Golden Bough*, which sought "explanations" of "primitive" religious belief and behavior in the context of a "sophisticated" modern Western sensibility.[83]

Wittgenstein's analysis of religious belief reported in students' notes on the appropriately grouped *Lectures and Conversations on Aesthetics, Psychology, and Religious Belief* focuses on the function of an announced belief in a Last Judgment—a belief that, according to Paul Englemann, Wittgenstein took quite seriously, but in his own way.[84] Such a belief functions for a person, says Wittgenstein, to provide a kind of "guidance for life." "It will show, not by reasoning or by appeal to ordinary grounds for belief, but rather by regulating for all in his life."[85] "Evidence" adduced in support of it will be, at best, only indirectly the sort of evidence that supports ordinary "cognitive" beliefs. This does not mean, as some have claimed, that Wittgenstein is a "fideist" in the sense of claiming extraordinary or incorrigible cognitive grounds for religious beliefs. If one says that one does not hold such a belief, as Wittgenstein said that he would in the circumstances described in the lecture, one is not "disagreeing"; one is saying that one "does not see things that way."

Both the aesthetic and the religious are "ways of seeing things." As Stanley Cavell puts it, when Wittgenstein says that fruitful philosophical investigation leads to "perspicuous representation," or that the solution of a problem consists in the "vanishing" of a problem, he means that "there is no longer any question or problem which your words would match. You have reached conviction, but not about a proposition; and consistency, but not in a theory. You are different, what you recognize as problems is different." (The "world of the happy man is different from the world of the unhappy man," Wittgenstein said.) "And this is the sense," says Cavell, "and the only sense, in which what a work of art means cannot be *said*. Believing it is seeing it."[86] Wittgenstein said that

> When E [Paul Englemann] looks at what he has written and finds it marvelous—[Englemann had said that rummaging through his old papers or reading his grandfather's letters made him think they were worth publishing, but when he looked at them individually he was sure they were not]—he is seeing his life as a work of art created by God and, as such, it would certainly be worth contemplating, as is every life and everything whatever. But only an artist can so represent an individual thing as to make it appear to us like a work of art. A work of art forces us, as we might say, to see it in the right perspective, but, in the absence of art, the object is just a fragment of nature. *We* may exalt it through our enthusiasm, but that does not give anyone else the right to confront us with it. But it seems to me too that there is a way of capturing the world sub specie aeterni other than the work of the artist. Thought has such a way—so I believe—it is as thought flies above the world and leaves it as it is, from above, in flight.[87]

Both Heideggerian and Wittgensteinian themes inform appraisals of the aesthetic in relation to the religious—or beauty in relation to holiness—in late-twentieth-century philosophy. The never-finished "movement" of thought, in the context of ever-increasing awareness of the indefinite variety of "forms of life" and of cultures, expressed in an indefinite variety of language games, has led to a reassessment of the nature and role of philosophizing. If philosophy can no longer aspire to be, or secondarily to reflect, "the mirror of nature," philosophy may nevertheless, suggests Richard Rorty, engage in "edifying conversation" with other cultural enterprises.[88] But can its only conversation, in the last analysis, be about or within linguistic "texts"? We shall see that Jacques Derrida thinks so, and that Derrida also radically questions the possibility of fixed or focal "presence" (Heidegger) in the texts that are "the world." We will address some of the implications of these claims in Chapter Six. In that chapter we will also examine the views of the Russian critic Mikhail Bakhtin, who proposed the employment of the "dialogical principle" in the ongoing conversation of criticism and philosophy with other disciplines and other genres. First we seek to enhance appreciation of cultural pluralism by examining in an even more condensed fashion than has been exhibited in the preceding chapters what we will label "Eastern thought."

CHAPTER FIVE

Holiness and Beauty in Eastern Thought

THE TITLE of this chapter is an expression of provincialism. If it is in any sense justified, it is only because it may seem to many to fit naturally within the parameters of much current discussion of our topic. Yet one must ask at once what and where is "the East," what and where is "the West," and from whose perspective were these geographical labels of cultures derived. We will be following the all-too-typical pattern of lumping together under the label "the East" an array of ancient and rich cultures stretching from the Indian subcontinent and Southeast Asia through the Central Asian and Chinese mainland, and thence through Korea to Japan. Each of these cultures has its own distinctive historical configuration, and each has produced a plethora of phenomena that I have been calling "aesthetic" and "religious." Yet the agenda for the discussion we have been following has been set by "Western" thinkers, and Western scholars have been engaged in critically responsible attempts to understand "Eastern" cultures for only a few generations.

A similar limitation of focus is indicated in the use of the term "thought" in the chapter title. In the preceding chapters we have learned that thought always occurs in cultural contexts that embrace many other human activities. The use of the term in this chapter, however, may serve as a further reminder that our goal in this study is to uncover the *conceptual* designations of holiness and beauty entailed in philosophical, religious, and aesthetic developments. We are interested in questions of *theory*, with only such attention to concrete historical practice as may be needed to assess the adequacy of theory. Thus just as we have not attempted in the preceding chapters to offer a history of "religious art" in relation to a history of religious thought in the West, we do not attempt, in this chapter, to survey the riches of Indian, Central Asian, Chinese, Korean, or Japanese art in relation to the history of the various religious traditions that appear in these cultures. Our focus is on what may be functional equivalents in the East of what has been called "aesthetics" and "theory of religion" in the

West and on the relation between the two. The use of these two terms by some recent Asian thinkers stems from the introduction into Asia of Western patterns of thought in the past two centuries.

It is notoriously difficult, if not impossible, to translate the term/ concept "religion," as we have seen it emerge in aspects of Western thought discussed in the preceding chapters, into an Asian language. Dharma? Shūkyō? Tao? "Terms such as 'philosophy,' 'religion,' and so forth," writes Hajime Nakamura, "may well turn out to be provincial clichés that need to be carefully reexamined and reinterpreted from the perspective of a broadly based cross-cultural cognitive anthropology."[1] Nakamura himself concludes that a word such as "tao," which may be translated "way" or "way of life," is perhaps the most useful. When John A. Hutchison and I wrote an introduction to religion we, too, chose the title *Ways of Faith*.[2]

What, then, about the terms "beauty" and "holiness"? Again there may be no terms clearly equivalent to Western usages in the Asian traditions we will consider. I believe, however, that it is helpful to continue, in this chapter, to use the term beauty as a surrogate for "aesthetic excellence," in whatever ways the latter may be conceived. Similarly, as we continue to employ the term holiness, it is as surrogate for what may be less felicitously called "ultimateness," in a sense that has an affinity with the analyses by Tillich and others outlined in Chapter Three. When we seek to identify the relation of holiness to beauty in aspects of Asian thought, we are seeking to identify the relation of aesthetic excellence to ultimateness, in whatever ways these may be conceived in these richly complex traditions.

The tenuousness of such conceptual distinctions in Asian thought may be illustrated in two personal experiences of the author. A number of distinguished representatives of Asian traditions participated in the East-West Philosophers Conference at the University of Hawaii in 1949. Most of the senior Western philosophers there represented varieties of idealistic or naturalistic traditions. Several younger participants suggested that some attention should be paid to Western theistic philosophy and theology. The chairman, a Westerner, said this would be out of order, because the subject of the conference was philosophy, not religion. At this point a saintly and distinguished historian of Indian philosophy rose and said, "Please explain the distinction; we do not understand it." Many years later, in 1961, I was asked to address the faculty of a liberal Hindu college near New Delhi on the nature and role of the academic study of religion. After I had talked about theories of religion and the distinction between studying *about* religion and studying religion "religiously," a similarly saintly professor of Sanskrit rose and said, "but we do not *study* religion—we *experience* it. If our guest has some religious experience he would like to share with us, we will hear him gladly." The attitude expressed in these personal encounters were expressed less directly in the examination of religious and philosophical topics during many years of discussion in the Columbia University Seminar on Oriental Thought and Religion.

How, then, may we proceed? One might address our topic in terms of its relevance to various religious traditions: Hindu, Jain, Buddhist, Taoist, Confucian, and so forth. Here let me acknowledge a notable omission in the materials we seek to examine in this perhaps already-overly-ambitious volume: Islam. Islam has affinities with some features of "Western" as well as some features of "Eastern" traditions. The varieties of its expression of a common faith were suggested in the brief account of Clifford Geertz's studies in Chapter Three. The omission of it here is perhaps justified by (1) problems of the accessibility and the character of Islamic thought that could plausibly be construed to be discussion of aesthetics and religion in the sense set forth in the preceding chapters, and (2) the influence on Islamic thought of both those Western sensibilities examined in Chapters One and Two and sensibilities that we shall seek to discern in the present chapter. Islam shares Semitic origins with Judaism and Christianity, and, like these faiths, its conceptuality was deeply influenced by Greek thought-forms as it developed formal philosophical and theological systems. Its insistence on a radical monotheism, however, has made it even more wary of visual images and their possible idolatrous seductions than has been the case in some Jewish and Christian traditions. At the same time it has celebrated the riches of the Arabic language, both as a medium of conceptual expression and as possessing a physical form of aesthetic excellence. Like the Chinese and Japanese traditions we examine below, it has prized the decorative values of calligraphy in "Arabesque." It shares with both Western and Eastern traditions an esteem for poetry in both content and performance as a favored means of inspiring and expressing religious devotion—especially in Sufism and other forms of Islamic mysticism. And it has developed distinctive architectural styles that are consonant with its religious vision.

We should also note the fact that many Easterners are wary of the "-isms" in terms of which others describe their traditions. "Hindu" is a term coined by Muslims at the time of their incursion into the rich cultures of the Indus River valley, just as "Christian" is a term coined by people of Greek sensibilities in Antioch. "Buddhist" is perhaps a natural appellation for the Way discovered and promulgated by Gautama. *"Shen-tao"* may be more straightforward: the way of the gods. And "Confucian" has a certain integrity, indicating a tradition originating (according to tradition) with K'ung Fu-tse, Master-Teacher Kung—though Confucius himself is portrayed as saying that he wished only to recover the "ways of the ancients" of the Early Zhuo (Chou) dynasty. Then there is simply "the way" of the Way—"Taoism."

In any event, students of Eastern aesthetic phenomena indicate that the forms and styles of such phenomena are influenced more by general features of the various cultural milieux than by specific religious considerations.[3] Geographical, ethnic, and regional factors play larger roles than do systematic or ideological goals of religious traditions. Thus there may be more similarities between Hindu, Jain, and Buddhist art in South India at a particular time than between Hindu art of South India and that of North India—or, certainly, than between Southeast Asian Buddhist art and Chinese or Japanese Buddhist art. Yet religious considerations of subject matter clearly play a role in the articulation of relations of aesthetic excellence to ultimateness. We shall, therefore, proceed geographically in our analysis, considering in turn Indian, Chinese, and Japanese expressions of the relation of holiness to beauty in the religious traditions of those areas.

I shall try to avoid generalizations, yet I would like to hazard two comments about Eastern aesthetic/religious phenomena as a whole that may be sustained by the exposition that follows. One is that many of the most influential comments on the nature of art and artistic creation in Eastern thought have been made by persons who were themselves artists—poets, painters, musicians, dancers. Theoretical reflection emerged from individual practices. There have been relatively few attempts to develop general theories of aesthetics relevant to all "matters of taste," and there has only recently been some reflection—in the style of the West—on "the nature of religion as such." This grounding of theory in personal practice may itself be a contribution to responsible reflection on the character of aesthetic excellence, in a world that seeks enrichment through positive affirmation of pluralistic resources. In the East, comments on beauty and holiness have been judged in terms of both the character and the practice of the persons offering the comments.

A second generalization provides a context for the first. The Asian cultures from which we shall select materials relevant to our topic have been, at least until the recent past, much more highly integrated than has Western culture since the Renaissance. Political, economic, aesthetic, and religious factors have been more subtly intertwined in the East than in the West. Beginning with Weber, Western social theorists have attempted to delineate some of the factors that enter into differences of cultural patterns in East and West, and the topic is one that contemporary scholars engaged in comparative cultural studies debate at length. Much of the debate now centers on theories of "secularization" and its implications for cultural change. Some employ the term modernization rather than secularization. Modernization, in turn, is often equated with "Westernization," a term that includes both "Western" scientific thought and technology and Western political and economic theory. Clifford Geertz, among others, however, has shown that indigenous traditions possess internal resources for both engendering and adapting to cultural change.

With respect to the topic of our study, it does seem clear that many of the views we shall consider in this chapter reflect a sense of cultural wholeness that was increasingly absent in the thought of many whose views we considered in Chapters Two, Three, and Four—unless their concepts of other cultures themselves betray an unexamined set of cultural assumptions! It is in part a recognition of these differences that led Ananda K. Coomaraswamy, one of the pioneering and most influential interpreters of Oriental art to Western audiences and readers, to maintain that there is a "Christian and Oriental, or True, Philosophy of Art,"[4] which may be found in Oriental as well as in classical Greek, Roman, and Christian cultures of the West before the latter became both diffused and internally differentiated in movements epitomized in the Enlightenment. He found this "true philosophy of art" in Platonic and Aristotelian components of Medieval Western thought and culture, as well as in Indian, Buddhist, and Confucian classics. It is, he thought, "a doctrine of art intrinsic to the Philosophia Perennis." Central to the doctrine is the view that all art is essentially iconographic, and that authentic art forms and objects embody and transmit "spiritual" meanings. Authentic experience of a work of art, in turn, entails appropriate preparation of the artist and the viewer, reader, or hearer for a transaction that transforms both the artist and the one engaged in an act of "appreciation." "The supreme achievement of individual consciousness is to lose or find (both words mean the same thing) itself in what is both its beginning and its end," he said. The object-subject of apprehension moves the will and attracts the intellect of the artist; its form is the agent of that formation expressed in and through the artwork and apprehended by the appropriately prepared perceiver.

There are, Coomaraswamy believed, universal themes or motifs that are expressed in varying ways in all great art, whether verbal or nonverbal. In traditional cultures, he said, there is a continuity between those values associated with the fine arts and those associated with the crafts of daily life. In these cultures, whose ideal forms are variously portrayed by Plato, Aristotle, and Augustine, and in Vedic,

Buddhist, and Confucian writings, there is a harmony of social function flowing from a common vision of human good. In commending a classical philosophy of art Coomaraswamy believed that he was also offering a critique of both modern aesthetic theory and aspects of modern culture. Modern aesthetic theory, he said, errs in placing the ground and goal of aesthetic experience in the life of feeling; true art is ultimately ideational and cognitive. Prizing aesthetic satisfaction as an end in itself is a modern form of idolatry or dehumanization. Ultimate human apprehension of the real also transcends even the experience of the beauty of the good; it is completed in contemplation, which should both guide and perfect human life.

Although many questions may be raised about Coomaraswamy's theory of "true" art, the theory does reflect the ideal of a holistic culture—an ideal that, he believed, had been embodied in both Eastern and classical Western cultures, including the classical culture of "Christendom." It is a view of culture that we will find exemplified in many of the concepts of the relation of the aesthetic to the religious in the expositions that follow. Coomaraswamy's generalizations must be modified, however, with respect to his comparison of classical Greek, classical Christian, and classical Eastern cultures. In Greco-Roman culture the practice of public and private piety reflected the need for a variety of foci of worship to meet different needs of persons and communities on different occasions. These practices, however, were not undergirded by a monolithic and systematic conceptual scheme of theology, or conducted under the aegis of one religious institution. Philosophers could employ the concept of *theos* in metaphysical speculation and could also be critical of some popular worship practices and of popular understandings of the myths they enacted. There was, however, no official theology espoused by an officially recognized monolithic religious institution.

With the establishment of Christianity as the official religion of the Roman Empire, however, a relation of religion to culture was enacted that differed from both the classical Greco-Roman practice and that of the Eastern cultures we will examine in this chapter. Conceptual articulation of ultimateness was focused exclusively in a theology grounded in the authority of canonical scriptures and an officially defined tradition expressing the import of this authority for changing cultural configurations. The Christian church emerged as a religious institution with specified relations to the state as a political institution. Each institution was seen as having primary responsibility for various aspects of life; in matters of ultimateness, however, the church was supreme. In Eastern cultures there has been no comparable differentiation and specification of a monolithic religious institution in relation to a monolithic political institution. Just as it is, I believe, misleading to speak of Hindu or Buddhist or Confucian "theology," so it would be misleading to speak of Hindu or Buddhist or Confucian "churches." Western assumptions about the relation of religious thought to an officially defined theology, expressing the conceptuality of a monolithic religious institution, have made it difficult for many Westerners to understand the relations of aesthetic excellence to ultimateness in Eastern cultures.

In the preceding chapters we could focus on the thought of individuals who shared a common cultural history. In this chapter we must describe in more general terms some of the conceptuality of religious traditions that, while maintaining important continuities, modified the expression of this conceptuality in differing cultural settings. Regional differences also entered into the aesthetic expressions of the conceptuality. Our exposition will proceed regionally, therefore, with special attention to distinctive features of religious traditions in the chronological order of their impact upon the culture of each region. We must bear in mind throughout the exposition the fact that Western models of "church" or "churches" and of "theology" or "theologies" are largely inapplicable to the materials we will be examining. And, given the scope of the data we shall attempt to interpret, we shall have to be even more arbitrarily selective, and our exposition will have to be even more condensed, than was the case in the preceding chapters.

INDIA

The Hindu Tradition

The richly complex religious tradition first labeled "Hinduism" by outsiders is essentially the tradition shared by persons of the Indian subcontinent who do not explicitly identify themselves with some other tradition, or who declare themselves to be adherents of no religious tradition. Its origins go back to the incursion of Aryan peoples from Central Asia and the Near East into the Indian subcontinent, perhaps early in the second millennium before the Common Era. (Chronological periodization of Indian history was the result of the work of British and other European scholars of the nineteenth century, as was the systematic study of Indian art forms.)[5] The rich indigenous culture that the Aryans encountered is often designated "Dravidian"; it, in turn, was the inheritor of a remarkable Indus valley culture labeled Mohenjo-Daro. The Aryans adopted some key concepts of the Dravidian way of life. One is *samsara*, the conceptualization of spatio-temporal existence as an indefinitely ongoing process of change, evolutionary or devolutionary. *Samsara* is governed by the law of *karma*, or law of causality—causality that informs not only the world of nature but also the world of human conduct. Consistency demands that conduct in "this life" is understood to be the result of former conduct in this or in previous lives. The goal of life is so to live in accord with *karma* that ultimate release from the "wheel of samsara" may occur: this is *moksha*, or deliverance. Who and where and when one is, is the result of how and where and when one has been. Who one will be, will be the result of *how* one is who one is in the present life. There are many paths through which one may generate "good *karma*" that will move one toward the goal of *moksha*. The process of moving toward or away from the goal will continue until the goal is reached—through however many "lifetimes" may be needed.

But what is the ultimate reality that is both "beyond" and "within" the process of *samsara*? Dravidian devotion had focused on a range of polytheistic powers approached in appropriate ritual. Indo-Aryans sang their wonder in that collection of poetic books called the *Vedas*—a term cognate with such other Indo-Aryan words as the Greek *oida* and the Germanic *wissen*: wisdom. Subsequent Hindu thought would embrace these books as canonical. In the *Brahmanas* the conceptuality and the ritual became more complex, and finally in the *Upanishads* (a term meaning "sitting-near," or at the feet of a sage) Aryan speculative thought, beginning perhaps around 500 B.C.E., designated the ultimately real as *Brahman*—trans-spatio-temporal Unity, the source and goal of spatio-temporal existence. The spatio-temporal world itself is *maya*, a term, unfortunately, frequently translated "illusion." *Maya* is as real as the spatio-temporal world is real, but *maya* is not the ultimately Real, or Brahman. Brahman within the spatio-temporal world is atman, usually translated—again, perhaps unfortunately—"soul."

At this point two concepts that are central to consideration of the relation of aesthetic excellence to ultimateness appear. Brahman, being "beyond" spatio-temporal reality, cannot be described in that spatio-temporal reality that is language. The least inappropriate linguistic expression regarding Brahman is that Brahman is *neti, neti*: "not this, not that" item or "substance" of spatio-temporal reality. But Brahman may also be "pointed to" in conceptual absolutes. Thus Brahman is said to be *sat-chit-ananda*: perfect existence, perfect consciousness, perfect *bliss*. "Perfect bliss" is the metaphysical goal of what would later be differentiated as specifically aesthetic experience—though with qualifications to be noted below.

Brahman, being beyond all human characteristics, is also therefore beyond specifically personal/impersonal adjectival designation. One may conceive of Brahman as *nirguna*, "without qualifications," or as *saguna*, "with (personal) qualifications." The former is the conceptuality of Advaita Vedanta—the "wisdom of unqualified nondualism"; the latter is the conceptuality of Vishistadvaita Vedanta, "qualified nondualism." Both are orthodox, though the former has been predominant in philosophical circles. Brahman as personal is manifested in a pantheon of gods and goddesses, the chief of whom, for *bhakti* (religious devotion), are Brahma, Shiva, and Vishnu. Each of these, in turn, may appear in *avatars*, or manifestations of manifestation, in specific times and places.

But why does Brahman, the causeless trans-spatio-temporal Real, manifest itself in the world of *maya* and *samsara*? Why time from the eternal, the many from the One? A traditional answer in Hinduism is one that has implications for the relation of aesthetic excellence to ultimateness. *Maya*, it is said, is the *lila*—the "sport" or "dance" of Brahman. The spatio-temporal world is characterized by tensions and resolutions, by rhythms of discord and harmony. Dance is a primordial art; music articulates the infinite variations on themes emanating from the dominant One; rhythm may be, as S. K. Saxena suggests, an art form in itself.[6]

Between the fourth and third centuries before the Common Era there emerged two great epics that were to offer verbal aesthetic articulation of basic Hindu conceptuality in a manner that would provide for all future generations major narrative, poetic, and dramatic sources for the molding of Hindu devotion through aesthetic creations: the *Ramayana* and the *Mahabharata*—the epics of the love of Rama and Sita, and of the "Great Bharata Civil War." What the works attributed to Homer were for Greek art and thought, so these works have been for Indian art and thought. The troubled but ultimately triumphant love of Rama and Sita provides a model of faithfulness, courage, and blissful fulfillment. The Great Bharata Civil War is an emblem of all human strife and its tragic or nontragic resolutions. More important, attached to the Mahabharata is the account of an episode whose recital would come to be called "the Lord's Song"—the *Bhagavadgita*.

The 'Gita recounts the counsels of Krishna, an *avatar* of Vishnu, to Arjuna, a warrior, on the eve of battle. In response to Arjuna's questions Krishna expounds the three major *margas*—paths, or *yogas* (forms of discipline; the term is cognate with the English *yoke*, as used in the King James Version of the Bible, where Jesus is reported to enjoin his disciples, or discipline-receivers, to "take His yoke upon them")—that lead to *moksha*, or release from *samsara*. These are the Way of Works: of "duty for duty's sake"; of knowledge of the Real attained through disciplined meditation; and of *bhakti*, devotion to a personal god or goddess. Each is a valid way, to be followed according to one's *karma*, individuality, and temperament. The way of *bhakti* focuses on one's *ishta-devata*, one's "chosen deity." It is during the portrayal of this Way that Arjuna asks Krishna to reveal himself in all his glory. The ensuing theophany is noted by Rudolf Otto as a singular example of evocation of the sense of the numinous. In the course of it Khrishna proclaims that he creates and pervades the whole universe, and that human rational, moral, or other means of apprehension of the divine are functions of *atman*, or cosmic soul. Beauty is an aspect of the divine. "For whatsoever . . . is beautiful . . . understand thou that to go forth from a fragment of my Splendor." "I am the splendor of splendid things."[7] The term translated "splendor" here resonates with "sublimity" as this term is used in examples of Western thought noted in Chapters Three and Four. The interest of contemporary Indian philosophers in the notion of the sublime is typified in S. K. Saxena's essay of Hegel's concept of the sublime.[8]

Since all of *maya* is ordered by the law of *karma*, the circumstances of individual lives within which individuals may move toward *moksha* are so ordered. And within each individualization of circumstance there are ordered steps toward that goal. If one is, in accord with past *karma*, born among the "twice-born"—those who have experienced individual human existence at least once before—one may enter into a graded series of *ashrams* or stages of life. The first of these is studenthood (*Brahmacharya*); the second is householderhood (*Grihastra*); the third is that of meditative withdrawal from the world (*Varnapastra*, "forest dweller"); and the last is that of the *sannyasin*, one who returns to the world but lives in the world as one not of the world. Progress through these stages may require an indefinite number of lifetimes. In the householder stage, which is an integral part of the journey to liberation, one fulfills economic, social, and other vocational duties. In this stage one's life is guided by three goods: *dharma* (religious duty), *artha* (worldly welfare), and *kama* (sensual pleasure). *Kama* is an essential ingredient of that good life that may lead to further stages of liberation. It includes skill in and appreciation of aesthetic creation, as well as skill in the art of love. The celebrated handbook of the latter is the *Kama Sutra*.[9]

The Hindu path to liberation includes, therefore, all the goods that may be labeled "aesthetic." They are among the means of liberation leading to spiritual fulfillment. And what is that? It is the realization *"tat tvam asi"*—that That (Brahman) art Thou (*atman*, individualized in personhood). It is the realization (making real) of the unity of "the soul" and the One, of self and Self. But what is the character of aesthetic excellence in relation to this goal?

Rasa is the Sanskrit term that is frequently translated "beauty"—but there are some thirty definitions of the term in Sanskrit dictionaries.

In the Rig-Veda it signifies the juice of the soma plant used in sacrificial ritual. In the Atharva-Veda its use is extended to denote the sap of grain and, more significantly, to mean "flavor" or "taste." Upanishadic abstraction extended this to "essence," and in the *Taittirya* and *Maitreya* Upanishads it is assimilated to "self-luminous consciousness," the experience of the joy of Brahman as *ananda*.[10] As such it is the goal and guide of poetic instruction, musical composition and performance, painting, and all the other arts. What, then, is it, and how is it evoked?

Rasa is, among other things, a felicitous blend of specified feelings and emotions. Elaborate taxonomies of these were developed by artists/aestheticians/critics. Various blends were in turn associated in standardized ways with colors, sounds, poetic and dramatic figures, and divinities. Is it, then, subjective—a "sense" or "sensibility" of the artist and/or the viewer or hearer; or is it objective, inhering in the artwork as such? "The essential quality of aesthetic experience," writes Eliot Deutsch in explicating the concept, "is neither subjective nor objective. It neither belongs to the art-work nor to the experiencer of it; rather it is the process of aesthetic perception itself, which defies spatial designations, that constitutes *rasa*. This view that the locus of *rasa* is nowhere, that *rasa* transcends spatio-temporal determination, is, I believe, the only way open to us to understand the nature of aesthetic experience."[11] *Rasa* is fully amenable to neither the formalistic nor the expressivist interpretations favored by some Western aestheticians. Yet, as Kant suggested in his emphasis on "disinterested pleasure" as a mark of aesthetic experience, in the experience of *rasa* the art object controls the experience, and the experience lays claim to universality. It thus imposes great obligations on both the artist and the hearer/reader/viewer. "The *rasa* is a generalized emotion, that is, one from which all elements of particular consciousness are expunged: such as the time of the artistic event, the preoccupation of the witness [audience], the specific or individuating qualities of the [artwork] itself."[12]

The artist, as Coomaraswamy noted, must go through appropriately disciplined preparation, and the perceiver must also be appropriately prepared if the experience of *rasa* is to occur. The experience is one of *mimesis*, but, as Deutsch writes, "it is an 'imitation' of a very special kind, for *rasa* does not imitate things and actions in their particularity, in their actuality, but rather in their universality, their potentiality."[13] In this respect, as Coomaraswamy claims, the experience is more open to Aristotelian than to Kantian interpretation.

Aesthetic experience, therefore, is essentially a "relishing" of certain generalized emotions which are "objectified" in vital form. Art is at once bound to life and *is* for itself. A work of art that occasions *rasa* is closely related to common experience, drawing as it does its own vitality, its aesthetic content, from those basic life emotions and situations that persons every-where endure. Form in art has meaning only in relation to content; in fact, there is form, the *rasa*-theory suggests, only when both for the artist and the "spectator" there is a lived, deeply felt content. But a work of art is not a mirror of life; it is . . . *alaukika*, extraordinary. . . . Aesthetic experience, according to the theory, is thus not something that is merely given, a fortuitous happening; it is an attainment. [14]

Donna M. Wulff[15] has described the role of *rasa* as a means to ultimateness in the thought of two medieval Indian thinkers: the Kash-mir Shaivite philosopher Abhinavagupta (10th–11th c. C.E.) and the Bengali Vaishnavite Rupa Gosvemi (first half of the sixteenth century C.E.). For Abhinava *rasa* is a means of transition "from ordinary mun-dane consciousness, with its egocentric limitations, to the universal and unmediated consciousness that is absolute freedom, which he of-ten equates with *ananda*" [Brahman as "bliss"]. For Rupa the basic un-derlying emotion in religious devotion is *love* for Khrishna. In the ex-perience of *rasa* this love is "transformed into a refined 'sentiment' or attitude that can, like Krishna himself, be perpetually relished."[16] "His concept of devotion," writes Wulff, "is fundamentally an aesthetic one."[17]

Is there, then, finally any distinction between aesthetic and reli-gious experience, if aesthetic excellence is conceived as *rasa*? The acme of experience as *rasa* is *santarasa*, which, according to Abhinava, is, as Deutsch puts it, "just that transcendental realization of unity that is joy-ful and peace-ful. It is grounded in the Self and is realized as a kind of self-liberation."[18] And, ultimately, "*Santa* is silence."

> What is silence in art? A work of art is constantly speaking, as it were, and yet it is mute, standing silent in its own concentrated being. The painting, the poem, the play is a center of silence and requires for its right apprehension an inner quietude, a silencing of desires and thoughts. Si-lence in art is not empty . . . rather the art-work that is right for itself participates in a silence which is the profoundest truth of being, the si-lence which is a dynamic harmony of all being and becoming. Silence in art, then, is not a mere absence of sound. *Santarasa* is a plenitude, it is surcharged with creative energy. The silence calls us out of ourselves to the concentrated being of the work itself. [19]

But even the "highest" form of aesthetic experience is not identical with the highest form of religious experience:

> herein lies the essential difference between aesthetic experience in its highest form and pure spiritual experience: the art-work calls our atten-

tion to it and controls our experience with it; the experience is temporal (albeit transforming); in spiritual experience the call is from that which is Real without division of object or time. The art-work, in the fullness of its experience as *santarasa*, points to Reality and participates in it. In pure spiritual experience there is only the Real. To the enlightened—but only to the enlightened—all experience is *santarasa*[20]

Contemporary Indian philosophers, building on the classical concept of *rasa*, have expressed affinities with a variety of Western aesthetic theories. Both G. Hanumantha Rao[21] and S. K. Saxena admire the work of Suzanne K. Langer (*Feeling and Form*). The basic framework of their reflections, however, is consonant with the general "Hindu" conceptuality briefly outlined above. And the most influential metaphysical expression of that conceptuality is that of Advaita Vedanta, which is described in its relation to aesthetics by T. M. P. Mahadevan in his *Philosophy of Beauty*.[22]

Buddhist Tradition

Gautama Siddhartha, "Sakyamuni"—"sage of the Sakya clan"—was born in 563 B.C.E. and entered "parinirvana" in 483 B.C.E. Coomaraswamy asserts that the date of Gautama's death is "the first quite definable landmark in Indian history."[23] It is also the case that remains of Buddhist art are among the earliest artworks now accessible on the Indian subcontinent, though the scope of Hindu monuments is much greater.

Gautama was born into a noble family (and hence among the "twice-born") and was trained in his youth and young manhood to assume the responsibilities of the noble householder. According to tradition, however, in the third decade of his life he experienced four "appearances" that radically called into question the adequacy of his current station in life: disease, old age, death, and a monk who seemed to have found equanimity in the midst of life that is characterized by these perennial elements. Then followed the "Great Renunciation," withdrawal to the forest, and a life of meditation. Extreme ascetic measures brought no insight. But one day, seated in meditation under a banyan tree, he experienced the Enlightenment of the Four Noble Truths: (1) All is *dukkha*: sorrow, dis-ease, incompleteness, transience. This is the given nature of life in *samsara*. (2) *Dukkha* is caused by craving or "thirst"—the desire to find fulfillment through attachment to the "goods" of *samsara*. (3) If, then, desire can be eliminated, sorrow will cease. (4) Desire may be eliminated by following the "Eightfold Path" of the way of life that embodies simplicity, truthfulness, nonviolence, and moderation. Thus Gautama became the Buddha, the Enlightened One. He did not, however, keep his enlightenment to himself, though he might then have entered *nirvana*. In an act of compassion, which was to become exemplary in later forms of Buddhism, he shared his insight with monks in the Deer Park in Benares. Thus was established the *sangha*—the order of those who follow the Way.

Gautama shared with his contemporaries much of the basic conceptuality outlined in the preceding section: *samsara, karma, moksha*. He refused, however, to speculate on the nature of the Ultimately Real as origin and goal of life, or on the state of life after *moksha*. "Such questions," he said, "do not tend to edification." Focus should be on the realization of the Noble Truths and following the Eightfold Path. And he did not think of himself as a "savior" or "deliverer"; he was a "pathfinder" who shared the path he had found; others "must be islands unto themselves."

Though the path discovered by the Buddha enjoined moderation and was called "the Middle Way," emphasis on detachment from the penultimate goods of *samsara* led to moderately ascetic practices among his followers. Also, although he eschewed metaphysical speculation about the Real and the nature of the ultimate state of enlightened life, he did address the nature of the self. It is not, he taught, an underlying "substance" of individuality; rather, like all else, it is an organic process of transience, *anatta*. At any given point in the ongoingness of penultimate reality, a self is the outcome of "dependent origination"—of those psychological, moral, and other factors that, as Whitehead would say, "concresce" in a given form of selfhood. The goal is so to live through these that one may eliminate their causal power, achieving the state called *nirvana*—literally, "quenching" or "blowing out." Whitehead said that "Buddhism is the most colossal example in history of applied metaphysics . . . a metaphysics generating a religion," in contrast with Christianity, which is "a religion seeking a metaphysic."[24] It may be more accurate to say that the doctrine of Gautama is a psychology that generated a metaphysic exemplified in a religious Way.

Buddhist teachings were carried to Sri Lanka during the reign of the Buddhist emperor Asoka in the third century B.C.E.; to Nepal, Tibet, and China by the first six centuries of the Common Era; to Java in the sixth century, and somewhat later to Burma, Thailand, and Indochina. The Buddhism of Southeast Asia, it is claimed, has remained closest to the teachings of Gautama. It is called "Theravada," or "the doctrine of the Elders." As the faith made its way into Nepal, Tibet, and China, however, the concept of "Buddahood" and the "Buddhanature" was enlarged to incorporate some other themes from the Hindu background and to place the Way in the framework of a more cosmic vision. Thus Gautama was seen as the appearance in "this age" of Buddhahood manifested in other ages, and to be manifested in ages to come, by a number of *Bodhisattvas* and expressed in essence by a number of *Dhyani* Buddhas. Aspects of Gautama Buddha's life and character were also given more universal status. We shall note the consequences for our topic in later discussion of the relation of holiness to beauty in the Buddhist traditions of China and Japan, which are part of "Mahayana" Buddhism—the Buddhism of "the larger container."

Meanwhile, we must ask what aesthetic theory and aesthetic religious practice characterized early Indian and Sri Lankan Buddhism? Given the ascetic emphases of Gautama's teaching, it is not surprising that there was an early suspicion and distrust of all allurements of "this world" of the penultimately real. Places of meditation and *stupas* containing relics—viewed simply as reminders of the teaching—were austere. Later some renderings of natural phenomena like creepers or wreaths of flowers were permitted as decoration, but they were not viewed as aesthetic means to the ultimate. Gradually, however, stylized symbols were admitted as aids to devotion and commitment to the Way: the elephant as a symbol of the renunciation period; the "Bodhi" tree as a symbol of enlightenment; the wheel as a symbol of the *dharma* of teachings. No figure of Gautama Buddha appeared, however, because such an appearance would not have been in keeping with the doctrine of *anatta* or "no-self," or with the role of Gautama as (self-less) "Pathfinder." There might be images of purported "footprints" left by the "Pathfinder." And even when more complex aesthetic creations were permitted in the preparatory ante-chambers of meditation halls, the inner sanctuary itself was bare—an appropriate symbol in itself of that "emptiness" or "silence" that, for many Buddhists, lies at the heart of enlightenment.

Gradually, however, some symbols of penultimacy were endowed with an aura of holiness by those who came for enlightenment, especially by pilgrims who took copies of them as talismans of devotion. Increasingly the figure of the Buddha himself became the focus of *bhakti*. But even this focus of devotional meditation lacked the varied forms celebrated in the Hindu tradition that saw many "names and forms" of *samsara* as possible means to realization of *moksha*; that celebrated the goods of *kama* as sacraments of the divine; or that saw *rasa* as pointing to ultimateness. The Buddha images that emerged as foci of devotional meditation were severely stylized and impersonal. The major one is that of the Buddha seated in classic yogic posture, manifesting the serenity of enlightenment. There were also images depicting various *mudras*, gestures or postures evoking the sense of the Enlightened One as Teacher (touching the fingers of one hand with the index finger of the other); Protector (hand raised with palm forward); Witnesser to that victory over ignorance (*avidya*) which is enlightenment (hand touching the earth); and so forth. Images of the Reclining Buddha could recall the last sermon and *parinirvana*, the transition into *nirvana*. Perhaps most appropriate for both early and later doctrine are representations incorporating the lotus blossom. The lotus, symbol of delicate purity rising through water (fluidity of *samsara*) from roots in the "mud" of *dukkha* and *avidya*, was/is a "natural" symbol of the Buddha-ideal. Even the seated Buddha in yogic posture could rest on that symbol.[25]

Is there a distinctively Buddhist aesthetic theory involved in all this? In general, many of the features of the theory of *rasa* outlined above are employed in early Buddhist reflection on artistic creation, art forms, and aesthetic apprehension. But how could a tradition whose earliest aesthetic expressions were appropriately "aniconic" accommodate in theory the later incorporation of iconic elements? How could a Way of meditative insight into psychological-metaphysical truth assimilate strong iconographic elements? In a sense, of course, if "icon" is equated with meaning or subject matter, iconographic expression of the meaning of the Four Noble Truths, and of the way of life flowing from them, is appropriate. But what about aesthetic apprehension and artistic creativity as such, or the nature and role of "expression," and the relation of expression to form, and other issues addressed in both classical Hindu expositions of *rasa* and various modern aesthetic theories?

Alex J. Wayman has suggested that in Buddhist analyses of the links of "dependent origination," both "passive" and "active" attitudes on the part of one seeking enlightenment are entailed.[26] Whereas some affective and other components of the causal elements in *avidya* are to be simply passively "lived through" in recollection, others are to be perceived and assessed through a sense of "fitness" that is similar to, if not identical with, the sense of fitness expressed in artistic creation. Freedom and restraint are both part of the enterprise of psychological analysis and meditative apprehension and of the enterprise of artistic creation. We shall see this parallel further illustrated in some reflections on the relation of the aesthetic to ultimateness in the thought of some Chinese and Japanese Buddhists. But just as we saw that there is no equation of even the acme of aesthetic apprehension with the experience of *moksha* in Hindu thought, so Wayman points out that although

my study of the Buddhist Dependent Origination, divided as it is into the determinacy and relatively free series, indicates that there is neither incompatibility between the two, nor requirement of their conjunction, and that in this Buddhist sense, one may have both passive enjoyment and creative imagination, as possibly does the creator of a work of art, [nevertheless,] whether it be the seeming freedom of aesthetic contemplation or the genuine freedom of creative imagination, neither are [sic] equivalent to the Buddhist "liberation" (moksha) or "release" (nirvana). This is because for this liberation it is necessary to have cessation of Dependent Origination.[27]

And perhaps the least inadequate "symbol" of this goal is, as was suggested in our analysis of rasa, silence or "emptiness" (sunyata).

CHINA

The Confucian Tradition

The origins of Chinese culture extend back to the beginnings of the third millennium before the Common Era. Fu Hsi, the legendary "inventor of writing," and Shen Yung, the legendary originator of agriculture and commerce, along with the semidivine emperors Yao, Sun, and Yü, the founder of the first—the Xia (Hsia)—dynasty,[28] are figures of this period who played large roles in subsequent Chinese thought and imagination. The Hsia dynasty was followed by the Shang (Yin) and, eventually, in the tenth century B.C.E., by the Zhou (Chou), whose virtues were to be extolled by Confucius. The Chou succumbed to internal division and external incursions, and it was in the "Spring and Autumn Period" of revival and decline that Confucius (551?-479 B.C.E.), Lao-tse, and other founders of the Confucian and Taoist traditions, lived.

From the ancient dynasties came some basic components of classical Chinese aesthetics and religion. Of prime significance for aesthetics is the fact that the Chinese language is itself ideophonic or logographic, originating in characters that were more or less literal representations of their referents. Terms and characters "picture" concepts. Picturing is therefore built into the language as such, but in a manner far more complex than that envisaged by Wittgenstein. The art of calligraphy became a master art. The picturing wrought through poiesis, in turn, would be of fundamental importance in Chinese sensibility and tradition. When painting emerged as a nonlinguistic form of picturing, its canons would be set in terms of the ideals of poetry. Collections of discursive writings from the first two millennia of Chinese history would also be canonized as the classical points of departure for authentic Chinese positions in all areas of thought.

Five major collections constitute the traditional "Confucian classics." The I Ching, or "Book of Changes," sets forth elements of the ancient art of divination. The *Shu Ching* consists of speeches and reports of the legendary rulers. The *Shih Ching*, or "Book of Poetry," played a large part in later aesthetic reflection, and the *Li Chi*, or "Book of Rites," played a similar role in later philosophical and religious thought. The fifth classic, the *Ch'un-ch'iu*, or "Spring and Autumn Annals," is a chronicle of events affecting the state of Lu, Confucius's native state, from 722 to 481 B.C.E. A sixth classic, a "Book of Music," is also sometimes mentioned, but there is no such separate work extant, though an essay on music is found in the *Li Chi*

From the ancient period come also some basic elements of traditional Chinese conceptuality. They are epitomized in the triad heaven-earth-humans. Heaven begets, earth nurtures, and humans are the connecting link between heaven and earth, of equal dignity and importance. The harmony between members of the triad reflects a balance between *yin* ("active" or engendering) and *yang* ("passive" or nurturing) forces. For a time the heavenly powers were conceived theistically, with Shang-Ti, the "Lord on high," as their ruler. The emperor, in turn, was the earthly exemplification of this heavenly rule, the "Son of Heaven." Gradually, there was less emphasis on a personalized "Lord of Heaven" and greater emphasis on *T'ien*, "Heaven," as such—the power that governs the cosmic moral order. *T'ien* might at times be thought of as possessing intelligence and will and as the arbiter of human destiny, and popular religion would continue to center on various gods and goddesses. But there would not be in Chinese classical thought the extensive and systematic metaphysical and theological speculation that engaged the Greeks in their classical period.

Like Plato, Confucius dedicated himself to study of the Good and sought to impart the results in counsels to statesmen or any who would seek it. He was not the first teacher in China, but he was apparently the first to accept students on the basis of their intellectual curiosity and aptitude rather than on the basis on their ability to pay—in this respect like Plato's teacher, Socrates. For years he wandered from state to state, seeking to inculcate his ideals. Shortly before his death he was invited to return to his native state of Lu, where he died in peace and with belated recognition of his tireless devotion to liberal learning in the service of society. His tomb is once again venerated in the Chü Fu district. And his teachings, *The Analects*, were added to the five classics of his culture.[29]

Although Confucius's interests were primarily ethical and political, there are at least three concepts central to his teaching that are basic in Chinese aesthetic reflection. One is *yi*—nonutilitarian obligation, duty, or respect: the doing of the work for the work's sake and respect for the work as an expression of duty or obligation. Another is *jen*.

The character for this important concept depicts human-and-human; unfortunately it has sometimes been literally translated "man-to-man-ness"! A more felicitous translation is "mutuality" or, simply, "humaneness"; it is the expression, in human or other relationships, of the ideal of willed *harmony*. It has also been translated "love" and compared with Greek, Christian, or other understandings of love—but this translation lends itself to forced interpretation if not manipulation. The third concept is *li*—translated "propriety" or "sense of fittingness." It is in terms of *li* that the appropriate ordering of human relationships may occur, in the service of the ideal of human harmony (*jen*), enacted from—and sanctioned by—a sense of duty (*yi*). The ordering of human relationships in accord with the "natural" functions of age, sex, and position in society requires a sense of *li*—a sense of the right thing to do in relation to the right person at the right time. In this respect it resonates with Aristotle's understanding of virtuous action.

Confucius's ethic has been called an "aesthetic ethic" because of the importance in it of a sense of "good taste." This is far too simplistic. It is the case, however, that Chinese aesthetic ideals include a prizing of harmonious renderings of materials, just as harmonious human relationships are viewed as various configurations of *li*. And there would emerge in later Confucian thought an insistence on *respect* for the aesthetic ideal in itself, apart from social functions, and for aesthetic creation as a distinctive achievement, in whatever art form it may be exemplified.

Confucius, in some respects like Gautama and in some respects like Socrates, eschewed speculation on the nature of ultimateness. The primary human task, he thought, is to achieve ethically and rationally ordered individual and social life. This emphasis has led some Western thinkers to question whether the Confucian tradition is a "religious" tradition, assuming that religious traditions must be theistic and that their major concerns must include firm views about the nature of the ultimate. Herbert Fingarette, in *Confucius: The Sacred as Secular*,[30] and Rodney Taylor, in *The Way of Heaven: An Introduction to the Confucian Religious Life*,[31] have, among others, sought to rectify this view. Confucius thought of himself as seeking to live in accord with "the will of Heaven." He worked, he said, with confidence that "though men might not know him," "Heaven knew him." He also laid great stress on proper observance of those religious rites that celebrate what Santayana and others have termed "natural piety," including filial piety. His successor Hsün-tse would defend these in terms of their humanistic and naturalistic value; others would offer defenses that may be more open to theistic interpretation. In the main stream of the Confucian tradition, in any case, reflection on aesthetic excellence in relation to ultimateness would not require exclusively specific formulations of the latter.

The Taoist Tradition

The legendary founder of the Taoist tradition, Lao-tse, is an appropriately shadowy figure, remembered in terms of illustrative anecdotes and parables rather than in terms of systematic teaching and political or social programs. The canonical memory is the *Tao Te Ching*, the "Book of the Tao and Its 'Virtue.'" Of nearly equal importance for the tradition is the work associated with Chuang-tse, the *Chuang Tzu*, a book of aphoristic sayings designed to evoke a sense of *Tao* and its ways.[32] And what is *Tao*? To ask the question in this way is to ask for a definition, and *Tao* cannot be defined, discursively articulated in terms of finite references, nor can it be fully qualified adjectively or adverbially, as positive or negative, active or nonactive. All attempts at such qualifications may be countered by a reminder of their opposites. If one speaks of action, *Tao* "does nothing," yet through it all things are done. If one speaks of strength, *Tao* is "weak," yet the way of *Tao* conquers all. To live in accord with *Tao* is to live with unpredictable spontaneity. It is not captured in specific ethical or political systems, as in Confucianism. Thus the Taoist Way (literally, the "way of the Way") would commend itself to those who, in an ordered society, sought a more authentic spontaneity—and to all who, in times of social chaos, sought constancy of personal worth through behavior of personal integrity.

It was in the Ch'in dynasty (265–420 C.E.) that both major Chinese art forms and important aesthetic theories emerged. At that time Taoist individualism, naturalism, and spontaneity found expression when ink replaced oil and the brush replaced the reed as medium and instrument of visual composition. While these were used for Buddhist religious painting, strong Taoist elements entered singularly into "mountain and water," or landscape painting. "Of the several forms of painting, landscape has been regarded as the crowning art of China," write Wing-tsit Chan and William Theodore de Bary. "It is here that the cardinal principles of Chinese art are embodied and the greatest of Chinese artistic talents immortalized. . . . The Taoist glorification of nature opened a new vista to artists and imbued them with a new sense of freedom. As a result, landscape advanced from a secondary position as simply the background of portraits to a position of equal and eventually of even greater importance." Landscape painting could express both the Confucian ideal of cultivated harmony and the Taoist ideal of spontaneous harmony. And, as Chan and de Bary affirm, "the harmony of the human spirit and the spirit of nature became the ultimate goal of Chinese art."[33] We have seen that the ideal of harmony also infused that sense of ultimateness that could be called "religious."

We must beware, however, of assimilating Confucian and Taoist understandings of aesthetic excellence and ultimateness too simply into Western conceptions of the beautiful and the holy. The association of *Tao* with nature has led some contemporary writers to suggest an affinity of the classical concept of *Tao* with certain concepts of natural science, and especially of physics. An informed critique of these and similar attempts to assimilate "Eastern mysticism" and "Western science" (or "Western religion") may be found in Richard H. Jones's *Science and Mysticism*.[34]

Chinese Buddhist Traditions

The interpenetration of classical Chinese and Buddhist cultures from the second through the tenth centuries of the Common Era is a paradigmatic example of constructive cultural adaptation and change. The two cultures differed radically in language, ethos, worldview, and historical experience. Yet within a few centuries a process of cultural enrichment occurred that resulted in neither a simple absorption of Buddhist culture by Chinese culture nor a radical revision of the basic conceptuality of either. The experience has been a model for subsequent Chinese confrontations with aspects of Western culture, including, most recently, Marxist ideology. It is highly relevant to the problems and opportunities created by contemporary awareness and appreciation of global cultural pluralism. It confirms in many ways the analysis of ideational change presented by the philosopher Alasdair MacIntyre in his *Whose Justice? Which Rationality?*[35] as well as the anthropological analyses of cultural change presented by Clifford Geertz.

It has been said, not entirely facetiously, that in the sense that "Christianity is Judaism's foreign office," so "Buddhism is Hinduism's foreign office." It was traditionally thought that, in the case of China, basic Hindu concepts like *karma*, *samsara*, and *moksha* were introduced solely through their appropriation in Buddhist thought. Recently, however, evidence has come to light of specifically Hindu religious art in China by the Song (Sung) dynasty (960–1279).[36] Buddhism itself entered China through the trade routes from Central Asia. It is first mentioned in the second century C.E. in Kiangsi province; the first translation of Buddhist scriptures occurred in the third century C.E. Not surprisingly, the translator, Dharmarakshá, found it useful to adapt some Taoist terminology for his purposes. By the sixth century Emperor Wu of Liang officially embraced Buddhism. In the North, Buddhist universalism appealed to non-Chinese invaders; in the South, Buddhism provided new ground for the legitimacy of new rulers, as well as egalitarian opportunities for study and meditation. In all areas Buddhist charitable work in medicine and social welfare, exemplifying the Buddhist ideal of compassion, appealed to all segments of society.

The Golden Age of Buddhist influence occurred in the first two hundred years of the Tang (T'ang) dynasty (618–906). At this time, writes Arthur F. Wright, "Supported by lavish donations of the devout, guided by leaders of true piety and brilliance, graced by the most gifted artists and architects of the age, Buddhism was woven into the very texture of Chinese life and thought."[37] Buddhist ritual became an integral part of state and imperial observances. According to Wright,

> In the artistic and cultural life of the great capital at Ch'ang-an, Buddhism was omnipresent. The gilded finials of innumerable temples and pagodas, the tolling of temple bells, the muted chanting of sutras, the passing to and fro of solemn processions were the palpable signs of Buddhism's ramifying influence in the life of the empire. The pagodas and the temple compounds testified to the long, slow blending of Indian and native elements into a new Sino-Buddhist architecture, whose glories we see reflected today in the buildings of the Horyuji monastery in Japan. The images and paintings which filled the great buildings were, similarly, a culminating fusion of elements from the native tradition and elements from Indian, Persian, Greco-Roman, and Central Asian sources. The Buddhas and Bodhisattvas who looked down from their pedestals on congregations of the devout had Chinese faces with expressions of calm compassion which were distinctively Chinese translations of the Buddhist vision of life and time.[38]

Differing emphases in the conceptual articulation of the commodious Buddhist way of life and deliverance also emerged in the Chinese milieu. Abstract concepts were translated into concrete analogies. The Ch'an (Japanese Zen) school emphasized enlightenment through meditation, either instantaneously or through a long process of meditational discipline. The Amitabha (Chinese O-mi-t'o, Japanese Amida or "Pure Land") emphasized salvation through faith in the grace of the "Lord of the Western Paradise." The T'ien-t'ai (Japanese Tendai) school proclaimed an eclectic ecumenism sanctioned by the Lotus Sutra. Its ideal was the classical Chinese ideal of harmony, through a recognition of historical relativism expressed in terms of "phases" of expression of Buddhahood in various cultures at various times. Popular devotion also prized the compassionate posture of Kuan Yin (Japanese Kannon, Indian Avalokiteśvara), the god/goddess of mercy, sometimes called "the Madonna of the East." We will encounter further expressions of these schools when we turn to Japanese aesthetics and religion below.

Neo-Confucianism

From the late ninth century onward the pervasive power of explicitly Buddhist concepts declined or rather was eclipsed through the incorporation of certain concepts transmitted through Buddhism and Taoism within revised and revitalized Confucianism. In the Sung dynasty the emphasis was once again on the ethical bases of a well-ordered state, inculcated through a system of rigorous examinations for all public officials. The philosopher Chu Hsi revived interest in revised versions of the Confucian classics. Basic Confucian concepts were expanded to accommodate speculative interests; thus *li* came to be understood as Cosmic Principle. And in the Ming dynasty Wang Yang-ming (1472–1529) stressed "mind" as the ultimate reality "within," to be realized through disciplined meditation. "Quiet sitting," preferably in places of natural beauty, became an integral part of the self-cultivation of the sage, and sagehood itself came to be understood as a religious goal.[39]

In this period of Neo-Confucian revitalization an influential theory of painting appeared, the *wen-jen-hua* theory, associated with the writings of Su Shih (1037–1101), Huang T'ing-chien (1045–1105), and Kuo Jo-haü (dates not certain). Painting was understood by all of them to be the work of cultivated literati who were also adept in poetry and other verbal arts, which provided some of the ideals of painting as such. There was an emphasis on landscape painting as essentially expressive rather than illustrative, articulating the "spirit resonance" (*ch'i i-yün*) of the artist. The viewer was to "see the artist in the artwork," and the artist, like the sage, was to view his or her vocation in the context of self-cultivation. The mastery of painting was understood to be a means of "mastery of mind"—a spiritual achievement. The concept employed in articulating this goal was the *tao*. Furthermore, the process of self-cultivation that may center on painting was said to require moral as well as intellectual preparatory discipline.[40]

The Neo-Confucian prizing of "quiet sitting" in the cultivation of sagehood, and the emphasis in *wen-jen-hua* aesthetic theory on landscape painting and on "seeing the artist in the work," exemplify a recurrent theme in both Chinese and Japanese religious and aesthetic sensibility and theory: the centrality of nature, and of the arts of human design and expression of nature, in both cultures. Not only the art of landscape painting, but also the art of landscape architecture, has been prized in both China and Japan. We have noted the equality of value expressed in the classical Confucian triad heaven-earth-humans. We have noted the Taoist emphasis on nature and "naturalness" that played an important role in the emergence of landscape painting as a paramount genre long before its emergence as an independent genre in Western art history—which was roughly in the seventeenth century C.E. We have seen how Buddhist emphasis on meditation, particularly in the Ch'an (Zen) school, was paralleled in the Neo-Confucian practice of "quiet sitting." Just as the logographic pictorial character of Chinese (and written Japanese) language influenced the understanding of *poiesis*, and the ideals of poetry influenced the canons of visual art, so also "picturing" through artfully designed landscapes and landscape paintings is a paradigmatic expression of ultimateness through aesthetic excellence in both China and Japan. Gardens may both express and form ideals as they mediate harmonies and compose the mind or spirit. In contemporary China and Japan they can be, even for persons who consider themselves to be "modern" and therefore "secular," foci of both aesthetic sensibility and "natural piety."

Unfortunately, there is not space for a consideration of distinctive Korean expressions of aesthetic excellence in relation to ultimateness. We may simply note the importance of the Korean "bridge-culture" in the transmission of Chinese and other sensibilities to Japan, to which we now turn.

JAPAN

It is appropriate, for a number of reasons, to conclude our analysis of the relation of aesthetics to religion in Asian cultures with a brief account of examples from Japan. Japan is an island country that has received migrations of peoples and cultural influences from other islands of the Pacific as well as from the Asian mainland. Its relation to Asia has been compared with that of the British Isles to Europe. Although it has absorbed and adapted many ideas from outside, it has managed at the same time to develop an enriched indigenous culture with its own integrity. The relation of Japan to China is perhaps symbolized in the Japanese language: Chinese characters are adapted for written expression, but oral communication in the two languages is different. Since the nineteenth century Japan has also pursued, more vigorously than many of its neighbors, the study and appropriation of Western cultures and technology. It has now emerged as one of the most prosperous industrial powers of the world. With the new cosmopolitanism has come an increased interest in certain forms of Western philosophy and art. The work of Martin Heidegger, for instance, has engaged Japanese scholars—and, as we have seen, in Heidegger's thought the ontological, the poetic, and the numinous are closely intertwined. Similarly, various forms of expressionism in art have interested Japanese artists. Structural and poststructural literary criticism has evoked a response similar to that of some Western scholars who see in the latter "signals of transcendence." And the people who love *haiku* admire the poetry of Emily Dickinson and make pilgrimages to her grave. What indigenous aesthetic and religious sensibilities are involved in this response? To get an idea of these sensibilities let us briefly note some of the major religious traditions and aesthetic theories that have played central roles in Japanese culture.

Shinto

The earliest and indigenous religion of Japan is Shinto (from *shen-tao*, "the way of the gods"). Its canon incorporates myths celebrating natural forces and kinship ties. The eighth-century C.E. classic, the *Kojiki*, arranged these myths in an account of the creation of the Japanese islands as a special work of the gods and of the descent of the Japanese imperial family from the sun goddess Amaterasu. The shrine of the sun goddess at Ise may have been founded as early as the third century C.E. Shinto rituals were designed to express reverence for both the powers and the beauties of nature and to celebrate social ties culminating in loyalty to the emperor. Both the *Kojiki* and a companion chronicle, the *Nihongi*, stress the divine origin of all things Japanese and of the Japanese people themselves, in a graded hierarchy.

After Buddhism entered Japan in the sixth century, Shinto and Buddhism were brought into a complementary, though at times precarious, relationship. "Ryobu" or "mixed" Shinto developed the view that ancient Shinto deities were appearances in Japan of the deities of Mahayana Buddhism. During most of the course of Japanese history the two traditions have coexisted peacefully, meeting different needs of individual worshipers for different occasions in life. Shinto worship itself is aesthetically restrained and primarily nonverbal, occurring in aesthetically simple arrangements in aesthetically pleasing locales. A distinguished scholar of Shinto, a member of the faculty of Tokyo University, said to the Columbia University Seminar on Oriental Thought and Religion some years ago that Western scholars of religion find it difficult to understand Shinto because they do not understand aesthetics.

Japanese Buddhist Traditions

Buddhism was introduced into Japan in 538 C.E. or 552 C.E. by Chinese monks. In subsequent centuries each of the major forms of Chinese Buddhism found expression in distinctively Japanese forms. Each of these has played a role in the development of aesthetic theory, and each has prized aesthetic excellence as propaedeutic to ultimateness.

Zen (Chinese Ch'an), however, has had the greatest impact on the arts. In Zen Buddhism, all scriptures and sutras are looked upon as "fingers pointing to the moon" of self-realization of the Buddha-nature inherent in all individuals. In the course of its history it has developed various meditational techniques, physical and mental. Famous among the latter are *koans*, pithy locutions designed to shock the mind into a way of knowing that goes beyond or behind logical categories and subject-object distinctions. The emphasis in Zen on simplicity, restraint, and discipline is reflected in the development of the traditional Japanese tea ceremony, flower arrangement, and Nō drama, each of which, as we shall see, is an expression of basic Japanese aesthetic concepts as well as "fingers pointing to the moon" of ultimateness.

Confucian Influences

Buddhist monks brought to Japan a reverence for the Chinese classics, and protocols of Confucian political and social propriety were assimilated into Japanese practices. In the *Heian* period (794–1191) Chinese aesthetic accomplishments set the standards of cultural achievement. These standards are reflected in Lady Murasaki Shikibu's *The Tale of Genji*, which is perhaps the *first* novel. But, just as Neo-Confucianism in China assimilated many Taoist and Buddhist themes, so Confucian scholars of the Tokugawa period (1600–1868) embraced Wang Yangming's "mind school" of meditation. In the eighteenth century Kaibara Ekken espoused the disciplined study of nature and of human beings as parts of nature. Thus Confucian as well as Buddhist and Shinto ideals became elements of the Japanese understanding of both aesthetic excellence and ultimateness.

There was also a strong sense of the transience and relativity of all forms of sensibility, and of conceptual distinctions that claim exhaustiveness. Thus in the eighteenth century Tominago Nakamoto espoused a form of historical relativism and advocated historical criticism as a means of understanding the origins and distinctive emphases of the religious traditions of Japan, suggesting that they might have in common a form of "ethical culture" reminiscent of the "natural religion" prized by some European intellectuals of the Enlightenment.

In all these developments there are forms of religious eclecticism and of rational inquiry that epitomize a distinctively Japanese approach to matters of aesthetic excellence or beauty and ultimateness or holiness. In the major terms of the Japanese aesthetic vocabulary, there are echoes of Japanese religious sensibility. We have noted that both aesthetics and religion entail ways of apprehending and of articulating reality. The Japanese term *aware* signals a distinctive mode of apprehension that is akin to a sense of wonder—intrinsic to Zen—at the givenness of things. In old texts it is used as an exclamation of surprise or delight—of what, as Donald Keene puts it, "an early Western critic of Japanese literature called the 'ahness of things,' though gradually it came to be used adjectively, usually to mean 'pleasant' or 'interesting.'" [41] The affairs of the hero of *The Tale of Genji* engage him because he finds them "interesting." In this and other works of literature the term also expresses, as Keene puts it, "a gentle sorrow, adding not so much a meaning as a color or a perfume to a sentence. It bespoke the sensitive poet's awareness of a sight or a sound, of its beauty and its perishability." [42] "Perishability" evokes a Buddhist sense of the impermanence of all things.

To *aware* was later added the term *miyabi*, literally "courtliness" but in general "refinement." "*Miyabi*," writes Keene, "was perhaps the most inclusive term for describing the aesthetics of the Heian period (794–1191). It was applied in particular to the quiet pleasures which, supposedly at least, could only be savored by the aristocrat whose tastes had been educated to them—a spray of plum blossoms, the elusive perfume of a rare wood, the delicate blending of colors in a robe." [43] Here are echoes of Confucian cultivation of refinement guided by *li*.

In the Kamakura period (1192–1336) the concept of *yūgen* became dominant. It, too, calls to mind the Zen Buddhist sense of that which cannot be articulated discursively. "Yūgen," writes Keene, "was a word used to describe the profound, the remote, the mysterious, those things which cannot be easily grasped in words." [44] Although it may be found in many forms of Japanese medieval art, "the Nō theater," says Keene, "was the medium which carried it to the highest degree." [45] And Nō drama combines a Confucian sense of ritual with the indirect evocation of mood so characteristic of Taoism and Zen.

We have noted the role played by landscape architecture, in conjunction with landscape painting, in both Chinese and Japanese aesthetic and religious sensibilities. Japanese gardens are generally more highly stylized and compact than are the less ordered and more spacious public gardens of China. In both countries the effects of water on stone are employed to evoke aesthetic and religious emotions. Zen meditation centers make singular use of artfully spaced and deployed stones to focus apprehensions that elude verbal formulation or conceptual description. Eliot Deutsch employs the concept *yūgen* to interpret the experience of the rock garden of Ryoanji:

> The garden is not symmetrical insofar as asymmetry implies symmetry as its standard of measure. The garden is not symmetrical and it is not asymmetrical; it is irregular in just that unique way which comes from the splendid fusion of chance and determination. . . . One cannot apprehend

a garden in the same manner as a painting or a piece of sculpture, for a garden makes available too many perspectives. . . . Unlike most works of art, no amount of familiarity with this Zen Rock Garden can provide one with any solid assurance as to what it is that one will meet in experiencing it; for the work drives one into oneself. . . . The Rock Garden of Ryoanji is not a finished thing; it manifests yūgen and is thus an open invitation to contemplative being.[46]

Toward the end of the medieval period another aesthetic ideal, that of *sabi*, joined *yūgen*. "*Sabi*," says Keene,

suggested not only "old" but the taking of pleasure in that which was old, faded, or lonely. . . . [I]t is most profoundly felt in the tea ceremony. . . . The tea hut is extremely bare and almost devoid of color. If a flower is arranged in a vase, it is usually a single, small blossom of some quiet hue or white. The tea utensils are not of exquisite porcelain but of coarse pottery, often a dull brown or black and imperfectly formed. The kettle may be a little rusty. Yet from these objects we receive an impression not of gloominess or shabbiness but one of quiet harmony and peace. . . . [T]he love of imperfection as a measure of perfection in pottery and other forms of art and nature is very old with the Japanese. . . . [The] love for the fallen flower, for the moon obscured by rain, for the withered bough is part of *sabi*.[47]

This quality, notes Keene, is superbly captured in many brief and allusive poems called *haiku*. We again note a sense of the impermanence of things. This is not bemoaned; the Buddhist sense of *dukkha* is simply an affirmation of "the way things are." This sense is further expressed in the Japanese term/concept *ukiyo*, "the floating world" of waves, of woodblock prints, and of the transient passions.

Many Japanese are now asking what is "floating" and what is enduring in Japanese culture. Intense involvement in world affairs and fascination with alternative cultural patterns and possibilities have precipitated extensive debate about what from Japan's past should be preserved and celebrated in a nation expressing increasing autonomy and heightened pride in things uniquely Japanese. This debate in Japan epitomizes a more general debate about the ends of art and of religion that is occupying scholars in many countries. In the next chapter we turn to a summary of some of the issues involved in that debate, and to some major alternative positions that are emerging from it.

CHAPTER SIX

The Contemporary Debate about the End(s) of Art and the End(s) of Religion

W E HAVE NOW completed our account of the relations of art and aesthetics to religion and theories of religion in the views of representative thinkers and movements in both Western and Eastern cultural traditions. In this chapter we will examine some major issues in recent discussion of these relationships. We will note that both modern understandings of aesthetics and modern understandings of religion are subject to extensive and fundamental criticism. A vivid consciousness of the plurality of cultures, and of the plurality of approaches to the delineation and appraisal of aesthetic and religious phenomena, calls many assumptions of previous discussion radically into question. We will seek to appraise both the difficulties and the opportunities afforded by this situation and will describe some revised understandings of our topic that may facilitate responsible and constructive inquiry and appreciation.

In 1978 a group of ninety scholars from twenty-nine countries published the conclusions of a ten-year study of "Main Trends in Aesthetics and the Sciences of Art," undertaken on behalf of the United Nations Educational Scientific and Cultural Organization. Mikel Dufrenne, coordinator of the study and editor of the report, said in the Foreword:

> The semantic field of art is very uncertain. How can it be delimited? On the one hand, it so happens that art does not have, always and everywhere, the same status, content, and function. . . . [T]he diversity of political, social and ideological backgrounds results in very considerable differences in the situation and meaning of art from one society to another. On the other hand, quite apart from any socio-cultural presuppositions, . . . today the word "art" is highly suspect and the extent of the concept is very vague . . . it is not only the "theories" of art which hesitate to determine its essence; it is also the practice of artists, who continually give the lie to any definition.[1]

Although theories of aesthetics encompass more than art, which is frequently discussed in terms of the philosophy of art, our study has shown that the "semantic field" of aesthetics is also "very uncertain" at the present time. Our review of the historical origins of aesthetic theory culminates in a present situation characterized by indecisiveness and conflict among a wide range of alternative views. We have also seen that the emergence of theories of religion in the Enlightenment has culminated in comparable diversity and imprecision in specification and employment of the concept religion in current discussion. The assumption that there is a distinctively aesthetic category, beauty, has long been under attack. Proposals of a distinctively religious category—the sacred, the Holy, the transcendent—are similarly criticized. As we shall see in this chapter, more recently notions of "alterity" or "otherness" are put forward by those who would discern "sediments of the sacred" in current culture criticism. In 1962 Wilfred Cantwell Smith proposed an end to the use of the concept of religion. More recently Arthur Danto has announced "the end of art" as a result of its "philosophical disenfranchisement."[2]

We proceed, then, to examine the ground for and the cogency of the argument that we have now come to the end of art and the end of religion. We then ask what, if the argument is compelling, could be the next move of those who are interested in what up to now has been called art and aesthetic theory or religion and theory of religion, in the light of the parallel histories and current dilemmas of these two areas of scholarly investigation and human concern?

We begin with consideration of the structure of the UNESCO study of major current trends in aesthetics. If a similar study of major trends in current thought about religion were undertaken, a remarkably similar structure could well be deemed appropriate. An indication of the similarity of structure is suggested in the current organization of academic study of art or art history, on the one hand, and religious studies or the history of religions, on the other. In some academic institutions there are Departments of Art, embracing a range of historical studies, a range of critical studies, and an area of "studio studies" addressed to the practice of art. Similarly, in some academic institutions there are Departments of Religion, or of Religious Studies, that seek to coordinate historical, textual, social-scientific, psychological, philosophical, and theological approaches to the study of religion. Although such departments may strenuously assert that they do not, as such, *practice* religion or teach *how* to practice it, they do seek to *"study"* its practice. In others, and in some of the scholarly literature of the field as a whole, the umbrella term is "history of religions." In some quarters this term, interestingly enough, is designed to indicate that the study includes attention to "non-Western" religions. Elsewhere, the term bespeaks a general primacy of what is considered to be a "historical" approach to the wide range of issues encompassed in the discipline, though the specific character of that approach remains debatable.

The UNESCO study of aesthetics begins with an acknowledgment of diversity of cultural ideologies. The "East" in this case embraces countries of Eastern Europe and elsewhere in which Marxist theory plays a dominant role, as well as "Third World" countries now struggling to define and preserve national identity and cultural integrity while appropriating "Western" technology. In many if not most of these latter areas, as we have previously noted, the awareness of "art" as a distinctive cultural enterprise and product, and more especially of "aesthetics" as systematic critical reflection on art and other forms of aesthetic experience, is a relatively recent component of critical inquiry.

The situation is parallel, we have seen, to that which obtains with respect to religion. "Classical" cultures do not designate certain things "artworks," certain persons "artists," and certain values "aesthetic." Similarly, in such cultures there is not an area or segment of life that is thought of as the culture's "religion," though Eliade and others, we have seen, find *homo religiosus* preeminently in "archaic" cultures, and Coomaraswamy finds genuinely "religious" art in Eastern and in Classical and Medieval Western cultures, where the split between the sacred and the profane does not extend to those who celebrate each culture's point of convergence of ethos and worldview, to borrow Clifford Geertz's formula. Dufrenne, in the UNESCO study, notes that "Literature and the arts have of course existed in such countries from time immemorial . . . (but) they have existed without awareness of their existence, without asserting any claim to specificity or independence; they were completely integrated with a culture which itself had an integrating force, and the 'aesthetic' purpose was indistinguishable from religious, social, and utilitarian purposes." Dufrenne also goes on to note that the newly emerging differentiated consciousness "does not remain neutral, for . . . art immediately becomes a sensitive area in the confrontation of Western societies with those of the East or with the Third World countries. It also becomes a cultural policy issue."[3]

The "policy issue" is frequently formulated indigenously in Marxist terms, mainly because Marxism engenders self-consciousness about "ideology" and "imperialism." "But," Dufrenne continues, "these opponents do not use the Marxist doctrine in the sense of a Western or foreign contribution; they assert it as a progressive philosophy, capable of expressing the universal and of promoting a truly international culture. It is this desire for universality that they set over against Western culture, and not a national culture belonging to the past from which, even though they do not reject it, they believe the new culture can only be saved in so far as it can be excelled."[4] Furthermore, notes Dufrenne, "it is also for the West to ascertain whether the universal can be reconciled with the particular and to contribute, for its part, to furthering the universal without any suspicion of imperialism."[5]

The theme of pluralism and universality or comprehensiveness—pluralism of methods, of subject matter, and of cultural achievements and allegiances—sets the agenda for matters discussed in this chapter. We go on to note that the UNESCO group found it "natural" to manage its study through an analytical summary of current work exemplifying various distinctive "approaches": historical, comparative, sociological, psychological, anthropological, and semiotic. Philosophical schools and issues were seen to be implied or presupposed in each.

New trends in the history of art are said to include, first, those schools of art history that seek to place the history of art in the broader framework of the history of ideas and of civilization. Second, and in some quarters seen as opposed to this, is the work of those who view the history of art as uniquely the history of forms and structures of artworks. There is, however, growing awareness of the need for a more comprehensive approach, because, as Béla Köpeczi of the University of Budapest puts it, "a history of art that attempts to explain the aesthetic phenomenon by external factors, or a history of art that only attempts to examine its 'interior development,' are fragmentary, since they fail to resolve the problem of the relationship between the work of art and the history of mankind from which it cannot be dissociated."[6] Köpeczi singles out existentialist and Marxist views of "the general history of mankind" for brief analysis, but he also notes the issue posed by M. Al'Patov:

> It has been observed that works of art created in different times and in different places of the world are related in a surprising way in many essential features; sometimes they resemble each other more closely than do works pertaining to the same school or period. Proponents of the chronological tradition deride such links, which 'transcend barriers' (sic). They only admit relationship where there has been actual contact between schools and artists or the positive influence of one school on another. However, affinities between Pierro della Francesca and the painting of ancient Egypt, between sculptures at Chartres and early Greek sculpture, between Russian ikons and portraits in the Favum, are undeniable and tangible facts which art historians should take into account.

Al'Patov speculates that "it is perhaps due to the fact that art is subject to the same intrinsic logic and laws as those which cause all men at all times and in all places to find an identical solution to the same mathematical problem. In any case, study of such similarities helps us understand and visualize the history of art not only as a long progression, as a series of links in a chain, but also as a brotherhood of artists of genius, as a unique whole, in which classical and barbarian artists of Africa, Asia, and Europe have been able to co-exist in peaceful rivalry."[7]

In the field of religion, someone like Eliade would see comparable convergences of "manifestations of the sacred" as universal apprehensions of *homo religiosus*; Jungians would speak of archetypes.

The issue raised is intrinsic to all comparative approaches to art and aesthetics or to religion. René Étiemble, addressing the comparative approach in aesthetics, notes that although the comparative approach is largely a twentieth-century phenomenon, publications and organizations that seek to nurture it have recently multiplied. Goethe's original notion of *Weltliteratur* was extremely limited in scope. Only in the 1960s and 1970s have many Eastern European and most Oriental literatures been included in the notion. Even so, current debate still includes the question of the legitimacy of the comparative concept itself, and methodological issues dominate vigorous discussion. Étiemble, however, believes that "the existence of so many different attitudes and methods gives us grounds for hoping . . . that the best comparativists will . . . succeed in going beyond the artificial distinction between *national* and *cosmopolitan* and in dealing correctly with the most important questions raised by their discipline from a point of view now historical, now sociological, and now aesthetic."[8] It would obviously be easy to transpose the question of "world literature" into the question of "world religions" and the comparable methodological issues into those of "comparative religions."

A representative and thoughtful study in the area of "comparative aesthetics" is offered by Eliot Deutsch,[9] of the University of Hawaii, who is knowledgeable in the fields of both Western and Oriental philosophies and religions. Comparing Ma Yüan's painting, "Bare Willows and Distant Mountains," from the late-twelfth-century to the early-thirteenth-century Song (Sung) dynasty, with Pieter Breughel's "The Massacre of the Innocents," Deutsch adduces four "dimensions of aesthetic relevance for comparative criticism, with the aim of providing an answer to the question: what kind and quality of knowledge do we need to have of an art-work from another culture and of the culture itself in order that we may get to the art-work in its full aesthetic potential?"[10] These four dimensions are as follows:

(1) a recognition and sympathetic understanding of the *Weltanschauung* that informs an individual work—in this case noting the view of the relation of humans to nature assumed by Breughel, as compared

with that assumed by Ma Yüan. Although this may be difficult for some to achieve, "the fault lies with us and not with the ideas themselves."

(2) an understanding of the "cultural-authorial aesthetic preference" of a culture, which is always closely related to its *Weltanschauung*. Here Deutsch has in mind the *range* of options offered to judgments of taste in a particular culture. These may be determined in part by the *materials* principally used in a culture's artworks (e. g., paper or silk and brush and inks in China; paper, canvas, paints of many media and colors in the West; wood, bronze, other metals or ceramics; marble or other stone). The "aesthetic preferences" engendered by these and other factors "may be assimilated as an organizing mode of perception, and, when so assimilated, may contribute to our apprehension of the aesthetic quality of the individual work of art."[11]

(3) an apprehension of the formal content of the artwork—"the realized composition or design, the resolution of contrasts and tensions, the inner vitality that is the art-work in formal terms, e.g., the linear rhythm and spontaneity of Chinese art, related to calligraphy, as compared with the more measured verticality of much Western art prior to the modern period." The formal content of an artwork is, however, in the last analysis unique to that specific work. "It is the particular art-work as particular, as absolutely irreplaceable, in its own vital being of line and color, pattern, harmony, contrast, tension which is the formal content of aesthetic experience—East and West."[12]

(4) a recognition of the range of meaning and the variety of symbolic values in a work of art that are directly wedded to its formal content. Here Deutsch adumbrates a basic issue that receives different resolutions in different fundamental philosophies. These values may be expressed in "natural" or in varieties of "conventional" symbols. And there are also, he believes, "essential" symbols. "This type of symbolism is not so much in the work as it is the work itself as it participates in—and as it has its *presentative* reality in—spiritual being. Through its formal content and other dimensions of aesthetic relevance, the art-work—if it is a good work—is perceived here in its fullest qualitative efficacy as a unique concentration of meaning and value. The essential symbolic level is achieved when the art-work as such uncovers and reveals spiritual being in its own aesthetic being."[13]

These "dimensions of relevance" for comparative aesthetics specified by Deutsch could well be transposed, with modification, to the study of "comparative religion." In the first place, such study must include an understanding of the relation of religious traditions to specified *Weltanschauungen*. Indeed, Ninian Smart has recently proposed that religions be treated as "worldviews" in comparative studies.[14] This would lead, then, to an account of the range of options offered for religious experience, thought, and action within a religious tradition, as these have emerged in the history of that tradition and are exhibited in its current life.

The third "dimension of relevance" for the comparative study of religion is analogous to the role of formal analysis in comparative aesthetics. It entails critically sensitive apprehension of the confluence of meaning and value in representative expressions of the religious traditions compared. There might be a comparison, for instance, of the celebration of the Eucharist in a thirteenth-century European monastery or in a twentieth-century "people's church" of Latin America, with the celebration of Passover by a Jewish community in thirteenth-century Spain or in twentieth-century Israel; or the observance of Ramadan in Ottoman Islam or in twentieth-century Teheran compared with the observance of *holi* in India during and after the British Raj. Comparisons of this sort are as difficult as they are—or may be—illuminating. As Deutsch put it, the difficulties may lie not in the concepts but in ourselves.

Such comparisons should involve more than, for instance, Geertz's analysis and appraisal of Balinese shadow plays and Moroccan maraboutism. They would require not only a knowledge of the relation of the tradition represented to *Weltanschauungen* and the range of religious experience afforded by the tradition in its specificity, but also aesthetic sensitivity of the sort employed in formal analysis, broadened into basic human sensitivity to complexly nuanced expressions of basic human "ultimate concerns." Such sensitivity or sensibility may be suggested in van der Leeuw's version of phenomenological understanding, but it should articulate more than the essentially aesthetic "loving gaze" that van der Leeuw specifies as the uniquely human empathetic capacity. [15] And, as is the case in aesthetic formal analysis as interpreted by Deutsch, comparable analyses of expressions of religious faith must recognize the irreducible singularity of each expression, in its structure and in its ambience. Such recognition may be implied in Wilfred Cantwell Smith's insistence that each confluence of "cumulative tradition" and personal or communal faith occurs in uniquely individual personal or communal constellations. [16]

The fourth "dimension of relevance" suggested by Deutsch, transposed from comparative aesthetics to comparative religion, may be more readily apparent to those who believe that both aesthetic and religious phenomena "reveal spiritual being" (Deutsch) in their own characteristic ways. Representatives of varying religious traditions and philosophical schools employ different synonyms for "spiritual being" and the modes of its normative disclosure. Representatives of theistic religions, for instance, characteristically speak of "God" and "revelation." In current Christian appraisals of the significance of other "revelations" (if any) for Christian revelation, a rubric widely employed is "theology of religions." In this enterprise divergent views of the significance of other faiths for Christian truth-claims are offered. These range from what William Ernest Hocking called "the way of radical displacement" to the "way of radical reconception," and from the exclusivist claims of some Christian theologians to the emphasis on dialogue with other faiths now extensively commended in the literature of the theology of religions. The Christian doctrinal stance recommended for such dialogue may be "Christo-centric" or "theo-centric."[17]

In the case of nontheistic religions, or religions in which theistic and nontheistic options are offered, as is the case in some forms of Hinduism and Buddhism, the frameworks for comparison are more broadly philosophical. Such frameworks have been employed in the East-West Philosophy Conferences and other gatherings at the University of Hawaii, under the sponsorship of the East-West Philosophy Center. They also inform the procedures of some groups now espousing and conducting "Buddhist–Christian dialogue." Less specific philosophical frameworks, and a wider variety of hermeneutical devices, are employed in relevant groups within the International Association for the History of Religions. Critical understanding and rigorous application of carefully specified "dimensions of relevance" comparable to those appropriate for aesthetic analysis of what Deutsch calls "essential symbols" in artworks could bring new dimensions to the comparative study of religion, whether this is taken on under the auspices of theology, philosophy, or the history of religions.

In each case descriptive and normative judgments must be both carefully distinguished and responsibly related. Concepts and procedures must be both faithful to the traditions compared and unambiguously available for comparative discussion. We have only recently arrived at the point where the problems and the possibilities of the theology of religions or of comparative religion may be clearly seen and responsibly addressed. It is my conviction that those who are interested in comparative aesthetics and those who are interested in comparative religion or the theology of religions have much to learn from each other that could be of great profit to all.

We continue our analysis of the UNESCO study of aesthetics, as compared with current trends in the study of religion, by noting that similar parallelism of structure and procedure is exhibited in Jacques Leenhardt's summary, in the UNESCO study, of the sociological approach employed in current work in the "sciences of art." "We can identify," he says, two main streams in research in the sociology of art and literature. On the one hand is the sociology of the work of art, a book, a picture, film, etc., when the sociologist traces its existence in society. This leads him to investigate the components of the creator's social environment, its routes and internal laws. Secondly, the work of art itself may be treated as a subject, considered in its sociological context and therefore viewed in the making. In this case it is no longer its existence in society which is investigated, but rather the sociological conditions for its creation.[18]

The student of religion might think of these two foci of research as the religious institution, organization, or movement, on the one hand, in its social inception and the routes it has followed in society; and, on the other, the religious innovator or innovation: the prophet or prophetic phenomenon, or the priest and the priestly phenomenon, interpreted according to Durkheim, Weber, or Parsons.

In the light of these isomorphic structures of contemporary reflection on art and aesthetics and current reflection on religion and theory of religion, we turn now to a question that is foundational for both enterprises: Is there a categorical concept that has unique employment in the field of aesthetics or philosophy of art, as Kant maintained, and a categorical concept that is uniquely distinctive of the field of religion, as Eliade and others maintain? Examination of a recent carefully argued and thoughtfully nuanced argument for the restoration of the concept of beauty as the distinctive normative category of aesthetics is relevant to issues involved in claims for a distinctive category in religion such as the sacred, the holy, "otherness," or the transcendent.

Mary Mothersill believes that Kant discovered the foundations of aesthetics when he saw that there are no *principles* of taste, in the sense of assertions exhibiting logical entailments, and yet there are genuine judgments of taste, which may be either true or false.[19] There are, however, three "avoidable difficulties" in Kant's otherwise correct account of aesthetic judgment, she believes. His general formulation could have been the following: "Although there are no principles of taste, there must be some 'grounds of judgment' to which we appeal in 'our hope of coming to terms.' " The normative character of judgments of taste might be construed in terms of assertion rather than as command (Kant's "all men ought to . . ."). The normative factor, however, is not strictly derived from an ascribed property of the aesthetic object or from the quality of "pleasure" characterizing one's "feeling"; it has rather the force, in the form of an assertion, of an appeal, a recommendation, or an invitation. (Its logical *structure* is that of assertion; its logical *function* is that of recommendation.)

Second—and this observation is highly relevant to the comparable designation and establishment of phenomena as "sacred," "holy," and so forth, in foundational judgments in religion—Kant combined, without also distinguishing, analysis and description. He was thus driven to support the kind of formalism that would open both his general account of aesthetic judgment and his specific claims for "beauty" as the distinctively aesthetic category to warranted criticism. Phenomenological *description*, Mothersill reminds us, is *not* conceptual *analysis*, though they may be fruitfully combined if they are also carefully distinguished. What reflection may isolate (i.e., a concept) need not be present, in isolated form, in consciousness.[20]

Third, says Mothersill, Kant needlessly added to the concept of beauty another concept, "the sublime," in his analysis of aesthetic experience and judgment. His notion of the sublime, she notes, was drawn from the literary culture of his day and the character of his own response to certain things in nature. But "agreeable terror" is also an affect, and "negative pleasures" are pleasures.

> If it were established that the judgment of taste could be shown to be true without being . . . an empirical generalisation over preferences and . . . without recourse to principles of taste, the wish to construe it as an implied command might vanish. If it were recognized that everything beautiful is expressive and that the only affects excluded are those which in kind or by reason of intensity are incompatible with pleasure, then it would no longer be desirable (or indeed, possible) to exclude judgments based on affective response. This would relieve the theory from its commitment to "formalism." Moreover, once it is allowed that what is beautiful may be awe-inspiring or melancholy or tempestuous—that a phrase such as Yeats' "a terrible beauty" has legitimate application . . . the "sublime" would find its place within the general rubric of beauty.[21]

This move would blunt the criticism of those who claim that phenomena appropriately labeled "ugly" on a narrowly *formalist* notion of beauty could not be encompassed in the concept of beauty. It is criticisms such as these, along with the difficulties entailed in relating the concept to the wide variety of aesthetic phenomena for which it is claimed as categorical—"natural," literary and visual art, music, and so on—that have led many modern aestheticians and critics to eschew the concept of beauty in aesthetic appraisal. Mothersill suggests that the many alternatives offered—such as aesthetic, literary, artistic, visual, or musical "*merit*," or "aesthetic or artistic *value*"—must actually function *logically* as synonyms for beauty, with respect to the *logical* role that that concept would play in a revised Kantian analysis. In this role, Mothersill claims, the concept of beauty (or its synonyms) is indispensable, because "there is a particular complex capacity, that of taking various items to be beautiful, which is central to our form of life. . . . A description of a person who lacked (totally) that capacity would find its place, if anywhere, in the literature of psychopathology." Beauty, she continues, is a "good"; it may characterize items of any kind; and it is "caused by pleasure and inspires love."[22]

These remarks may recall some convictions of Plato in his vision of the relation of beauty to the Good, though the specifically aesthetic category of beauty, as developed by Kant and modified by Mothersill, was, as we have seen, not a part of Plato's philosophical vocabulary. The question remains, in any case, whether a comparable case for a distinctively religious category can be made on similar logical ground. We have seen that Hume and Kant locate aesthetic judgments in the domain of taste, and that Schleiermacher, Otto, Eliade, and others relate religious judgments to a unique sensibility that has affinities with the affections and their expression in a notion of taste. If religious sensibility, like spatio-temporal sensibility, yields no "principles" with logical entailments, may there nevertheless be religious judgments that are true or false? If there are no "principles" of religious discernment underlying all truth-claims in judgments asserting the status and application of the concept of the holy or the sacred, must there not, as Mothersill asserts with respect to the application of the concept "beauty," be some "grounds of judgment" to which we appeal in our hope of "coming to terms"? Is there "a particular complex capacity"— that of taking various items to be holy or sacred—that is "central to our form of life"? Or could "our form of life" evolve, or have evolved, into forms in which a capacity to take some items to be sacred or holy is no longer present? It could be noted, parenthetically if not cynically, that many people who take a number of things to be sacred or holy do "find their place in the literature of psychopathology," although Foucault reminds us to ask who establishes the canon of such literature.

Two issues are involved in the appropriation of Mothersill's revised Kantian argument for the restoration of the concept of beauty to normative status in aesthetics for the establishment of a categorical concept for religion. One is designation of the character of the religious concept in itself; the other is the logical form of justification employed in establishing its validity and use. The character of the concept, in all traditions that employ it, is intrinsically distinguished from that of all other concepts employed in all other forms of reflection and discourse by both negative and positive adjectival and adverbial constructions. The concept is understood to express that which is "other than," "more than," or "transcendent of," anything that can be expressed in any other concept or any combination of other concepts. If the concept is thought of as having a referent, that referent (Brahman, for instance) is said to be "neti, neti; not this, not that," in response to attempts to assimilate it, even analogically, to other concepts and their uses. In theistic religions God is said to be the "Wholly Other"; "negative theology" is said to have the highest positive value in attempts to conceptualize God, because more can be said about what God is *not* than can be said about what God *is*. Although it may then be affirmed that the "Wholly Other" has revealed its nature to humans in ways that are wholly or in part beyond both human conceptual approximation or control ("reason") and human merit (and therefore the supreme exemplification of "grace"), the "otherness" of what is revealed is affirmed along with the "otherness" of revelation as a mode of apprehension or disclosure.

This otherness may, in some traditions, be evoked if not approximated through analyses of foundational concepts like being, truth, beauty, or goodness, and the ascription to concepts that are said to "point to" the uniquely and distinctively "Other" of "absolute" status in relation to other employments of such concepts (e.g., Absolute Truth, Absolute Goodness, Absolute Beauty, Being-itself, the Ground and Power of Being, *sat-chit-ananda*). Always, however, there is communication of a sense of "something more" than can be expressed in the absolutes and the "in-themselves." Rudolf Otto, we have seen, maintains that "the Holy" comprises two "moments": the rational and the nonrational. The rational is the conceptual: the absolutes, omniscience, omnipotence, omnipresence. The nonrational is the numinous, the "Wholly Other" than conceptual, which is evoked rather than rationally or conceptually established. Although other analysts of religious phenomena have seen difficulties in various aspects of Otto's argument, and particularly in the stance from which he claims to adduce it, Otto's affirmation of a transconceptual ingredient in the distinctively religious category seems to be congruent with the data of traditions of thought and practice that normally count as "religious." Others would use different language, depending on the ground and purpose of their analyses.

A concept that links the aesthetic with the transcendent character of the distinctively religious category is expressed, in the Hebraic and Christian traditions, in the term "glory." Analogous terms appear in other traditions. The Christian theologian Hans Urs von Balthasar composed a comprehensive Christian theology that he called an "aesthetic" theology, utilizing the concept of glory as the controlling concept. [23]

Some linguistic analysts have expressed the "otherness" of the distinctively religious category in terms of its (appropriate) "logical oddness." The logical oddness of the category is also reflected in the oddness of the modes of argument traditionally employed to establish its validity, in terms of both meaning and application. These have ranged from esoteric instruction in techniques that are said to lead to mystical apprehension of the ineffable to a variety of philosophical arguments for, if not proofs of, "the existence of God." The recurring fascination of these arguments bespeaks their perennial significance. At the same time, mystics, fideists, and atheists join in affirming their inadequacy or inappropriateness.

The "case for theism" in modern Western religious philosophy has been made in terms of appeals to selected features of forms of experience: perceptual/cognitive, moral, and affective. The logical construction of an understanding of self and world is said to require the concept of God as the ground and goal of explanation; or the validity of moral law is said to require theistic validation; or the ubiquity of specific affections or feelings (e.g., awe or wonder) is said to imply or require a unique source or object of such feelings.

It is in the views of those thinkers who ground religious apprehension primarily in affective experience, we have seen, that the theories of religion implied or employed are most closely related to aesthetic theory—from Edwards to Schleiermacher, Otto, Eliade, and Tillich. Even theories of religion that stress cognitive or volitional experience factors include a role for affective factors that is unique to theories of religion. The role of feeling in Kant's proposed harmony of pure and practical reason is therefore of special relevance for an account of "religious judgment" that utilizes the structure of a revised Kantian analysis of aesthetic judgment. A viable argument for the unique character of the category distinctive of religion, and for the validity of its application to specified ranges of data, must show how the unique role of feeling in the derivation of the concept and its application is related to cognitive assertions and volitional imperatives.

Kant, we have seen, could ascribe only the status of "regulative idea" or ideal to the concept of God in its cognitive use for "pure reason." But he found the concept to be a clear implicate of "pure practical reason" and its exhibition of the moral law. Kant himself ascribed no privileged status to aesthetic experience—even the experience of the sublime—for apprehension of the divine, though he may have pointed to such apprehension in his notion of "aesthetic ideas."

Suppose, however, that the form of argument that Kant used in his analysis of aesthetic judgment, as this argument is revised by Mothersill, were transferred to argument for the concept of the divine and specification of its range of application. Like "beauty" for Kant and Mothersill, "the divine" or surrogate would be affirmed to be distinct from concepts of truth and goodness, but it would also be affirmed to be distinct from beauty—or even, without remainder, from "being." It would, in short, be affirmed to articulate those features of "otherness" or "moreness" that many analysts of the concept have found intrinsic to its meaning. It would exhibit *appropriate* "logical oddness."

Oddness of meaning would appropriately entail oddness of argument employed in establishing the range and procedures of justification and application of the concept. The "odd" thing about Kant's attempt to harmonize the dictates and dilemmas of "pure" and "practical" reason was his appeal to a form of *feeling* as providing a synthesizer of thought and action. Yet judgments of feeling (taste) neither yield nor presuppose principles—that is, assertions that, though nondemonstrable, exhibit logical entailments that may be formulated in true or false propositions. So he was driven to the language of imperatives in his analysis of the "four moments" of aesthetic judgment. Suppose, with Mothersill, we reconstrue these imperatives to be in fact, *from one point of view*, assertions. As assertions they would exhibit, to those who took them to be assertions, all the logical characteristics of other assertions about the real that are deemed to be logically warranted. Now suppose that we also reconstrue the "logical" cases for theism, or its logical/ functional equivalent in nontheistic religious traditions, to be assertions, *for purposes internal to the tradition* and from the point of view of the tradition.

"Proofs" of the existence of God would then be construed as genuine proofs in their logical form, and they would lead to assertions that are either true or false. An important "oddity" about them, however, has long been noted by many who have put them forward in the defense or explication of faith: although they may be logically "clean," they are convincing and religiously efficacious only to those who have additional ground for belief. Their employment is in the service of "faith seeking understanding" and in rendering intelligible the content of faith to those who would understand it. As is the case with aesthetic judgments as interpreted by Mothersill, for those who are in different circles of faith, or no circle of faith, the theistic "proofs" and the assertions they entail would be best understood as recommendations or invitations, expressed in the language of assertion. They would also be appropriately thus understood by those within the faith circle of a religious tradition who wish to employ them for explicitly apologetic purposes. For a John Henry Newman they might reflect the structure of "the grammar of assent"; for a Paul Tillich they might pose the existential questions that invite theological "answers." Critics, in any case, would not misconstrue their unique logical form and function, and therefore deny that which they are not designed to affirm. Like critics of the concept of beauty and its application in aesthetics, critics of the concept of the divine (or the holy) could be led to more re-

sponsible understanding and appreciation of the character of the category distinctive of religion, and of the logical form and force of its
employment.

Let us now address the question whether "a complex capacity to
take certain items to be beautiful" (or sacred or holy) may no longer
be present in our form of life, or at least in that form of life experienced by people who also understand themselves to be living in a
postmodern age.

Arthur Danto, in any case, believes that in our postmodern form
of life (if and where *that* exists) the usefulness of the concept art has
come to an end. Recalling Hegel's conviction that in the unfolding of
Spirit in history, art has had a necessary, but not culminating, role in
the movement toward the concrete universal, he suggests that Hegel
may have exhibited both philosophical insight and historical pre-
science with respect to the art world of postmodern culture. There
have been, he believes, two major models of art historical development in modern art historical theory. One is a "progressive" model,
based on the assumption that if ultimately in science everything can
be *known*, then ultimately in art everything can be *shown*. Central to
the employment of this model is the concept of *mimesis*, from its classical Aristotelian employment through its delineation by Auerbach to
its "illusionist" meaning for Gombrich. Like Aristotle, Danto claims
that *mimesis must include action*. With the coming of photography and
cinematography, not to mention "holistic" projection, many if not all
the goals of *mimesis* have been realized, and the very concept of "illusion" becomes problematic.

As the mimetic model is abandoned by many, Danto notes, "expressive" models are substituted. Here the emphasis falls, not on the
success of mimesis, but on the affective disposition or intent of the
artist and/or the affective experience of the artwork-as-transaction by
the viewer (or hearer)—or on the plurality of "symbolic forms." Specification and delineation of these affective/expressive factors and forms
are so complex and problematic, however, and their theoretical framework is so intrinsic to their appraisal, that generalized normative judgments are either impossible or completely relative to theoretical assumptions and personal or group preferences. Thus, says Danto, we
have come to a point where the "end of art," in the sense of the "goal
of art," is "to determine itself."[24] But if this has become the end (goal)
of art, perhaps we have then also come to the end (finish) of art.

The English sculptor, William Tucker, Danto notes, said "the 60's
was the age of the critic. Now it is the age of the dealer." But suppose,
Danto continues, "the Age of Art" *as such* has then also come to an
end. "Suppose it all has really come to an end, and that a point has

been reached where there can be change without development, where the energies of artistic production can only combine and recombine known forms, though external pressures favor this or that combination? Suppose it is no longer a historical possibility that art should continue to astonish us, that in this sense the Age of Art is internally worn out, and that in Hegel's stunning and melancholy phrase, a form of life has grown old"?[25]

The end of art in both senses thus indicated, however, may, Danto suggests, be the beginning of a "new freedom" that may both demand and facilitate the emergence of a new concept. "We have entered a period of art so absolute in its freedom," says Danto,

> that art seems but an infinite play with its own concept, as though Schelling's thought of an end-state of history as a "universal ocean of poetry" were a prediction come true. Art-making is its own end in both senses of the term: the end of art is the end of art. . . . The instances which fall under the concept are so various that it would be a mistake to identify art with any of them. Having reached this point, where art can be anything at all, art has exhausted its conceptual mission. It has brought us to a stage of thought essentially *outside* history. At last we can contemplate the possibility of a universal definition of art and vindicate thereby the philosophical aspiration of the ages, a definition which will not be threatened by historical overthrow. . . . A universal definition of art, a closed theory, must allow for an openness in the class of cases, and must explain this openness as one of its consequences. Post-modernism is the celebration of openness. The end of post-modernism is its explanation.[26]

Taking this statement at face value, we might well embrace it as one suggestive formulation of the task of those who would responsibly address the meaning of religion after the "end of religion." Could a "universal definition of religion," "a closed theory," allow for an "openness in the class of cases" and "explain this openness as one of its consequences"? We may leave open the question of face value in Danto's further assertion that the task, with respect to art at least, is basically a philosophical task, "because philosophy is something that will have no post-historical phase. . . . Nothing could be more dismal to contemplate than philosophizing without end, which is an argument that philosophy is not art and pluralism is bad for philosophy. The important question is what philosophers to breed for, and my answer is those who can give us the philosophy art has prepared us for." "I," says Danto, "am but their prophet."[27]

As we consider the relevance of Danto's position on the end of art to the question of the end of religion, it may be instructive to note some responses to Danto by fellow aestheticians. Richard Kuhns (a Columbia colleague of Danto) says that Danto's thesis rests on a mistake, "bedded in the assumption that art is subservient to the theories that make it meaningful."[28] Hegel's view, in particular, embraces an alleged history of art *as interpretation*, and it assumes a "god's-eye" view that is simply not available. "His theory, and Danto's use of it," says Kuhns, "are part of a cultural whole which itself is expressed in art." Furthermore, *our* culture includes not only the theories that Danto specifies as the dominant "models" for the interpretation of art history but also important psychoanalytic theories.[29] This type of theory would emphasize the *expression*, not only of the artist but also of the culture itself, in the artwork. It would see the role of art as central to "the conducting of persons into culture" and to the definition of the culture itself. Kuhns writes, "A person's sense of identity, or style, and of communal participation and obligation, is formed slowly and decisively, through the interaction with objects of art." This view of the function of art, it may be noted, is congruent with Geertz's view of the function of religion. In any case,

> it may be that Danto's vision of the end of art is a response to the mixing of traditions which makes us in a dim but puzzling sense inheritors of "the human" rather than the Greek, or Chinese, or native American, which once served to some people as "my own." If by "human" we mean, in part, being in possession of culture, then the post-historical cultural period means a revised sense of "humanness." Unlike the philosopher, who seeks to write the last manifesto, the artist lives in the ever-reborn belief that the task of art is the establishment of new manifestos on into the foreseeable future.[30]

Three themes are here articulated: One is the culture-boundedness of all cultural expressions, including those of aestheticians in cultures where such persons exist. Another is the centrality of art in performing functions that others would associate with religion. The third is the ineradicable open-endedness of cultural history, "for the foreseeable future." In any case, as David Konstan notes, "life and death make a tricky metaphor when applied to cultures, which are so versatile in selecting their own pasts." The "perspectivism" that is assumed in analyses like Danto's, and exhibited in the art world as analyzed from Danto's point of view, "is not a sign that art is dead, but a continuation of a dialectical development of art in terms specific to the contradictions of the world as we now experience it." Konstan continues, "The note of pique in Danto's treatment of modernism is symptomatic of a conservatism that is tolerant for want of energy, and of an unpardonable parochialism at a time when peoples and classes newly entered upon history are enriching and transforming all perspectives on art. . . .

The most important things to be represented are those that have not yet been seen."[31]

Thomas Martland, once a student in the Department of Philosophy of which Danto and Kuhns are members, maintains in his book *Religion as Art* that art, and religion *as* art, have had as their distinctive missions the "representations of things not seen" prior to their discernment in religious and artistic insight and their expression in the works of prophets and artists—or artists-as-prophets and prophets-as-artists. Both art and religion, Martland maintains, "present collectively created frames of perception and meaning by which men interpret their experiences and orient their lives."[32] The "frames of perception and meaning," however, are not primarily orientations that a culture already embodies and expresses at a given point in time. As Martland puts it,

> My thesis says that art and religion do not so much express fundamental feelings common to mankind as determine these feelings; they do not so much provide explanations of phenomena which men cannot otherwise understand as provide those data which men have difficulty understanding; they do not so much provide security or ways of adjusting to phenomena which men cannot otherwise handle as interpret the world in such a way that phenomena are delineated which men seem not to be able to handle.[33]

Whereas both art and religion, it might be said, perform "priestly" functions of "conducting us into life" (Kuhns) and celebrating the "confluence of ethos and worldview" in a specific culture at a specific time (Geertz), Martland's thesis is that "what distinctively marks art and religion is not their serving things past, but their providing necessary equipment to move into the future."[34] He proceeds to argue his case by recourse to examples taken from a broad range of artworks, especially in the modern period, and from a range of data selected from Confucian, Hindu, Buddhist, Jewish, Christian, and Muslim traditions.[35]

Let us turn now to further consideration of a phenomenon that Danto sees as calling into question the usefulness of the concept of art as this has been traditionally employed, but which others see as faithfully reflecting the problematic ethos and (pluralistic) worldview(s) of "our" (postmodern) culture, thereby opening up the possibility of new apprehension and expression of the real in art, and perhaps new apprehension and articulation of the real in religion. We refer to the major role that *criticism* plays in current discussion of the arts, and the role it might play in discussion of religion that includes both "the culture of criticism" and "the criticism of culture," to borrow again Giles Gunn's felicitous combination of terms.

Of course the question—what is criticism?—is itself a perennial if not a foundational question for critical discussion, just as the question—what is philosophy?—is a perennial philosophical question, asked, perhaps, with new self-consciousness in current philosophical discussion. (Indeed, philosophy has been called, among other things, "the criticism of criticism.") At the risk of gross oversimplification and egregious omission of important nuances, one could say that criticism entails at least (1) careful and rigorous *analysis* of the item(s) critically addressed, employing a specified analytical procedure; (2) *interpretation* of the items critically addressed, through elucidation of their (analyzed) "contents"; and (3) evaluation or *appraisal* of that which is critically addressed. In the actual work of criticism, of course, these three elements are employed concurrently, with emphasis falling on one or another of them at various points, and with one or another of them exalted to a position of paramount importance in the total mix by critics of various persuasions.

It is certain forms of *literary* criticism that have been the subject of the most intensive and fruitful debate in recent discussion of basic issues germane to a cultural situation that is alleged to entail, among other things, both the end of art and the end of religion. This is the case in part because these modes of criticism bring to a focus important philosophical issues and important developments in the human sciences. The philosophical issues include the nature and significance of the critiques of traditional "foundational" models of philosophy by Nietzsche, Heidegger, and Wittgenstein.[36] Developments in the human sciences include developments in psychoanalytic theory and in anthropological and sociological theory, among others. All these are brought to bear on, and utilized in various ways in, critical positions that have a common point of departure, namely, what is taken to be a uniquely modern or postmodern awareness of the nature and role of *language* in the construction of selves, societies, and worlds, whether of the self of the "author" and/or that of the "voice" of the text, or of the world exhibited in the text. This awareness of and focus on language stems, in turn, from developments in the "science" of language: linguistics. In the work of Saussure and others the character of word as *sign*, employed in the work of *signifying* and articulating *signifieds*, underlies the enterprises of *semiotics* (analysis of signs) and *semantics* (analysis of meanings achieved in the work of signs).

The significance of these modes of literary criticism extends to many fields. The fruitfulness of a "semiotic," if not semantic, model of cultural analysis was suggested in our brief account of the views of

Clifford Geertz in relation to some of the central concerns of this book. Giles Gunn believes that issues articulated in, and both the challenges and possibilities posed by, the "new new criticism" must be addressed in any responsible appraisal and reaffirmation of the "moral," if not the religious, functions of literature. Others have focused more specifically on what they take to be new openings to transcendence occasioned by and expressed in that form of criticism—if it *is* a "form of criticism"—discussed under the rubric "deconstruction."[37] The scope and focus of this book permit or warrant only an audaciously brief account of this "school," "movement," or simply "comment" (see below) and the possible ground for seeing in it some "signals of transcendence," to borrow Peter Berger's phrase, that are uniquely appropriate to our time.

To speak of deconstruction is to ask what has been "constructed" and how. In the semiotic idiom, what have been—and all that can be—constructed are texts. But in the semiotic idiom, texts are also all that is. Literary texts are specific constellations of that "textualizing" that constitutes all our views of self, society, and world—or rather, simply all that constitutes selves, societies, and worlds, since "views" are also texts exhibiting salient features of what, in the "viewing" context, constitutes the "texts viewed." All texts occur in contexts, and all contexts are expressed in texts. A function of criticism is to elucidate text/context within a given contextual/textual milieu. But what *method* of analysis should be employed in this enterprise? The "structuralist" school of criticism maintained that a method comparable to that employed in the specification of linguistic structures in linguistic systems (Sassure), or structures of human perception and action in social or cultural systems (Lévi-Strauss), is paradigmatic. Basic to its program was the assumption that there are a finite number of constant components of all linguistic or social phenomena, and that these components are related in a finite number of types of relations, binary or others.

Jacques Derrida calls radically into question this basic assumption. In the spirit of Nietzsche, he questions the status of the "transcendental signified" in the phenomenological program of Edmund Husserl. Although he agrees with Heidegger that the "foundational" "onto-theological" metaphysical thinking that has dominated Western philosophy since Plato and Aristotle bespeaks an "idolatry" of thought-forms available to a given historical milieu, he also maintains that Heidegger himself succumbed to the lure of foundationalism in his call for a recall of Being. (Heideggerians may reply that when Heidegger speaks of the absence-in-presence or presence-in-absence of Being he is enunciating a task for thought that takes full account of the "alterity" spoken of—if it can be spoken of—by Derrida, but without what many perceive to be the nihilistic indefinite "play" of texts/contexts in Derrida's program, if it is a "program.")

This leads us to ask what alterity is or is not, can or cannot be, "said to be," in Derrida's criticism. Derrida agrees with the basic semiotic assumption that we cannot avoid or escape language; that self, society, and world are constituted by language. But the history of the ways in which we have presumed to think that our language has captured once-and-for-all a reality (world) "outside" language, in an isomorphism of concept and world, reveals both the seduction and the impossibility of what Derrida terms "logocentrism." There is also the seduction of believing that we have found in the workings of language itself some fixed and constant givens or structures. Then the "philosophy of presence" reasserts itself. Derrida, it should be noted, does not deny or denigrate any of those relatively useful structures of discourse, of varying scope, that in fact enable us to "understand," "express," "interpret," and "get on in" the world—scientific, literary, or other. "Deconstruction," as Joseph Margolis puts it, is rather "the general strategy that exposes, in a thousand tactics, the myth of the fixed, essential, timeless, and naturally accessible structure of an independent reality that [our] would-be-total networks have 'found out.' "[38]

All such tactics deny the power of *différance*. This term, central to Derrida's position, utilizes the differing meanings of the French verb *differer*: differentiating, deferring, differing. All texts are marked by different differentiating marks. These may be simply different markings—different words, different patterns and forms of discourse internal to and formative of the text singled out for attention. But each mark both affirms what is "present" and depends for that affirmation on a sense of what is thereby "absent." In the search for the absent, or in the further linkages of "presents," "closed" or total meaning ("closure") is ineluctably and indefinitely *deferred*: text leads to context leads to text leads to context. "Deconstruction," therefore, notes Margolis,

> permits us to recover the power of *différance*, unnoticed by us in the ongoing and multiple busyness of generating systems of concepts and words with which to net the world—unnoticed because it cannot be noticed, the source of what we generate but not itself a generative process at all, because *it is not* (in a deeper sense than that in which the would-be intelligible world is not) and because if we say that *it is*, in that sense in which the things of the intelligible world are said or thought to be, then it *would* be designated by terms in the same way *they* are, which is to say the same way in which (falsely) we suppose reality to be perfectly caught in words.[39]

The recovery of "what cannot be said," and what makes possible our saying whatever can be said, is effected through what Derrida terms *writing* (not graphics in distinction from speech, but that which makes spoken/written discourse possible). It is *writing* that "indicates, suggests, recalls, enables us to recover—but does *not* signify—a radical alterity that is the origin of the power of every conceptual scheme; hence also of the limited, deconstructible power of every particular such scheme."[40]

There is a perennial temptation to discern in the "traces" of writing that constitute all discourse constant patterns of absence itself. "Weak deconstruction" pursues this quest, and it is not to be abjured or denigrated so long as it is aware of what it is and is not doing. Some pursue it on the model of psychoanalytic dream interpretation or other therapeutic techniques (Lacan); others, on different models. But deconstruction in the full and radical sense is *not* decipherment, notes Margolis; "deconstruction primarily directs all would-be (or actual) analyses and interpretations of texts and theories (as texts) to the *recovery* of the unsayable power of *différance*." This also means that deconstruction is not a *method*. Perhaps, suggests Margolis, it is "only a *comment* on whatever way we have of generating and interpreting texts (which remains a mystery)."[41] "This, then," continues Margolis,

> is the unsayable wisdom of *différance*, a kind of terror or perhaps joy or perhaps longing or perhaps misgiving or perhaps grim determination or perhaps indifference. . . . Perhaps this is to say that Derrida is the theologian who has escaped the grip of the onto-theological; but who, [by] a kind of paradox and perverse vengeance, has actually managed to invent an onto-theology that is not a member of the class of such theories just because it is a member, or perhaps it is a member because it is not. In any case, Derrida's theory of deconstruction leaves the world as it is and was as far as the interpretation of particular texts is concerned; but it emphatically does not leave the world as it is and was, as far as our grasp of why it is and must be left as it is and was. Whether we are thereby made sadder or more joyful or more indifferent is a contingent matter that hardly disturbs the thesis.[42]

The conviction that Derrida's sense of "radical alterity" is a possible "signal of transcendence" appropriate to our time is not, for Gunn and others, a "contingent matter." What Derrida called, in *Of Grammatology*, "the crevice through which the yet unnameable glimmer beyond the closure may be glimpsed"[43] is to be found, says Gunn,

> in language, and more particularly in all that language masks, hides, disavows, especially in the act of disavowing it. Through this crevice one can obtain a glimpse of a light shed by what Derrida has named, in his essay on Levinas, the "unforeseeably" or "infinitely" or "absolutely-other," which Levinas locates at the center of all religion and which Derrida aptly defines as "the religiosity of the religious." Comprising that dimension of

experience which is "resistant to all categories," the "absolutely-other" discloses itself in what our concepts fail to encompass. . . . Derrida is careful to state that this encounter with this "transcendence beyond negativity" cannot be experienced through direct contact but through separation, rupture, differentiation, puzzlement. Yet the encounter is available, accessible, indeed unavoidable, at the heart of experience, and it takes the form of a radical question that experience puts to language, "at the point where neither no nor yes is the first word but an interrogation."[44]

The language of interrogation is the language of question-and-answer, and the language of question-and-answer is the language of dialogue. It is in the "dialogical principle" that we find the key to understanding language, self, society, and world; and through it we may glimpse transcendence, in the view of the Russian critic Mikhail Bakhtin (1895–1975). Bakhtin, who was a member of one of those sensitive, cosmopolitan, and productive circles of "liberal" thinkers in Russia before the Revolution, and who both accepted and criticized various features of post-Revolutionary Russian thought and society, is increasingly recognized as one of the most fascinating and suggestive critics of the poststructuralist and postmodern era.[45]

Like Derrida, Bakhtin affirms that interpretation is infinite. "There is no first and last discourse, and dialogical context knows no limits (it disappears into an unlimited past and in our unlimited future). Even *past* meanings, that is those that have arisen in the dialogue of past centuries, can never be stable (completed once and for all, finished), they will always change (renewing themselves) in the course of the dialogue's subsequent development. . . . Nothing is absolutely dead; every meaning will celebrate its rebirth."[46] Relative stability is achieved in different ways in different forms of inquiry and expression. Natural science studies objects as idealities, in abstract systems. The human sciences study objects/subjects that respond and are temporally/spatially unique. These sciences are subject to trends toward formalistic objectivism, on the one hand, or Romantic subjectivism, on the other.

Human selves are inherently social, in constant interaction with other social selves, says Bakhtin. "I-for-myself" is an unknowable abstraction. Furthermore, the "facts" of natural science are "reiterative." Whereas natural science yields "knowledge" in a carefully specified sense and in accord with carefully specified protocols, the human sciences yield "understanding." Linguistics, which provided one of the models for structuralism, is based on the model of natural science; what is needed for understanding, including an understanding of what natural science is, is a meta- or trans-linguistics. Natural science is *logical*; the human sciences, and an understanding of what natural science is, must be *dialogical*, because human selves, including selves of scientists, are inherently social.

Like Derrida, Bakhtin sees language, whose basic unit he calls "utterance," as constantly moving toward, or being moved toward, a putatively fixed "center." This occasions the "monologic" idea of one common authoritative unity. "Monologism" is the Bakhtinian equivalent of Derrida's "logocentrism." But language is also centripetal, constantly breaking out of its unities to express what has been left out—what has been forgotten or what is new. The "old" appears as newly relevant, and the "new" becomes the given of future dialogue. This "heteroglossial" texture of language is celebrated in "the carnivalesque." (One of Bakhtin's major literary studies was of Rabelais.) The most authentic exhibition of dialogic "polyphony," however, is found in the novel—and for Bakhtin Dostoevsky is the paradigmatic artist of the polyphonic novel.

Again as is the case with Derrida, the concept of "the other" plays a decisive role in Bakhtin's philosophical anthropology. Individual consciousness, he says, requires an "other" for its identity. "Self-portraits" in painting, he says, are "always ghostly." The self-portrait of autobiography is also elusive if not illusionary. But "I" and "Thou" are always distinct, and the relationship is asymmetrical; the differences are correlated with the needs of each. "The morphological parallelism of the pronouns—'mine,' 'yours,' 'his'—leads us to a false analogy between entities that are radically distinct and irreducible, [such as] 'my love' and 'his love,' 'my life' and 'his life,' 'my death' and 'his death,' " notes Todorov.[47] Bakhtin puts it this way: "In the life that I experience from within, I cannot, in principle, live the event of my birth and my death; to the extent that they are *mine*, they cannot become events in my own life. . . . The affective weight of my life as a whole does not exist for me. Only the other is in possession of the values of being a given person."[48] "I can only die for others; conversely, for me, only others die. . . . In all the cemeteries there are only the others."[49]

Todorov concludes his exposition of Bakhtin's position with the following quotation from Bakhtin:

Man, life, destiny, have a beginning and an end, a birth and a death; but not consciousness, which is infinite in its very nature, since it can reveal itself only from the inside, that is for consciousness itself. Beginning and end take place in an objective (and objectival) universe for others, but not for the consciousness involved. It is not a case of not seeing death from the inside, by analogy with the fact that we cannot see the back of our neck without a mirror. The back of the neck exists objectively and others can see it. But there exists no death from the inside; it exists for no one, not for the dying, not for others; it has absolutely no existence. The absence of a conscious death (death-for-oneself) is as objective a fact as the absence of conscious birth. Therein resides the specificity of consciousness. [50]

The use of the term translated "consciousness" in this quotation might falsely suggest an affinity with Hegel. But Bakhtin, strenuously and at length, insisted that *dialogue* is not *dialectic*. It is the inherently open-ended question-and-answer, give-and-take, of human engagement with and in the world. In that dialogical process, matters that are or were "foundational" in one context may emerge as derivative in another, and vice versa. The process is exhibited in the "reiterations" of scientific inquiry as well as in the changing patterns of perception and expression in cultural analysis and cultural achievements. In the contemporary world we are freshly aware of indefinitely rich resources for ongoing dialogue. In the next and final chapter I will propose the appropriation of the "dialogical principle" exhibited in Bakhtin's critical theory, through a modification of John Dewey's notion of "inquiry." This dialogic neo-pragmatism, I propose, may facilitate constructive continued debate about the end(s) of art and religion in the postmodern world.

CHAPTER SEVEN

Beyond the End of Art and the End of Religion

W HAT IS THE conclusion of the contemporary debate about the end(s) of art and the end(s) of religion that we reviewed in the preceding chapter? Have we come to the end of art and the end of religion in modern sensibility? The answer is—yes, and no. We have come to the end of conceptualizations of art and aesthetic theory typified in Western philosophies of art and art history of the nineteenth and the first half of the twentieth centuries. We must come to the end of that conceptual disarray in the current art world to which Danto has called attention.

We must also move beyond those aspects of modern theories of religion that betray their culture-boundedness. Our review of the historical background and development of some of these theories, and of the complex data of Eastern traditions, makes this clear. Just as Arthur Danto announced the end of art, so Wilfred Cantwell Smith has called for the end of religion. Smith performed a great service in calling attention to the complexities of the relation of personal piety to cumulative traditions. We are now increasingly aware of these complexities. Smith's critique of previous ambiguities, however, does not eliminate the need for more sophisticated theoretical reflection on a perennial component of human culture.

We have just recently come to the *beginning* of more critically comprehensive reflection on art, with appropriate consideration of those dimensions of art to which Danto's critics have effectively called attention. In the Introduction to this book I affirmed that all critical reflection on art entails, explicitly or implicitly, a theory of aesthetics. Our review of the UNESCO Committee's report on the current state of aesthetics shows that reflection on aesthetic theory in a global context has just begun, and that exciting possibilities of creative insights lie ahead.

We have also just recently come to the *beginning* of more critically comprehensive theories of religion that are appropriately informed, not only by philosophical and historical but also by anthropological and sociological perspectives, and by modern or postmodern critical theory. These emerging theories of religion will address responsibly the rich possibilities inherent in modern awareness of methodological and cultural pluralisms. Can universalizing strategies that had their birth in Western cultures embrace without distortion the unique human achievements of all cultures? This is the paramount question that must be addressed in both aesthetics and religion in a world beyond the end of art and the end of religion.

The character of the tasks confronting both those who would develop more adequate theories of art and aesthetics and those who would develop more adequate theories of religion is exemplified in current philosophical debate about foundationalism and the current debate in critical theory about deconstruction. The most promising perspectives for both these tasks are, I believe, those provided by a dialogic neo-pragmatism whose character I will sketch below.

Where, then, do we go from here?

First, a word to the academy: Both the study of aesthetics and art and the study of religion are—or could be—microcosms of that macrocosmic enterprise we call liberal education. Both fields are—or should be—inherently multimethodic and intercultural or cross-cultural. Each brings—or could bring—to a distinctive focus a wide range of humanistic and social-scientific methods of inquiry. But both fields, in their anxiety to define and establish themselves as bona fide members of the academy, suffer from methodological imperialisms and cultural provincialisms. Only formal analysis, or critical interpretation, really counts as art criticism, it is said on the one hand. Only historical, or textual, or sociological, or philosophical, or theological understandings of religion really count, it is said on the other hand. Only the art of x period in the West, or of y period elsewhere, can set a canon, some say. The whole idea of "periods" and of a "canon" is ridiculous, others say. Only the uniquely theological expressions of religions that had their birth in the confluence of Semitic and Hellenistic cultures are really accessible to Western scholars, some say. Only if we get out of our cultural binders and put off our cultural blinds can we really see what "religion as such" is, say others. And still others continue the debate about whether there really are such things as "art" and "religion" around which fields of study can be organized. Fields require parameters, and the parameters of these "fields" are unclear if not nonexistent, it is claimed. Why not let the "established" disciplines of the academy deal with the putative phenomena in ways that are clear to other fields?

These positions, I maintain, are anachronistic in the academy of the postmodern age. Disciplinary boundaries have become appropriately blurred, like the shifting texts of deconstructive critical analysis. The interplay of contexts in the study of aesthetic and religious "texts" is uniquely germane to the life of the academy of our day. But it can be so only if students of aesthetics and art and students of religion pursue their work with a vivid awareness and positive affirmation of the inherently multimethodic and intercultural character of their enterprises.

More specifically to the point of this book: students of aesthetics and art and students of religion have much to learn from each other. Both the history of their disciplines and the exigencies of the current climate of the academy and the world it serves affirm this fact. Students of art must get over their suspicions of any apparently "religious" interpretation of their work and its subject matter. Students of religion must get over fears of "mere aestheticism." They must abandon the conviction that the only legitimate interest of students of religion in art is or should be an explication of the allegedly religious or theological significance of specified artworks. I hope that the historical review offered in this book, and its suggestions of the fruitfulness of certain convergences in the study of art and aesthetics and of religion at the present time, will put these fears and convictions to rest and inaugurate an era of mutual stimulation and enhancement.

The possible audacity of these remarks will no doubt be appropriately chastened by some who may discover what they believe to be lacunae or inaccuracies in my condensed historical analysis and questionable argument in my presentation of sample appropriations of methods employed in one field for the benefit of the other. So, I will now be even more audacious and speak not simply to the academy but to the world it is called to serve. That world, I have been reiterating, is for the first time in its history many worlds in one, and at least some of its inhabitants are aware of that fact. (William James, we recall, remarked that "the world is one—in more ways than one.") Among the riches of each of its cultures are achievements that we now label aesthetic and religious. Any viable understanding of that world must include these as central if not definitive expressions of a humanity that can and should no longer be thought of as merely Greek, Hebrew, Hindu, African, European, or American. Yet the riches of that common humanity can be appropriated only by those who are aware of the distinctiveness of their own culture in the context of awareness of culture as universal. One might well begin this awareness with art and religion, and their interplay, in each case. And to begin with these relations requires at least an acknowledgment of both the problems and the possibilities outlined in this book.

I concluded this survey of Western views of our subject with a sampling of modern philosophies and did so because I believe that it is philosophy that has had, and might continue to have, the task of providing both synoptic vision and the protocols of critical analysis and appreciation. These have been the dual tasks of philosophy from the time of its appearance in human culture, whether in Greece or India or China. In recent years there has been a battle between those philosophers who stress synoptic vision (seeing life and the world steadily and seeing them whole) and those who stress critical analysis (knowing what we mean when we say or do anything in particular). Each combatant has something important to offer the other if a truce could be arranged. There are signs that some parties on both sides might now be amenable to negotiation. Analysts are talking about "philosophy of mind" and metaphysicians and ontologists are attending to method. But, as is the case with art and religion, some philosophers are also now asking whether—or asserting that—philosophy has come to an end. Some mean by this that analysis has run its course. Others mean that metaphysics, in both the classical forms labeled by Heidegger "idolatrous" and the postclassical "recall of Being" via existential phenomenology, or even "the hermeneutics of suspicion" unveiling the realm of the suspicious, has evaporated in the postmodern world. Once philosophy asked what was left for it to do now that we have science: now it asks what is left for it to do now that all its traditional ways of doing are problematic.

I will be audacious again and say that philosophy must, and can, continue its traditional dual task of providing both synoptic vision and critical analysis. Philosophers have been led to believe that their "discipline" can no longer perform these tasks because the tasks are not as clear in scope of execution as they once seemed to be. It is said that the acids of modernity, as it expresses itself in methodological dilemmas and cultural relativisms, have dissolved the fabric of what was once called philosophy. I disagree. The philosophical spirit and the philosophical tasks come with being human. It is the bewildering richness of what we now glimpse humanity to be that challenges philosophy to continue to undertake both of its time-honored tasks in the service of humanity.

Can any of the old models serve, or be adapted to the "new" tasks? Yes. Good cases can be made for several: process philosophy, for instance. I propose a dialogic neo-pragmatism. This philosophy will be empirical in two senses: it will be grounded in a broad theory of experience, and it will be experimental in method. It will operate with a theory of experience encompassing, as Dewey put it, all that humans do and undergo: experience as sensory/perceptual/cognitive, moral, affective/aesthetic, religious—whatever experience is or turns out to be "experienced" to be. It will be wary of experiential imperialisms that exalt one or another of the forms of experience to definitive status for all purposes, and of methodological imperialisms that award privileged status to one way of rendering experience. It will emphasize continuities rather than discontinuities, and constellations rather than dichotomies. Experience will not be seen as something "other" than the world ("nature"? "the real"? "Being"?) but as in and of the world: the world in certain arrangements as experience; experience related to the world understood as the ground and terminus of experience. If the philosophy is genuinely empirical it will include the experience of what seem to be the limits of experience in all its "mundane" forms.

In another idiom philosophers might talk about the limits of language. They might talk about "alterity" or "thusness," or even "the transcendent"—if they do not forget the immanence of the transcendent and the transcendence of the immanent. They might talk about the Holy, or about God, or about "the supernatural-in-the-natural" or "the natural-in-the-supernatural." Natural/supernatural talk, however, does not seem very apt or relevant at the present time. Certainly philosophers will talk about the aesthetic in experience as consummatory and exemplary. They will talk about the religious in experience as orienting and enabling. Therefore they will talk about the holiness of beauty and the beauty of holiness as the confluence of the consummatory, exemplary, orienting, and enabling in experience.

The enriched and renewed empiricism, however, must be not only inclusively *experiential* but also *experimental.* The experimental program of inquiry as envisioned by Dewey should be enriched and expanded by the employment of Bakhtin's dialogical principle. This principle does not assimilate dialogue to dialectic, or to any other exclusively logical paradigm for human interaction in pursuit of maximum human good. It is, as Bakhtin affirmed, based on both a respect for the otherness of the other and an openness to the other's point of view, in an understanding of selves and cultures that is inherently dialogic in character. It engenders carefully specified procedures for construing the world in the many ways in which it may be construed. In this light scientific inquiry will be seen to exhibit a carefully nuanced way of pursuing the problem-and-resolution, question-and-answer procedure of an ongoing dialogic search for understanding. Other forms of interrogation and appreciation that promise fresh understanding and enjoyment will be employed in other pursuits of human ends. Of paramount importance in the nuclear age is the bringing of scientific and humanistic inquiry (or science as humanistic and the humanities as scientifically informed) to bear on the issue of whether experience itself (as we know it) will continue in the habitat of the planet earth.

The character of the expansion of Dewey's concept of inquiry to Bakhtin's concept of dialogue is suggested in Justus Buchler's concept of "query." "Method becomes inventive," writes Buchler, "when it takes on the property of query. Query is that form of human experience which originates partly in a compound of imagination and wonder. . . . Query is more prodigal than method as such. Method without query can destroy mankind and its own luxurious progeny. Method informed by query is the essential expression of reason. Reason is query aiming to grow and flourish forever."[1]

The inherent open-endedness of dialogical query means that there are no constellations of past experience that are considered to be permanently eclipsed in the ongoingness of cultural experience. The past, as Bakhtin forcefully reminds us, frequently becomes newly relevant to present situations. Pragmatism is sometimes equated with naive progressivism and with a concentration on means at the expense of envisionment of controlling ends. This view, I maintain, is based on a superficial acquaintance with traditional pragmatism. A dialogical neo-pragmatism will prize critically envisioned ends as well as means effectively related to those ends. And it will honor the notion of canon while perennially reexamining that which is deemed to be canonical in specific cultural configurations. Does this imply a form of "foundationalism"?

Joseph Margolis has addressed this question suggestively in his book *Pragmatism Without Foundations,*[2] in which he suggests that species survival itself may constitute a foundational concern of responsible inquiry. Although such inquiry will not claim incorrigible epistemic grounds, it will recognize the fact that there must be some sense of a common world of inquiry relevant to the foundational concern of species survival. Displacement of old foundations of either *theoria* or *praxis* must also be rationally constrained by the need to make sense of the relations of old views to new and of the interpreted record of the history of inquiry itself. At the same time there must be an awareness of the fact that no overview should be deemed universally valid for all time.

These conditions for a vision of pluralism, as an "-ism," seem both minimal and, as far as they go, convincing. But we must ask what is the essential content of the term "species" in the concept of species survival. What is minimally, and therefore foundationally, the *human* species? What is basically "human" and therefore "humane"? The "human sciences" have offered or presupposed differing answers to this question, and the rich variety of human cultures have exhibited many facets of what have been taken to be minimally human prizings and enjoyments. Among the worldviews espoused in these cultures are some that would not take biological species survival in and of itself to be the foundational commitment of human beings. There are people who—while affirming a religious obligation for the continuation of the species, but not at any cost—would affirm that "man's chief end is to glorify God and enjoy Him forever," in the context of a worldview that does not equate "forever" with biological survival of either persons or the human species. Others hold that (1) although *maya*, the penultimately real realm of space/time, is the *lila* (sport or play) of Brahman, the ultimately real that transcends space/time, and that (2) in the realm of *maya* or *samsara* the law of karma is never abrogated, (3) the goal of human existence is *moksha* or deliverance and the realization of union with Brahman (*tat tvam asi*).

To note these positions is not necessarily to commend them; indeed, many would hold that they are incommensurable. It is simply to note that in the riches of worldviews now becoming a part of global consciousness there may be more humanly significant visions of heaven and earth than are dreamt of in even the most "liberal" Western humanistic philosophies. These and other visions must be included in a responsible ongoing dialogue within our pluralistic world. This means, I believe, that as interreligious dialogue continues, any "world faith" that may emerge may, as William Ernest Hocking affirmed, appear to each of the existing faiths to be consonant with its foundational commitments, as enriched by enhanced experience.[3]

Does this mean the espousal of relativism rather than objectivism as a condition for fruitful dialogue? No. It means, as Richard Bernstein has suggested, a stance that is "beyond objectivism and relativism."[4] Bernstein shows that the concept of dialogue provides the key to understanding the philosophy of science of Thomas Kuhn, the hermeneutical philosophy of Hans-Georg Gadamer, the social-political philosophy of Jürgen Habermas, and the work of Hannah Arendt, as each of these thinkers addresses the problems of objectivism and relativism or foundationalism and contextualism.

The concept of dialogue would also enhance and deepen the import of the concept of "conversation" espoused by Richard Rorty in his delineation of the task of philosophy when philosophy can no longer be expected to provide the "mirror of nature."[5] In discussing the "consequences of pragmatism" he says that "in the process of playing vocabularies and cultures off against each other, we produce new and better ways of talking and acting—not better by reference to a previously known standard, but better in the sense that they come to *seem* clearly better than their predecessors."[6] Rorty also maintains, along with Bakhtin, that important roles will be played in the ongoing dialogue by genres that are called, not "philosophy," but "novels" (Bakhtin's favorite genre), "paintings," "musical compositions," "cinematic productions," and many other forms of conversation-making—including, I suggest, in certain religious traditions, "theologies" and "atheologies."

In the continuing dialogue, both within art history and the history of religions and between aesthetics and theory of religion, cultural change engenders an awareness of unexplored possibilities in neglected or newly discovered sources. Thus at the beginning of the twentieth century, European artists began to employ "primitive" forms and motifs and folkloric themes in a variety of ways that ranged from appropriation of motifs (e.g., Paul Klee's use of hieroglyphs) to the informing of vision (e.g., Picasso's integration of tribal masks with Cubist planar experiments). At the same time, artists such as the sculptor Constantin Brancusi retrieved the elemental forms prized by his native tradition, for transformation into a streamlined modern idiom. Now, near the end of the twentieth century, these appropriations of the "primitive" by early- and high-modern artists may seem in themselves naive; certainly the attempt to appraise them within the frames of art historical practice has provoked controversies strikingly akin to the critical practice of comparative religion.[7]

Thus we are again reminded of parallels between the internal dialogue of art history and aesthetics and the internal dialogue of the history of religions and theory of religion. In this book I have attempted to highlight these parallels as they have appeared in various historical and cultural configurations, and to suggest a philosophical stance that may facilitate fruitful discussion of the relation of aesthetics to religion in a global context. Through this discussion, concepts for expressing new visions of beauty and holiness may emerge.

Notes

INTRODUCTION

1. Mary Mothersill, *Beauty Restored* (Oxford: Clarendon Press, 1984).

2. Giles Gunn, *The Culture of Criticism and the Criticism of Culture* (New York: Oxford University Press, 1987).

CHAPTER ONE

1. The New English Bible (New York: Oxford University Press, 1961).

2. The Complete Bible: An American Translation, trans. J. M. Powie Smith and Edgar J. Goodspeed (Chicago: University of Chicago Press, 1948); The Holy Bible, Revised Standard Version (New York: Thomas Nelson, 1952).

3. The Holy Bible, trans. James Moffatt (New York and London: Harper and Brothers, 1926).

4. Gerhard von Rad, *Old Testament Theology*, Vol. 1, trans. D. M. G. Stalker (New York: Harper and Row, 1962), 364–365.

5. Ibid.

6. Ibid., 368.

7. Walter Eichrodt, *Theology of the Old Testament*, 2 vols., trans. J. A. Baker (Philadelphia: Westminster Press, 1965), 1:277.

8. Ibid., 1:282.

9. Ibid., 2:352.

10. Wilfred Cantwell Smith, *The Meaning and End of Religion* (New York: Macmillan, 1962), 59.

11. Ibid., 28.

12. Bernard Bosanquet, *A History of Aesthetics* (New York: Macmillan, 1892), 30.

13. Plato, *The Symposium*, vol. 3 in *the Works of Plato*, trans. Benjamin Jowett (New York: Dial Press, n.d.), 341–343.

14. Aristotle, *Nicomachean Ethics*, in *The Basic Works of Aristotle*, trans. Richard McKeon (New York: Random House, 1941), 1101–1107.

15. Robert J. O'Connell, S.J., *Art and the Christian Intelligence in St. Augustine* (Cambridge, Mass.: Harvard University Press, 1978), 47. O'Connell's study

is one of a small number of works devoted explicitly to Augustine's aesthetics. I have profited greatly from his work in the exposition that follows. Other studies of the subject include Karel Svoboda's *L'esthetique de S. Augustine et ses sources* (Paris-Brno, 1933); Sr. Joseph Arthur, *L'Art dans Saint Augustine*, 2 vols. (Montreal, 1944); Henri-Iréné Marrou, *Saint Augustine et le fin de la culture antique* (Paris, 1938). (These sources are cited in O'Connell, *Art and the Christian Intelligence.*)

16. *Saint Augustine On Music*, trans. Robert C. Taliaffero (Annapolis, Md.: St. John's Bookstore, 1939).

17. O'Connell, *Art and the Christian Intelligence*, 91, 101–102.

18. Kenneth Burke, *The Rhetoric of Religion* (Boston: Beacon Press, 1961), chap. 2.

19. For general treatments of this theme see Anders Nygren, *Agape and Eros* (New York: Macmillan, 1939), and Daniel Day Williams, *The Spirit and the Forms of Love* (New York: Harper and Row, 1968).

20. O'Connell, *Art and the Christian Intelligence*, 162.

21. Katherine Everett Gilbert and Helmut Kuhn, *A History of Esthetics* (Bloomington: Indiana University Press, 1953), 139–140.

22. Anthony Kenny, *Aquinas* (New York: Hill and Wang, 1980), 44.

23. Ibid., 46.

24. Jacques Maritain, *Art and Scholasticism* (New York: Charles Scribner's Sons, 1962), 4.

25. Ibid., 18.

26. Maritain, *Art and Scholasticism*, 28.

27. Karl Rahner, *Foundations of Christian Faith* (New York: Seabury Press, 1978).

28. Thomas Gilby, *Poetic Experience: An Introduction to Thomist Aesthetics* (New York: Russell and Russell, 1934). For a recent construction of a Thomistic interpretation of beauty, see Armand A. Maurer, C.S.B., *About Beauty* (Houston: Center for Thomistic Studies, University of St. Thomas, 1983).

29. *Pange Lingua*, in *The Hymnal 1982: According to the Use of the Episcopal Church* (New York: The Church Hymnal Corp., 1985), Nos. 329 and 330.

30. Perry Miller, ed., *Images or Shadows of Divine Things by Jonathan Edwards* (New Haven: Yale University Press, 1948), 20.

31. Ibid., 18.

32. Psalm 34:8 King James Version.

33. See Clyde A. Holbrook, *Jonathan Edwards, The Valley and Nature: An Interpretive Essay* (Lewisburg, Penn.: Bucknell University Press, 1987). For an excellent study of aesthetic themes in Edwards's thought see Roland A. de Lattre, *Beauty and Sensibility in the Thought of Jonathan Edwards* (New Haven: Yale University Press, 1968). I have drawn extensively on the work of de Lattre in the preceding exposition. In the works by Edwards himself, see especially *The Religious Affections*, ed. John E. Smith (New Haven: Yale University Press, 1959), and *The Nature of True Virtue*, with a Foreword by William Frankena (Ann Arbor: University of Michigan Press, 1960).

CHAPTER TWO

1. Alasdair MacIntyre, *After Virtue* (Notre Dame, Ind.: University of Notre Dame Press, 1981), 36–37.

2. Michel (Eyquem) de Montaigne, *Collected Essays*, trans. Donald M. Frame (Stanford: Stanford University Press, 1958).

3. G. W. Leibniz, *Monadology and Other Philosophical Writings*, trans. and intro. Robert Latta (London and New York: Oxford University Press, 1925); Daniel E. Munjello, *Leibniz and Confucianism* (Honolulu: University Press of Hawaii, 1977); David Hume, *The Natural History of Religion*, ed. H. E. Root (Stanford: Stanford University Press, 1957), and *Dialogues Concerning Natural Religion and Posthumous Essays* (Indianapolis: Hackett Publishing Co., 1980).

4. Michel Foucault, *The Order of Things: An Archeology of the Human Sciences (Les Mots et Les Choses)* (New York: Vintage Books, 1973), 61. (Trans. not given.)

5. Ibid., 55–57.

6. Ibid., 49.

7. This is the basis of the volume by Michael Mooney titled *Vico and the Tradition of Rhetoric* (Princeton: Princeton University Press, 1985).

8. Donald P. Verene, *Vico's Science of the Imagination* (Ithaca: Cornell University Press, 1981).

9. John D. Schaeffer, "Vico and Religion," *Religious Studies Review* 13 (October 1987): 322.

10. Mooney, *Vico and the Tradition of Rhetoric*, 263. Other works on Vico noted in Schaeffer's review essay include Giorgio Tagliacozzo and Hayden White, eds., *Giambattista Vico: An International Symposium* (Baltimore: Johns Hopkins University Press, 1969); Giorgio Tagliacozzo and Donald P. Verene, eds., *Giambattista Vico's Science of Humanity* (Baltimore and London: Johns Hopkins University Press, 1975); Leon Pompa, *Vico: A Study of the New Science* (Cambridge and New York: Cambridge University Press, 1974); Isaiah Berlin, *Vico and Herder: Two Studies in the History of Ideas* (New York: Random House, 1976); Giorgio Tagliacozzo, ed., *Vico and Contemporary Thought* (Atlantic Highlands, N.J.: Humanities Press, 1979); and Giorgio Tagliacozzo, ed., *Vico Past and Present* (Atlantic Highlands, N.J.: Humanities Press, 1981).

11. Wilbur Samuel Howell, *Eighteenth-Century British Logic and Rhetoric* (Princeton: Princeton University Press, 1971), 7.

12. For an excellent summary of these developments see Paul Oskar Kristeller, "The Modern System of the Arts," in his *Renaissance Thought II* (New York: Harper Torchbooks, 1965).

13. David Hume, *An Enquiry Concerning Human Understanding, Together with a Letter from a Gentleman to His Friend in Edinburgh*, ed. Eric Steinberg (Indianapolis: Hackett Publishing Co., 1977), 113.

14. Ibid., 114.

15. Ibid., italics mine.

16. Ibid.

17. David Hume, *A Standard of Taste and Other Essays*, ed. and intr. John W. Lenz (Indianapolis: Bobbs-Merill Co., 1965), 3–24.

18. Ibid., 6.

19. Ibid., 13.

20. Ibid., 17–23.

21. Ibid., 17.

22. Ernst Cassirer, *Kant's Life and Thought* (New Haven: Yale University Press, 1984), 171–172.

23. Immanuel Kant, *Critique of Pure Reason*, trans. Norman Kemp Smith (New York: St. Martin's Press, 1929, 1965), and *Critique of Practical Reason*, trans. Lewis White Beck (New York: Liberal Arts Press, 1956); James C. Meredith, *Kant's Critique of Aesthetic Judgment* (Oxford: Oxford University Press, 1911); Immanuel Kant, *Critique of Judgment*, trans. J. H. Bernard (New York: Hafner Press, 1951). Cf. Francis X. J. Coleman, *The Harmony of Reason: A Study in Kant's Aesthetics* (Pittsburgh: University of Pittsburgh Press, 1974); and Mothersill, *Beauty Restored.*

24. See Kant, *Critique of Judgment*, 82–106; cf. Samuel H. Monk, *The Sublime: A Study of Critical Theories in Eighteenth-Century England* (New York: Modern Language Association of America, 1935); R. W. Bretall, "Kant's Theory of the Sublime," in *The Heritage of Kant*, ed. G. T. Whitney and David Bowers (Princeton: Princeton University Press, 1939); Marjorie Hope Nicolson, *Mountain Gloom and Mountain Glory: The Development of the Aesthetics of the Infinite* (Ithaca: Cornell University Press, 1959); Edmund Burke, *Philosophical Inquiry into the Origin of Our Idea of the Sublime and the Beautiful* (New York: Harper Brothers, 1869); and Iris Murdoch, "The Sublime and the Good," *Chicago Review* 13, no. 3 (Autumn 1959): 43.

25. Meredith, *Kant's Critique of Aesthetic Judgment*, 80.

26. Coleman, *The Harmony of Reason*, 92.

27. Ibid., 87.

28. Ibid., 86.

29. Murdoch, "The Sublime and the Good," 49.

30. Bosanquet, *A History of Aesthetics*, 240.

31. Ibid., 242.

32. Michael Podro, *The Critical Historians of Art* (New Haven: Yale University Press, 1982), 4.

33. Ibid., 27.

34. Karl Friedrich von Rumohr, *Italiensche Forschungen*, ed. J. von Schlosser (Frankfort-am-Main, n.p., 1920), 18. Trans. and quoted in Podro, *The Critical Historians of Art*, 29.

35. Ibid., 30. Quotation from Rumohr, *Italiensche Forschungen*, 226.

36. Ibid.

37. Friedrich Schiller, *On the Aesthetic Education of Man in a Series of Letters*, trans. with intro. Reginald Snell (New York: Frederick Ungar Publishing Co., 1954).

38. See John Herman Randall, Jr., *The Career of Philosophy*, Vol. 2: *From the Enlightenment to the Age of Darwin* (New York: Columbia University Press, 1965), 232–236.

39. Robert F. Brown, *The Later Philosophy of Schelling* (Lewisburg, Penn.: Bucknell University Press, 1977), 16.

40. Randall, *The Career of Philosophy*, 261. In the brief exposition that follows I have drawn on the work of Randall and Brown, with the conviction that they make convincing cases for their general interpretations of the complex thought of a complex individual. More detailed presentations of aspects of Schelling's thought that are of special relevance to this study include the following works. Several are by other Columbia colleagues and students from whose study of Schelling I profited over a period of years: Schelling, *The Philosophy of Art*, trans. A. Johnson (London: John Chapman, 1845); *Schelling: On Human Freedom*, trans. James Gutmann (La Salle, Ill.: Open Court, 1936); *Schelling: The Ages of the World*, trans. Frederick de Wolfe Bolman, Jr. (New York: Columbia University Press, 1942; reprint, New York: AMS Press, 1967); Schelling, "System of Trancendental Ideaism" (Selections), trans. Albert Hofstader, in *Philosophies of Art and Beauty*, ed. Albert Hofstader and Richard Kuhns (New York: The Modern Library, 1964); *Schelling's Treatise on "The Deities of Samothrace,"* trans. and interpretation by Robert F. Brown, *Studies in Religion* 12 (Missoula, Mont.: Scholars Press, 1976); Victor C. Hayes, "Myth, Reason, and Revelation: Perspectives on and a Summary Translation of Three Books from Schelling's Philosophy of Mythology and Revelation" (Ph.D. diss., Columbia University, 1970); and Paul Tillich, *Mysticism and Guilt-Consciousness in Schelling's Philosophical Development*, trans. with intro. and notes by Victor Nuovo (Lewisburg, Penn.: Bucknell University Press, 1974), and *The Construction of the History of Religion in Schelling's Positive Philosophy: Its Presuppositions and Principles*, trans. with intro. and notes by Victor Nuovo (Lewisburg, Penn.: Bucknell University Press, 1974).

41. See *Schelling's Treatise on "The Deities of Samothrace,"* passim. See especially 51 and note 48, and 63.

42. Brown, *The Later Philosophy of Schelling*, 261. Cf. Tillich, *The Construction of the History of Religion in Schelling's Positive Philosophy*, and Hayes, *Myth, Reason, and Revelation*.

43. Randall, *Career of Philosophy*, 275.

44. Friedrich Daniel Ernst Schleiermacher, *On Religion: Speeches to Its Cultured Despisers*, trans. John Oman (New York: Harper Brothers, 1958), 9.

45. Smith, *The Meaning and End of Religion*, 45.

46. George Lindbeck, *The Nature of Doctrine* (Philadelphia: Westminster Press, 1984).

47. Schleiermacher, *Soliloquies*, trans. Horace L. Friess (La Salle, Ill.: Open Court, 1926).

48. Paul Bernabeo, "With Blended Might: An Investigation of Schleiermacher's Aesthetics and a Family Resemblance to His Views of Religion" (Ph.D. diss., Columbia University, 1982).

49. Schleiermacher, *Soliloquies*, 16.

50. Ibid., 34–35.

51. Schleiermacher, *Speeches*, 36; italics mine.

52. Ibid., 56.

53. Ibid., 51.

54. Schleiermacher, *The Christian Faith* (Edinburgh: T. and T. Clark, 1956).

55. Schleiermacher, *Speeches*, 138–139.

56. G. W. F. Hegel, Preface to Philosophy of Right, in *Hegel's Philosophy of Right*, trans. T. M. Knox (Oxford: Oxford University Press, 1942), 1–13.

57. *Hegel's Aesthetics: Lectures on Fine Art*, trans. T. M. Knox, 2 vols. (Oxford: Oxford University Press, 1975), 1:25. E. H. Gombrich names Hegel rather than Winckelmann "The Father of Art History" in a reading of *The Letters on Aesthetics of G.W.F. Hegel* (1770–1831), in *Tributes: Interpreters of Our Cultural Tradition*, trans. Angela Wilkes (Ithaca: Cornell University Press, 1984), 5. For a more general assessment of Hegel's importance for these and related issues see Hans-Georg Gadamer, "The Heritage of Hegel," *Reason in the Age of Science* (Cambridge, Mass.: Harvard University Press, 1981), 38.

58. *Hegel's Aesthetics*, 1:111.

59. Ibid., 1:2.

60. Ibid., 1:157.

61. Ibid., 1:175.

62. *Hegel's Philosophy of Mind, Being Part Three of the Encyclopedia of the Philosophical Sciences*, trans. A. V. Miller (Oxford: Oxford University Press, 1971), 563.

63. Arthur Danto, *The Philosophical Disenfranchisement of Art* (New York: Columbia University Press, 1986).

64. *The Critical Historians of Art*, 96. For an excellent discussion of the role of theory in recent art history see James Elkins, "Art History without Theory," *Critical Inquiry* 14 (Winter 1988): 354–378.

CHAPTER THREE

1. *Webster's Collegiate Dictionary*, 5th ed. (Springfield, Mass.: G. and C. Merriam Co., 1946), 241 def. 2.

2. Stephen Knapp and Walter Benn Michaels, "Against Theory," in *Against Theory: Literary Studies and the New Pragmatism*, ed. W. J. T. Mitchell (Chicago: University of Chicago Press, 1985), 11. For a useful summary of the status of theory in art history see Elkins, "Art History without Theory."

3. Philip Ashby, "The History of Religions," in *Religion*, ed. Paul Ramsey (Englewood Cliffs, N. J.: Prentice-Hall, 1965), 5. For a thoughtful discussion of some of these problems of definition, see Robert D. Baird, *Category Formation and the History of Religions* (The Hague and Paris: Mouton and Co., 1971). For a critically informed history of the discipline of comparative religion, see Eric J. Sharpe, *Comparative Religion: A History* (London: Gerald Duckworth and Co., 1975).

4. Sharpe, *Comparative Religion*, 161–163.

5. Rudolf Otto, *The Idea of the Holy*, trans. John W. Harvey (London: Oxford University Press, 1923), 177.

6. Ibid., 178.

7. Ibid., 144.

8. Ibid., 148.

9. Ibid., 63.

10. Ibid., 66–68.

11. Ibid., 69.

12. Ibid.

13. Ibid., 70.

14. Mircea Eliade, *The Sacred and the Profane: The Nature of Religion*, trans. Willard R. Trask (New York: Harper and Row Torchbooks, 1961), 10.

15. Elkins, "Art History without Theory," 356–357.

16. Eliade, "Literary Imagination and Religious Structure," in *Symbolism, the Sacred, and the Arts*, ed. Diane Apostolos-Cappadona (New York: Crossroad, 1986), 172–173. This is a useful anthology of some of Eliade's principal writings on the subject, along with critical essays.

17. Eliade, *Patterns in Comparative Religion*, trans. Rosemary Sheed (London and New York: Sheed and Ward, 1958).

18. For a comprehensive bibliography of Eliade's works to 1980, see Douglas Allen and Dennis Doeing, *Mircea Eliade: An Annotated Bibliography* (New York: Garland Publishing Co., 1980).

19. See, among Eliade's works, *Yoga, Immortality and Freedom*, trans. Willard R. Trask, Bollingen Series 56 (New York and London: Routledge and Kegan Paul, 1958); *Shamanism: Archaic Techniques of Ecstasy*, trans. Willard R. Trask, Bollingen Series 76 (New York: Routledge and Kegan Paul, 1964); and *Rites and Symbols of Initiation*, trans. Willard R. Trask (New York: Harper Torchbooks, 1965).

20. The most widely known summary of Eliade's analysis of the sacred in relation to history is *Cosmos and History: The Myth of the Eternal Return*, trans. Willard R. Trask (New York: Harper Torchbooks, 1959).

21. See, among other works by Eliade, *Images and Symbols: Studies in Religious Symbolism*, trans. Philip Maiket (New York: Sheed and Ward, 1961).

22. Eliade, "Shadows in Archaic Religions," in *Symbolism, the Sacred, and the Arts*, 5.

23. Ibid., 6.   24. Ibid., 86–103, 154–171.

25. Cf. Günter Spaltman, "Authenticity and Experience of Time: Remarks on Mircea Eliade's Literary Works," in *Myths and Symbols: Studies in Honor of Mircea Eliade*, ed. Joseph M. Kitagawa and Charles H. Long (Chicago: University of Chicago Press, 1969), 365–387, and George Utatescu, "Time and Destiny in the Novels of Mircea Eliade," ibid., 398–407.

26. Eliade, "Cultural Fashions and the History of Religions," in *The History of Religions: Essays on the Problem of Understanding*, ed. Joseph M. Kitagawa (Chicago: University of Chicago Press, 1967), 21–38. Reprinted in *Symbolism, the Sacred, and the Arts*, 17–31.

27. Gerardus van der Leeuw, *Sacred and Profane Beauty: The Holy in Art*, trans. David E. Green, Preface by Mircea Eliade (Nashville and New York: Abingdon Press, n.d.), v.

28. Ibid., vii.

29. Gerardus van der Leeuw, *Religion in Essence and Manifestation*, trans. J. E. Turner, with Appendices Incorporating the Additions to the Second German Edition by Hans H. Penner, Foreword by Ninian Smart (Princeton: Princeton University Press, 1986).

30. George Alfred James, "Phenomenological Approaches to Religion: An Essay in Methodology in the Study of Religion with Particular Attention to the Phenomenology of Religion of P. D. Chantepie de la Saussaye, William Brede Kristensen and Gerardus van der Leeuw" (Ph.D. diss., Columbia University, 1983).

31. van der Leeuw, *Religion in Essence and Manifestation*, 671.

32. Ibid., 673.

33. Ibid., 675.

34. Ibid., 680.

35. Ninian Smart, in the Foreword, ibid., xv.

36. Ibid., 684.

37. Ibid., 676.

38. Ibid., 686; italics mine. In the sequel we shall note the prophetic and creative function of art as interpreted by Paul Tillich, Thomas Martland, and others.

39. van der Leeuw, *Sacred and Profane Beauty*, 4.

40. Ibid., 7.

41. Suzanne Langer, *Feeling and Form* (New York: Charles Scribner's Sons, 1953).

42. van der Leeuw, *Sacred and Profane Beauty*, 265.

43. Ibid.

44. Ibid., 270.

45. Paul Tillich, *Systematic Theology*, Vol. 1 (Chicago: University of Chicago Press, 1951), and *The Dynamics of Faith* (New York: Harper Torchbooks, 1957), 14–16. For a comprehensive bibliography of Tillich's writings see Richard Grossman, *Paul Tillich: A Comprehensive Bibliography* (Metuchen, N.J.: Scarecrow Press, 1963). The authorized biography is Wilhelm and Marion Pauck, *Paul Tillich: His Life and Thought* (London: Collins, 1977).

46. In 1960 Tillich visited Japan. In reflections that he shared with friends after his return, he remarked that had he visited Japan earlier he would have given even greater attention to the relations of aesthetics to religion, and to the religious significance of aesthetic sensibility, in his reflections on religion and culture. His reflections on the relation of Christianity to other world faiths were summarized in his Bampton Lectures at Columbia, published as *Christianity and the Encounter of World Religions* (New York: Columbia University Press), 1963.

47. Paul Tillich, "Honesty and Consecration," *Protestant Church Buildings and Equipment* 13, no. 3 (September 1965): 15. Quoted in Michael F. Palmer, *Paul Tillich's Philosophy of Art* (Berlin and New York: Walter de Gruyter, 1984). Palmer's is the only full-scale study of Tillich's philosophy of art as such. I have profited from many of his insights in my brief exposition.

48. John Paul Clayton, "Tillich and the Art of Theology," in *The Thought*

of Paul Tillich, ed. James Luther Adams, Wilhelm Pauck, and Roger Lincoln Shinn (New York: Harper and Row, 1985), 278ff.

49. Paul Tillich, "Art and Society, Lecture I: Human Nature and Art," edited and reprinted in *Paul Tillich on Art and Architecture*, ed. and intro. John Dillenberger, in collaboration with Jane Dillenberger; trans. from the German by Robert Scharlemann (New York: Crossroad, 1987), 12. This volume is a valuable anthology of many of Tillich's principal writings on the subject. It reflects John Dillenberger's claim that "of all the theologians of our century, [Tillich] alone set the agenda for the role of the arts in theological work" (xxvi).

50. See J. A. Martin, Jr., "St. Thomas and Tillich on the Names of God," *The Journal of Religion* 37 (October 1957): 253–259.

51. Tillich, "Art and Society," 26.

52. Palmer, *Tillich's Philosophy of Art*, 178ff.

53. Emile Durkheim, *The Elementary Forms of the Religious Life*, trans. Joseph Ward Swain (New York: The Free Press, 1956). (Original copyright, London: George Allen and Unwin, 1915.)

54. See Edward B. Tylor, *Primitive Culture* (New York: Brentano's, 1924); and Robert R. Marrett, *The Threshold of Religion* (London: Methuen, 1914).

55. Max Weber, *Basic Concepts in Sociology* (New York: Philosophical Library, 1962); *The Protestant Ethic and the Spirit of Capitalism* (New York: Charles Scribner's Sons, 1958); *The Religion of China* (New York: Macmillan, 1964); *The Religion of India* (Glencoe, Ill.: The Free Press, 1958); and *Sociology of Religion* (Boston: Beacon Press, 1963).

56. Thomas F. O'Dea and Janet O'Dea Aviad, *The Sociology of Religion* (Englewood Cliffs, N.J.: Prentice-Hall, 1966, 1983).

57. Robert Bellah, *Tokugawa Religion* (Glencoe, Ill.: The Free Press, 1957); *Varieties of Civil Religion* (San Francisco: Harper and Row, 1984); and *Habits of the Heart* (Berkeley: University of California Press, 1985).

58. Clifford Geertz, "The Concept of Culture," in "After the Revolution," *The Interpretation of Cultures* (New York: Basic Books, 1973), 249–250.

59. Ernst Cassirer, *The Philosophy of Symbolic Forms*, trans. Ralph Manheim, Preface and Intro. by Charles W. Hendel (New Haven: Yale University Press, 1953); and Suzanne Langer, *Philosophy in a New Key* (New York: New American Library, 1956), and *Feeling and Form: A Theory of Art* (London: Routledge and Kegan Paul, 1955).

60. See Geertz, *Works and Lives: The Anthropologist as Author* (Stanford: Stanford University Press, 1988), vi. Additional references to Burke occur elsewhere in Geertz's work. Geertz notes that some others have also pursued the question of the relation of ethnography to literary style, namely, J. Clifford and G. Marcus, *Writing Culture: The Poetics and Politics of Ethnography* (Berkeley: University of California Press, 1986). For the work of Kenneth Burke see *The Rhetoric of Religion* (Berkeley: University of California Press, 1970), and George Knox, *Critical Moments: Kenneth Burke's Categories and Critiques* (Seattle: University of Washington Press, 1957).

61. Geertz, "Towards an Interpretive Theory of Culture," in *The Interpretation of Cultures*, 10.

62. Ibid.

63. Ibid.

64. Geertz, *Works and Lives*, 6.

65. Geertz, *The Interpretation of Cultures*, 30.

66. Kenneth R. Rice, *Geertz and Culture* (Ann Arbor: University of Michigan Press, 1980).

67. Geertz, *The Interpretation of Cultures*, 89.

68. Ibid., 91.

69. Ibid., 90.

70. Clifford Geertz, *Islam Observed* (Chicago: University of Chicago Press, Phoenix Edition, 1971; Copyright Yale University Press, 1968), 1–2.

71. Ibid.

72. See John Hutchison and James Alfred Martin, Jr., *Ways of Faith*, 2d ed. (New York: The Ronald Press Co., 1960), 14.

73. For an introduction to the major doctrines and forms of Islam see Frederick Mathewson Denny, *An Introduction to Islam* (New York: Macmillan; London: Collier Macmillan, 1985).

74. Michael Baxendall, *Painting and Experience in Fifteenth-Century Italy* (London: Oxford University Press, 1972, 1974).

75. Ibid., quoted in Geertz, "Art as a Cultural System," in *Local Knowledge* (New York: Basic Books, 1987), 102–105.

76. Geertz, "Art as a Cultural System," 119.

CHAPTER FOUR

1. For an exposition of this view, see Willard E. Arnette, *Santayana and the Sense of Beauty* (Bloomington: Indiana University Press, 1955). For further exposition of Santayana's aesthetic theory, see Jerome Ashmore, *Santayana, Art, and Aesthetics* (Cleveland: The Press of Western Reserve University, 1966).

2. Santayana, "Reason in Art," in *The Philosophy of Santayana*, ed. Erwin Edman (New York: The Modern Library, 1942), 255–259.

3. Santayana, *Interpretations of Poetry and Religion* (New York: Charles Scribner's Sons, 1900), 290.

4. Santayana, *Reason in Art* (New York: Charles Scribner's Sons, 1905), 103.

5. Santayana, "Reason in Religion," in *The Philosophy of Santayana*, 179ff.

6. Toward the end of his career Dewey remarked to his colleague Professor Herbert Schneider of Columbia, "Yes, I remember very well that this was our spiritual emancipation in Vermont. Coleridge's idea of the spirit came to us as a real relief, because we could be both liberal and pious; and his *Aids to Reflection* book, especially Marsh's edition, was my Bible." After the publication of his principal work on religion as such, *A Common Faith*, he said to Professor Schneider, "All I can do on religion is to say again what I learned from Coleridge way back in my childhood." John Dewey, as quoted by Her-

bert Schneider, in Corliss Lamont, ed., *Dialogue on John Dewey* (New York: Horizon Press, 1959), 15; John Dewey, as quoted by Herbert Schneider, in Oral History Interview, Summer 1966, Center for Dewey Studies, Southern Illinois University, Carbondale, Ill. For these references I am indebted to Professor Steven Rockefeller of Middlebury College. See also Rockefeller's essay, "John Dewey: The Evolution of a Faith," in *History, Religion, and Spiritual Democracy: Essays in Honor of Joseph L. Blau*, ed. Maurice Wohlgelernter (New York: Columbia University Press, 1980).

7. William Clebsch, *American Religious Thought* (Chicago: University of Chicago Press, 1973).

8. Charles Sanders Peirce, *Collected Papers of Charles Sanders Peirce*, ed. Charles Hartshorne and Paul Weiss, 6 vols. (Cambridge, Mass.: Harvard University Press, 1935), 6: secs. 344ff. Selected and conveniently grouped in Charles Hartshorne and William L. Reese, eds., *Philosophers Speak of God* (Chicago: University of Chicago Press, 1953), 259ff.

9. See Julius Seelye Bixler, *Religion in the Philosophy of William James* (Boston: Marshall Jones Co., 1926).

10. John Dewey, *Logic: The Theory of Inquiry* (New York: Henry Holt and Co., 1938), 104ff.

11. Cf. Wayne L. Proudfoot, "Interpretation, Inference and Religion," *Soundings: An Interdisciplinary Journal* 61 (Fall 1978): 378.

12. Moritz Schlick, "The Foundations of Knowledge," in *Logical Positivism*, ed. A. J. Ayer (Glencoe, Ill.: The Free Press, 1959), 223.

13. John Dewey, "Having an Experience," in *Art as Experience* (New York: Capricorn Books, 1959 [1939]), 55.

14. Ibid.

15. Ibid., 56.

16. Ibid., 57.

17. See Robert U. Roth, *John Dewey and Self-Realization* (Englewood Cliffs, N.J.: Prentice Hall, 1962), 44. Other interpreters who have—correctly, I believe—stressed the centrality of the aesthetic in Dewey's philosophy include John J. McDermott, *The Philosophy of John Dewey*, Vol. 2: *The Lived Experience* (New York: G. P. Putnam's Sons, 1971), 696; Erwin Edman, "Dewey and Art," in *John Dewey, Philosopher of Science and Freedom*, ed. Sydney Hook (New York: Dial Press, 1950), 40–49, 65; and George S. Geiger, *Dewey in Perspective* (New York: Oxford University Press, 1958), 19–20, 24.

18. Dewey, *Art as Experience*, 270.

19. Ibid., 105.

20. Ibid., 270ff.

21. Ibid., 25.

22. John Dewey, *Experience and Nature* (New York: W. W. Norton, 1929), 358.

23. John Dewey, *A Common Faith* (New Haven: Yale University Press, 1960 [1939]), 12.

24. John Dewey, *Human Nature and Conduct* (New York: The Modern Library, 1957 [1922]), 243.

25. Dewey, *A Common Faith*, 19.

26. Dewey, *Experience and Nature*, 202.

27. John Dewey, *Reconstruction in Philosophy* (Boston: Beacon Press, 1957 [1948]), 211. For a judicious and appreciative account of the relation of aesthetic to religious experience in Dewey, see William M. Shea, *The Naturalists and the Supernatural* (Atlanta: Mercer University Press, 1984), chap. 5.

28. Dewey, *Art as Experience*, 195.

29. Principal works of Whitehead that are relevant to our topic include the following: *Adventures of Ideas* (New York: Macmillan, 1933); *Aims of Education* (New York: Macmillan, 1957); *The Concept of Nature* (Ann Arbor: University of Michigan Press, 1957); *Process and Reality* (New York: Macmillan, 1929); *Religion in the Making* (New York: Macmillan, 1927); *Symbolism: Its Meaning and Effect* (New York: Macmillan, 1927). For a comprehensive bibliography see *Alfred North Whitehead: A Primary-Secondary Bibliography*, ed. Harvey A. Woodbridge (Bowling Green, Ohio: Philosophy Documentation Center, Bowling Green State University Press, 1977).

30. *Dialogues of Alfred North Whitehead*, as recorded by Lucien Price (Boston: Little Brown and Co., 1954), 255.

31. Whitehead, *Process and Reality*, 271.

32. Ibid.

33. Ibid., 392.

34. Ibid., 395–396.

35. F.S.C. Northrop, "Foreword" to Donald W. Sherburne, *A Whiteheadian Aesthetic* (New Haven: Yale University Press, 1961), xxvii. Professor Northrop himself employed a quasi-Whiteheadian concept of "undifferentiated aesthetic continuum" in his work in comparative philosophy. See Northrop, *The Meeting of East and West* (New York: Macmillan, 1946).

36. Sherburne, *A Whiteheadian Aesthetic*, chap. 6.

37. Ibid., 143.

38. Ibid.

39. Whitehead, *Adventures of Ideas*, 324–325.

40. Ibid., 257.

41. Whitehead, *Religion in the Making*, 16.

42. Among the theologians espousing "process theology" see, as representative, John B. Cobb, Jr., *A Natural Theology Based on the Thought of Alfred North Whitehead* (Philadelphia: Westminster Press, 1956); William D. Dean, *Coming to a Theology of Beauty* (Philadelphia, Westminster Press, 1972); and Daniel Day Williams, *The Spirit and the Forms of Love* (New York: Harper and Row, 1967). The philosopher who has most influentially espoused a theistic interpretation of Whitehead is Charles Hartshorne. See his *Man's Vision of God* (Chicago: Willett Clark and Co., 1941) and voluminous subsequent bibliography. For a sample of the results of Whiteheadian–Buddhist dialogue see Steve Odin, *Process Metaphysics and Hua-Yen Buddhism* (Albany: State University of New York Press, 1982).

43. Whitehead, *Adventures of Ideas*, 270.

44. Sherburne, *A Whiteheadian Aesthetic*, 180.

45. Whitehead, *Process and Reality*, 377.

46. Whitehead, *Religion in the Making*, 101.

47. In Chapter Three we noted the influence of the literary critic Kenneth Burke on the cultural anthropologist Clifford Geertz. For a study of Burke's views in relation to Heidegger's, see Samuel B. Shotwell, *Kenneth Burke and Martin Heidegger* (Gainesville, Fla.: University Presses of Florida, 1987). Influences on other literary critics will be noted below.

48. Principal works of Heidegger that relate to our topic include the following: *Being and Time*, trans. John Macquarrie and Edward Robinson, Jr. (New York: Harper and Row, 1962); *Discourse on Thinking*, trans. John M. Anderson and Hans Freund (New York: Harper and Row, 1966); *An Introduction to Metaphysics*, trans. Ralph Manheim (New Haven: Yale University Press, 1959); *On the Way to Language*, trans. Peter Hertz and Joan Stambaugh (New York: Harper and Row, 1971); *Poetry, Language and Thought*, trans. Albert Hofstadter (New York: Harper and Row, 1971); *What Is Called Thinking?* trans. Fred D. Wieck and Glenn Gray (New York: Harper and Row, 1968); *What Is Metaphysics?* trans. R.F.C. Hull and Alan Crick in *Existence and Being*, ed. Werner Block (Chicago: Henry Regnery Co., 1949); and *What Is a Thing?* trans. W. A. Barker, Jr., and Vera Deutsch (Chicago: Henry Regnery Co., 1967).

An excellent expository treatment of Heidegger's "The Origin of the Work of Art" and related writings is Joseph J. Kocklemans, *Heidegger on Art and Art Works* (Dordrecht: Martinus Nijhoff Publisher, 1985). There are a number of accounts of main themes in Heidegger's thought. In the exposition that follows I have found especially helpful Joseph J. Kocklemans, *Martin Heidegger: A First Introduction to His Philosophy* (Pittsburgh: Duquesne University Press, 1965) and his *On the Truth of Being: Reflections on Heidegger's Later Philosophy* (Bloomington: University of Indiana Press, 1984). I have not given extensive references to specific passages in Heidegger's texts because Heidegger's style and the developmental complexity of his thought seem to render this inappropriate and cumbersome. I have also not cited the German words he employs for many of his concepts, except for major terms like *Sein, Dasein, Befindlichkeit*, and so on, that are central to our purposes. The question of translation of Heidegger's numerous neologisms is complex and extensively debated.

49. See Kocklemans, *Heidegger on Art and Art Works*, 127–132.

50. Heidegger, "Hölderlin and the Essence of Poetry," in *Existence and Being*, 293–315.

51. Robert Frost, *In the Clearing* (New York: Holt, Rinehart and Winston, 1962). The line is from "The Pasture," *The Poetry of Robert Frost*, ed. Edward Connery Lathem (New York: Holt, Rinehart and Winston, 1969), 1.

52. Kocklemans, *On the Truth of Being*, 138–139.

53. See John Macquarrie, *Principles of Theology* (London: SCM Press, 1966); and Karl Rahner, *Foundations of Christian Faith* (New York: Seabury Press, 1978).

54. Heidegger, "What Is Metaphysics?" *Existence and Being*, 391.

55. James Alfred Martin, Jr., *The New Dialogue Between Philosophy and Theology* (New York: Seabury Press, 1966; London: A. and T. Black), 5.

56. Ibid., 203.

57. Hans-Georg Gadamer, *Truth and Method* (New York: Seabury Books, 1975), and *Philosophical Hermeneutics* (Berkeley: University of California Press, 1976); and Paul Ricoeur, *Interpretation Theory* (Fort Worth, Texas: Texas Christian University Press, 1976), and *The Philosophy of Paul Ricoeur: An Anthology of His Works*, ed. Charles E. Reagan and David Stewart (Boston: Beacon Press, 1978).

58. James A. Martin, *Philosophische Sprachprüfung der Theologie*, intro. and trans. Gerhard Sauter and Hans Günter Ulrich (Munich: Christian Kaiser Verlag, 1974).

59. See J. L. Austin, *How to Do Things with Words* (New York: Oxford University Press, 1962); A. J. Ayer, *Language, Truth and Logic* (London: Victor Gollancz, 1936); and Gilbert Ryle, *Dilemmas* (London: Cambridge University Press, 1954), and *The Concept of Mind* (London: Hutchinson and Co., 1949).

60. See *Essays in Aesthetics and Language*, ed. William Elton (Oxford: Basil Blackwell, 1954).

61. Ludwig Wittgenstein, *Tractatus Logico-Philosophicus*, trans. D. F. Pears and B. F. McGuiness (London: Routledge and Kegan Paul, 1961).

62. Cf. W.J.T. Mitchell, *Iconology: Image, Text, Ideology* (Chicago: University of Chicago Press, 1986). Mitchell discusses the "iconology" of Wittgenstein in relation to other forms of iconology.

63. Allan Janik and Stephen Toulmin, *Wittgenstein's Vienna* (New York: Simon and Schuster, 1973), 195.

64. Wittgenstein, *Tractatus*, 6.522.

65. Ibid., 6.54, 7.

66. See Steven L. Bindeman, *Heidegger and Wittgenstein: The Poetics of Silence* (Lanham, Md.: University Press of America, 1981). Brian McGuinness, authorized biographer of Wittgenstein, is among those who suggest that Wittgenstein was a mystic. He uses this term to highlight Wittgenstein's passionate search for truth or enlightenment and the ascetic single-mindedness with which he pursued that quest. See Brian McGuinness, *Wittgenstein: A Life: Young Ludwig, 1889–1921* (Berkeley: University of California Press, 1988). I suggest that in this respect Wittgenstein exhibited some of the ideals of the Hindu *jnana-marga* and that, in Hindu terms, he had an overriding sense of *dharma*. It is best, however, not to speculate on the appropriate placement of Wittgenstein's views in the nomenclature of religious traditions or in the complex concept of "mysticism."

67. Thus George Lindbeck, in *The Nature of Doctrine*, proposes a theory of religion that he calls "cultural-linguistic," drawing on Geertz's theory of culture and on what Lindbeck believes, following Paul Holmer, to be Wittgenstein's theory of "language games." His interpretation of Wittgenstein, however, is open to serious question.

68. Ludwig Wittgenstein, *Lectures and Conversations on Psychology, Aesthetics, and Religious Belief*, ed. Cyril Barrett (Oxford: Basil Blackwell, 1966), #26, 8.

69. Ibid., #35, 11.
70. Ibid., #32, 10.
71. Ibid., #20, 7.
72. Ibid., #19, 7.
73. libd., #23, 7–8.
74. Ibid., #36, 17.
75. Ibid., #37, 18.
76. Ibid., #38.
77. Ibid., #35, 27.
78. Ibid., #41, 28.
79. Ludwig Wittgenstein, *Culture and Value (Vermischte Bemerkungen)*, ed. G. H. von Wright and Heikki Nyman, trans. Peter Winch (Chicago: University of Chicago Press, 1980), no. 23 (1930–1934).
80. William Hordern, *Speaking of God* (New York: Macmillan, 1964).
81. Ludwig Wittgenstein, *Philosophical Investigations*, trans. G.E.M. Anscombe (Oxford: Basil Blackwell, 1963), #23.
82. Henry L. Finch, "Religious Language: Some Reflections on Three Texts of Wittgenstein." Paper presented to the Columbia University Seminar on Studies in Religion, February 12, 1973.
83. Ludwig Wittgenstein, "Bemurkungen Über Frazer's *The Golden Bough*," *Synthese* 17, no. 3 (September 1967): 233–255.
84. Paul Englemann, *Letters from Ludwig Wittgenstein*, with *A Memoir* (New York: Horizon Press, 1968), 78.
85. Wittgenstein, *Lectures and Conversations*, 54.
86. Stanley Cavell, *Must We Mean What We Say?* (New York: Charles Scribner's Sons, 1969), 88.
87. Wittgenstein, *Culture and Value*, 4–5 (1930).
88. Richard Rorty, *Philosophy and the Mirror of Nature* (Princeton: Princeton University Press, 1979).

CHAPTER FIVE

1. Hajime Nakamura, "The Meaning of the Terms 'Philosophy' and 'Religion' in Various Traditions," in *Interpreting Across Boundaries*, ed. Gerald James Larson and Eliot Deutsch (Princeton: Princeton University Press, 1988), 151. This essay is a useful discussion of many of the problems entailed by this issue, and the book as a whole contains essays that address fruitfully many issues involved in cross-cultural studies. An excellent example of such study, employing a psychological perspective, is Alan Roland, *In Search of Self in India and Japan: Toward a Cross-Cultural Psychology* (Princeton: Princeton University Press, 1988).
2. John A. Hutchison and James Alfred Martin, Jr., *Ways of Faith* (New York: The Ronald Press, 1953; rev. ed. 1960).
3. See Pramod Chandra, *On the Study of Indian Art* (Published for the Asia Society; Cambridge, Mass. and London: Harvard University Press, 1983).
4. Ananda K. Coomaraswamy, "The Christian and Oriental, or True, Phi-

losophy of Art," in *Christian and Oriental Philosophy of Art* (New York: Dover Publications, 1956), 23–61.

5. See Chandra, *On the Study of Indian Art*, 10ff.

6. S. K. Saxena, *Aesthetical Essays: Studies in Aesthetic Theory, Hindustani Music, and Kathak Dance* (Delhi: Chanakya Publications, 1981). See especially chaps. 5 and 6.

7. Quoted in Mulk Raj Anand, *The Hindu View of Art* (Bombay: Asia Publishing House, 1957), 5. For other translations see Eliot Deutsch, *The Bhagavadgita* (Lanham, Md.: University Press of America, 1968), XV:12, 119; X:41, 93; Franklin Edgerton, trans., *The Bhagavadgita* (Cambridge, Mass.: Harvard University Press, 1972), 74, 54; and R. C. Zaehner, trans., *The Bhagavadgita* (London: Oxford University Press, 1969), 97, 81. See also *The Bhagavadgita: Krishna's Counsel in Time of War*, trans. Barbara Stoler Miller (New York: Columbia University Press, 1986).

8. Saxena, *Aesthetical Essays*, chap. 3.

9. Richard Burton and F. F. Arbuthnot, trans., *The Kama Sutra of Vatsyayana* (London: Unwin Paperbacks, 1963).

10. Anand, *The Hindu View of Art*, 57.

11. Eliot Deutsch, *Studies in Comparative Aesthetics*, Monographs of the Society for Asian and Comparative Philosophy No. 2 (Honolulu: University Press of Hawaii, 1975), 2.

12. Edwin Gerow, "The Persistence of Classical Aesthetic Categories in Contemporary Indian Literature," quoted in Deutsch, *Studies in Comparative Aesthetics*, 5.

13. Ibid., 6.

14. Ibid., 11.

15. Donna M. Wulff, "Religion in a New Mode: The Convergence of the Aesthetic and the Religious in Medieval India," *Journal of the American Academy of Religion* 54 (Winter 1986): 673–685.

16. Ibid., 681.

17. Ibid., 683.

18. Deutsch, *Studies in Comparative Aesthetics*, 17.

19. Ibid., 18.

20. Ibid., 19.

21. G. Hanumantha Rao, *Comparative Aesthetics Eastern and Western* (Mysore: D.U.K. Murthy, 1974).

22. T.M.P. Mahadevan, *The Philosophy of Beauty* (Bombay: Bharatiya Vidya Bhavan, 1969).

23. Ananda K. Coomaraswamy, *The Arts and Crafts of India and Ceylon* (New York: Farrar Strauss and Co., 1964), 13.

24. Whitehead, *Religion in the Making*, 50.

25. For brief accounts of these and other features of early Buddhist art, see Coomaraswamy, *The Arts and Crafts of India and Ceylon*, and "Buddhist Primitives" in *The Dance of Shiva* (New York: The Noonday Press, 1957), 54–65; Anand, *The Hindu View of Art*, 20ff.; and A. Foucher, *The Beginnings of Buddhist Art* (London and Paris: n.p., 1917).

26. Alex J. Wayman, "The Role of Art Among the Buddhist Religieux," in *East-West Dialogues in Aesthetics*, ed. Kenneth Inada (Buffalo: Council on International Studies, State University of New York at Buffalo, 1978), no. 108.

27. Ibid., 12.

28. In my exposition of Chinese thought I have used initially the current pinyin rendering of dynastic names, with the traditional modern rendering in parentheses. In subsequent references to both dynastic and proper names I have used the traditional modern renderings because they are used in most of the sources cited and are probably still more familiar to most Westerners.

29. For a succinct account of Confucius's life and thought see Fung Yu-lan, *A Short History of Chinese Philosophy* (New York: Macmillan, 1948, and subsequent editions).

30. Herbert Fingarette, *Confucius: The Sacred as Secular* (New York: Harper Torchbooks, 1972).

31. Rodney L. Taylor, *The Way of Heaven: An Introduction to the Confucian Religious Life* (Leiden: E. J. Brill, 1985).

32. *Chuang Tzu, Basic Writings*, trans. Burton Watson (New York: Columbia University Press, 1964).

33. William Theodore de Bary and Wing-tsit Chan, "Taoism in Art," in *Sources of Chinese Tradition*, ed. de Bary, Vol. 1 (New York: Columbia University Press, 1960), 251–252. For a discussion of Chuang-tse on art, see Ellen Marie Chen, "Chuang-Tzu on Art and the Art of Living," *East-West Dialogues in Aesthetics*, 16–28.

34. Richard H. Jones, *Science and Mysticism* (Lewisburg, Penn.: Bucknell University Press, 1986; London and Toronto: Associated University Presses).

35. Alasdair MacIntyre, *Whose Justice? Which Rationality?* (Notre Dame, Ind.: University of Notre Dame Press, 1988): chap. 18, "The Rationality of Traditions"; chap. 19, "Traditions in Translation"; chap. 20, "Contested Justices, Contested Rationalities."

36. Beijing *China Daily*, June 21, 1988, 5.

37. Arthur F. Wright. *Buddhism in Chinese History* (Stanford: Stanford University Press, 1959), 70.

38. Ibid.

39. Rodney L. Taylor, *The Cultivation of Sagehood as a Religious Goal* (Chico, Calif.: Scholar's Press, 1978), and *The Confucian Way of Contemplation* (Columbia: University of South Carolina Press, 1988). The latter volume is an intimate view of the practice of a contemporary Japanese Neo-Confucian scholar of religious life.

40. Cf. Arthur F. Wright et al., *Confucianism and Chinese Civilization* (Stanford: Stanford University Press, 1959), and Susan Bush, *The Chinese Literati on Painting* (Cambridge, Mass.: Harvard University Press, 1971). For these references I am indebted to Mr. Ruichi Abe, a member of my seminar on aesthetics and religion, Columbia University, 1982. For a discussion of the concept of beauty in contemporary Chinese aesthetics, see Siu-chi Huang, "The Concept of Beauty in Contemporary Chinese Aesthetics," *East-West Dialogues in Aesthetics*, 28–43.

41. Donald Keene, "The Vocabulary of Japanese Aesthetics I," in *Sources of Japanese Tradition*, ed. William Theodore de Bary, Vol. 1 (New York: Columbia University Press, 1958), 172.

42. Ibid.

43. Ibid., 174–175.

44. Donald Keene, "The Vocabulary of Japanese Aesthetics II," in *Sources of Japanese Tradition*, 278.

45. Ibid.

46. Deutsch, *Studies in Comparative Aesthetics*, 26–27. For a further discussion of *yūgen* along these lines see Richard B. Pilgrim, *"Yūgen* and *Sabi* as Religio-Aesthetic Categories," *East-West Dialogues in Aesthetics*, 68–84.

47. Keene, *Sources of Japanese Tradition*, 280–281.

CHAPTER SIX

1. Mikel Dufrenne, ed., *Main Trends in Aesthetics and the Sciences of Art*, in *Main Trends of Research in the Social and Human Sciences*, Part 2, Vol. 1 (The Hague: Mouton Publishers/UNESCO, 1978), 491.

2. Smith, *The Meaning and End of Religion*, and Danto, *The Philosophical Disenfranchisement of Art*.

3. Dufrenne, *Main Trends*, 535.

4. Ibid., 539.

5. Ibid., 536.

6. Béla Köpeczi, in *Main Trends*, 578.

7. Ibid., M. Al'Patov, "Patrimonie artistique de l'homme moderne et problemes d'histoire de l'art," 654. Quoted by Köpeczi in *Main Trends*, 584–585.

8. René Étiemble, in *Main Trends*, 592.

9. See Deutsch, *Studies in Comparative Aesthetics*, 39–74, for the discussion that follows in the text.

10. Ibid., 42.

11. Ibid., 50.

12. Ibid., 62.

13. Ibid., 70.

14. Ninian Smart, "Pluralism, Religions, and the Values of Uncertainty," in *Hermeneutics, Pluralism, and Truth: The Seventh James Montgomery Hester Seminar*, ed. Gregory D. Pritchard (Winston Salem, N.C.: Wake Forest University Press, 1989).

15. van der Leeuw, *Religion in Essence and Manifestation*, 684.

16. Smith, *The Meaning and End of Religion*, 154–192.

17. See William Ernest Hocking, *Living Religions and a World Faith* (New York: Macmillan, 1940); John C. Hick, *God and the Universe of Faiths* (London: Macmillan, 1973); John Cobb, *Christ in a Pluralistic Age* (Philadelphia: Westminster Press, 1975); Karl Rahner, *Christian at the Crossroads* (New York: Seabury Press, 1975); Kenneth Cragg, *The Christ and the Faiths* (London: SPCK, 1986); and Paul F. Knitter, *No Other Name? A Critical Survey of Christian Attitudes Towards Other Religions* (Maryknoll, N.Y.: Orbis Press, 1985).

18. Jacques Leenhardt, "The Sociological Approach," in *Main Trends*, 93.

19. See Mothersill, *Beauty Restored*.

20. Ibid., 226.

21. Ibid., 245–246.

22. Ibid., 277, 271.

23. For a representative sample of von Balthasar's thought see Medard Kehl and Werner Loser, eds., *The von Balthasar Reader* (New York: Crossroad, 1982).

24. Arthur Danto, "The End of Art," in *The Death of Art*, ed. Beryl Lang (New York: Haven Publishing Co., 1984). For an elaboration of his basic thesis, see Danto, *The Philosophical Disenfranchisement of Art*.

25. Danto, "The end of Art," 8.

26. Arthur Danto, "Art, Evolution and History," in *The Journal of Aesthetics and Art Criticism* 44 (Spring 1986): 232–233.

27. Ibid., 233.

28. Richard Kuhns, "The End of Art?" in *The Death of Art*, 45.

29. Kuhns has developed such a theory in his *Psychoanalytic Theory of Art: A Philosophy on Developmental Principles* (New York: Columbia University Press, 1983).

30. Kuhns, "The End of Art?" 52.

31. David Konstan, "The Ends of Art," in *The Death of Art*, 91.

32. Thomas Martland, *Religion as Art* (Albany: State University of New York Press, 1981), 1.

33. Ibid., 12.

34. Ibid., 6.

35. For an appraisal of the cogency of Martland's case as developed in the work cited, see my review in *Annals of Scholarship: Metastudies of the Humanities and Social Sciences* 3, no. 1 (1984): 105–109.

36. On the comparison of Wittgenstein with Derrida on this topic see Henry Staton, *Wittgenstein and Derrida* (Lincoln: University of Nebraska Press, 1984).

37. See Mark C. Taylor, *Erring* (Chicago: University of Chicago Press, 1984), and *Altarity* (Chicago: University of Chicago Press, 1987).

38. Joseph Margolis, "The Mystery of the Mystery of the Text," in *Hermeneutics and Deconstruction*, ed. Hugh J. Silverman and Don Ihde (Albany: State University of New York Press, 1985), 140.

39. Ibid., 141.

40. Ibid., 142.

41. Ibid., 147.

42. Ibid., 149.

43. Jacques Derrida, *Of Grammatology*, trans. Gayatri Spivak (Baltimore: Johns Hopkins University Press, 1976), 10. Quoted in Gunn, *The Culture of Criticism and the Criticism of Culture*, 50. I agree with many others that Spivak's introduction to this book is one of the best accounts of basic themes and concepts in Derrida's work. I have not quoted extensively from the voluminous works themselves, for reasons of economy and effectiveness, but have

concentrated on interpretations, like Margolis's and Gunn's, that, among others, focus special attention on features of Derrida's work that are especially germane to the topic of this book.

44. Gunn, *The Culture of Criticism and the Criticism of Culture*, 50. The references are to Jacques Derrida, *Writing and Difference*, trans. Alan Bass (Chicago: University of Chicago Press, 1978), 95–96.

45. For an intellectual biography of Bakhtin, see Katerina Clark and Michael Holquist, *Mikhail Bakhtin* (Cambridge, Mass.: The Belknap Press of Harvard University Press, 1984). For a careful analysis and exposition of major themes in Bakhtin's thought see Tzvetan Todorov, *Mikhail Bakhtin: The Dialogical Principle*, trans. Wlad Godzich (Minneapolis: University of Minnesota Press, 1984). I am heavily indebted to these volumes for my brief exposition of Bakhtin, though my exposition radically truncates their more ample one and centers on themes especially germane to this study. I am grateful to Nathan Scott, as well as to Giles Gunn, for calling attention to the significance of Bakhtin for current criticism. For samples of Bakhtin's literary criticism see Bakhtin, *Problems of Dostoevsky's Poetics*, ed. and trans. Caryl Emerson, intro. Wayne C. Booth (Minneapolis: University of Minnesota Press, 1984), and *Speech Genres and Other Late Essays*, trans. Vern W. McGee, ed. Caryl Emerson and Michael Holquist (Austin: University of Texas Press, 1986).

46. Bakhtin, "Concerning Methodology in the Human Sciences." The quotation is from "k metalogii gumanitarnykh," in *Estetika Slovesnoga Tvochestva* (Moscow: S. G. Bocharov, 1979), 361–372. Quoted in Todorov, *Mikhail Bakhtin*, 110.

47. Todorov, *Mikhail Bakhtin*, 98.

48. Ibid. The quotation is from Bakhtin, "Avtor i geroj v estetichesko dejatel nosti," in *Estetika Slovesnoga Tvochestva*, 99.

49. Ibid., 316; quoted in Todorov, *Mikhail Bakhtin*, 98. For an English translation of Bakhtin's notes on "Towards a Reworking of the Dostoevsky Book" ("pererabotke knigi o Dostoevskom"), from which this quotation, as translated by Todorov, is taken, see *Problems of Dostoevsky's Poetics*, Appendix II, 283–302.

50. Ibid., 315–316. Quoted in Todorov, *Mikhail Bakhtin*, 98.

CHAPTER SEVEN

1. Justus Buchler, *The Concept of Method* (Lanham, Md.: University Press of America, 1985), 114. (Originally published by Columbia University Press, 1961).

2. Joseph Margolis, *Pragmatism Without Foundations* (Oxford: Basil Blackwell, 1986).

3. Hocking, *Living Religions and a World Faith*.

4. Richard Bernstein, *Beyond Objectivism and Relativism* (Oxford: Basil Blackwell, 1985).

5. Richard Rorty, *Philosophy and the Mirror of Nature*.

6. Richard Rorty, *Consequences of Pragmatism* (Minneapolis: University of Minnesota Press, 1982), xxxii-xxxvii.

7. In 1984, New York's Museum of Modern Art mounted an impressive exhibition of " 'Primitivism' in 20th-Century Art" that brought together, documented, and displayed exquisitely the variety of formal and cultural resources of and modes of such appropriation. A "blockbuster" show (with a correspondingly weighty catalogue), it drew a commensurate degree of attention. Much of the criticism focused on what were taken to be the tacit assumptions and implications of the show's subtitle: "Affinity of the Tribal and the Modern," which for many encapsulated an unexamined imperialism, both cultural and temporal. See *"Primitivism" in 20th-Century Art*, ed. William Rubin, 2 vols. (New York: The Museum of Modern Art, 1984); for incisive examination of the methodological and critical questions raised by the MOMA show, see James Clifford's "Histories of the Tribal and Modern," and Yve-Alain Bois's "La Pensée Sauvage," pendant essays that appeared in *Art in America* 73 (April 1985): 164 and 178ff. respectively. The dialogue continues.

Index

view of, 43–44; aesthetic ideas, concept of, 45–46; epistemology, 41–42; practical reason, view of, 42–43; overview, 41–46
Keene, Donald, 162–163
Kenny, Anthony, 24
Klee, Paul, 196
Knitter, Paul F., 214 n.17
Kockelmans, Joseph J., 209 n.58
Konstans, David, 180
Kristeller, Paul Oskar, 199 n.12
Kuhns, Richard, 179–181

Larson, Gerald James, 211 n.1
Leibniz, G. W., 33, 199 n.3
Lindbeck, George, 210 n.67
Locke, John, 4, 28, 29, 34, 42
logic, and rhetoric, functions compared, 36

McGuiness, Brian, 210 n.66
MacIntyre, Alasdair, 33
Macquarrie, John, 209 n.53
Margolis, Joseph, 184–185, 194
Maritain, Jacques, 25
Martland, Thomas, 121, 181
Miller, Perry, 29, 30
Mooney, Michael, 35–36, 199 n.10
Moore, G. E., 129
Mothersill, Mary, 5, 7, 172–174
Murdoch, Iris, 200 n.24

Nakamura, Hajime, 137
neo-pragmatism, dialogic, 192–196
Northrop, F.S.C., 120, 208 n.35

O'Connell, Robert J., 22, 197 n.15
Otto, Rudolf: the aesthetic and the religious, relations of, 72–74; history of religions, view of, 71–72; the holy, concept of, 69; the numinous, concept of, 70–71; overview, 69–75

Parsons, Talcott, 97
Peirce, Charles Sanders, 39, 110, 207 n.8

phenomenology of religion, 81–86
philosophy, tasks of, 192
Picasso, Pablo, 91, 103, 196
Plato, 4; art, view of, 12–13; beauty, nature and role of, 14–15; overview, 12–15
pluralism, cultural, 190–191; methodological, 190–191, 194
Podro, Michael, 48
poiesis, 12
primitivism, 196, 217 n.7
Proudfoot, Wayne L., 207 n.11

Rahner, Karl, 209 n.53, 214 n.17
Randall, John Herman, Jr., 38, 51, 200 n.38, 210 n.40
rasa, concept of, 145–148
religion: academic study of, 191; comparative, 169–170; concept of, 11, 54; "end" of, 7; sociology of, 172
religions, history of, 40, 63, 71–73
Ricoeur, Paul, 129, 210 n.57
Rockefeller, Steven, 207 n.6
Roland, Alan, 211 n.1
Rorty, Richard, 135, 195–196
Ryle, Gilbert, 129

sacred, the: in Eliade, 76–79; and profane beauty in van der Leeuw, 87
Santayana, George: beauty, concept of, 107; metaphysics, view of, 105–107; poetry, view of, 107–108; religion, view of, 108–109; overview, 105–109
Schelling, Friedrich Wilhelm Joseph: "Ages of The World" in, 53; centrality of art in, 52; overview, 51–54; "positive philosophy" and history of religions in, 53–54; systems or visions of, 51–53
Schiller, Friedrich von, 5, 49–50
Schlegel, Friedrich von, 5, 50–51
Schleiermacher, Friedrich Daniel Ernst: art and religion, view of, 57–58; overview, 54–58; religion, theory of, 56
Schneider, Herbert, 206–207 n.6
Scott, Nathan C., 216 n.45
Shea, William M., 208 n.27